I08I3028

IMAGES
of America

AROUND SAEGERTOWN

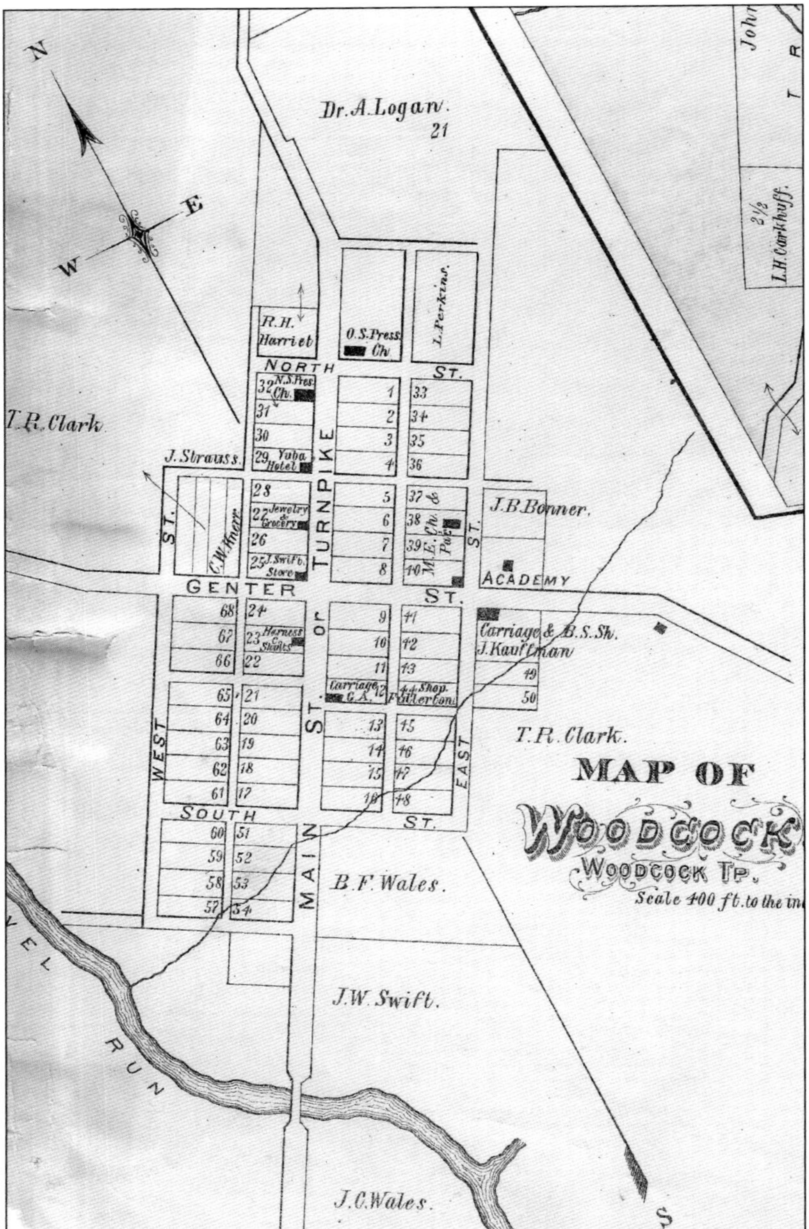

This 1876 map depicts the borough of Woodcock, one of the four main community centers discussed in this book. Few of the property owners are listed on this map, largely due to the size and detail involved.

On the cover: Pictured here are Saegertown School students. The beloved alma mater, starting when the current high school was opened in 1971, is as follows: "High above the valley, / dear old Saegertown. / To you we raise our voices, / school of great renown. / In your halls and classrooms, / new friends we have found. / So we're singing you our alma mater, / dear old Saegertown!" (Courtesy of the Crawford County Historical Society.)

IMAGES
of America

AROUND SAEGERTOWN

Joshua F. Sherretts

ARCADIA
PUBLISHING

ISBN 978-0-7385-5044-2

Published by Arcadia Publishing
Charleston, South Carolina

Printed in the United States of America

Library of Congress Catalog Card Number: 2007922543

For all general information contact Arcadia Publishing at:
Telephone 843-853-2070
Fax 843-853-0044
E-mail sales@arcadiapublishing.com
For customer service and orders:
Toll-Free 1-888-313-2665

Visit us on the Internet at www.arcadiapublishing.com

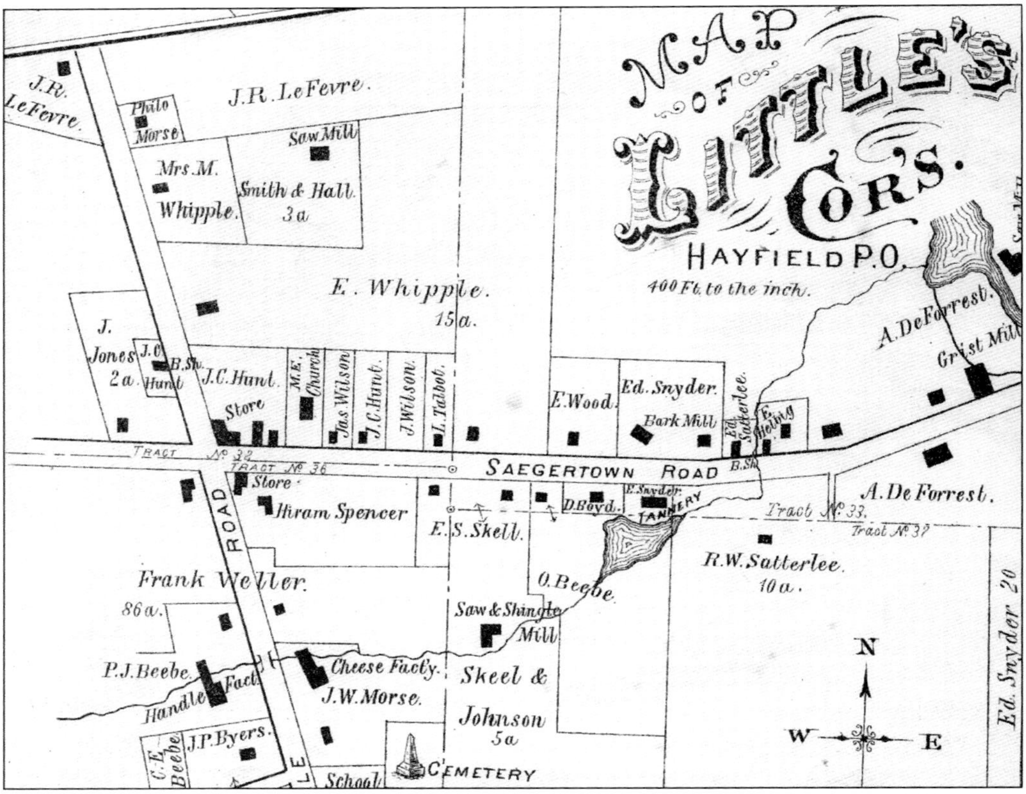

In another 1876 map, the village of Little's Corners is seen at its heyday in industry. Mills grace the streets of what was also known as Hayfield Post Office. There is great speculation on the identity of the original settler in Little's Corners; however, the Coon family arrived here in the first years of the 19th century.

Contents

Acknowledgments

I would like to thank Elizabeth Rice for her help and push to get this project started. Great appreciation and thanks go to the following for supplying photographs and information: Byham Miller Mizner Funeral Home, K. James Bertram, Hayfield Grange No. 800, Jim Reichel and the Hayfield Volunteer Fire Department, William B. Moore, Linda Z. Fink, Lea Baldwin, the Saegertown Heritage Society, and the staff and volunteers at the Crawford County Historical Society. Private individuals will be listed next to the photograph they provided for this work, but due to the immense number of photographs, organizations who lent photographs in large numbers as well as the many images received by Linda Fink will receive all credit here. Darcy Hammond deserves much appreciation for restoring a few of the photographs used in this book. Special thanks go to my mother, Joan Sherretts, as well as Donna Flory, Marie Loose, and Susan Scranton for their help in researching and preparing this work. Without them this would not have been possible.

INTRODUCTION

Saegertown and the area surrounding it is filled with history, much of which is unknown, even to those who live here. First settled in 1792 by Irish immigrants, Arthur and Patrick McGill, the land was chosen because of the beauty and utility of French Creek and the surrounding area. They established their claims slightly north of John Fredabaugh, a settler on Woodcock Creek, and brought their families from Northumberland County soon after, sharing the springs with local Native American tribes for many years. Patrick's house still stands as the oldest surviving in Crawford County.

Maj. Roger Alden, the first local agent for the Holland Land Company, bought land from Patrick McGill and John Fredabaugh and built a mill in 1801, starting a thriving community that carries on to this day. It was not complete, however, until Alden sold his assets to Daniel Saeger, who brought roughly 150 German immigrants from Lehigh County to settle the area. Although it was not thought of at the time, this act caused a cultural segregation that inhabited Saegertown for several decades afterward. Each group (German and Scotch-Irish) had different denominations of churches based on ethnicity and even sent their children to segregated schools.

The mineral springs found here were probably the most influential factor in Saegertown's rise to its early-1900s boom. From these waters, the Saegertown Bottling Works was started, hotels and inns of great class sprouted up everywhere, and business in the area skyrocketed. Figures such as John D. Rockefeller made the Saegertown Inn a vacation spot, putting the fair city on the map.

Several other attributes made Saegertown well-known and thriving. In 1854, the Crawford County Home was established. The first of its kind in Pennsylvania, the home and farm housed the poor and elderly in the county, having the resources to feed and offer them work on-site if they so desired in the many gardens and farm facilities. This opportunity extended into the more recent past. In 1868, the Benninghoff robbery occurred with the theft of roughly $500,000, believing it to be the largest oil funds robbery of all time. The Saegertown Band was invited to play in two presidential inaugurations due to its great reputation. Finally Saegertown Ginger Ale was found to be the best soft drink in the world at the 1900 Paris World's Fair. Included in this book are several images of the county home over the course of the last century and a half. A vast set of views of both the interior and exterior of the Saegertown Inn show its elegance as well.

During the 1930s, Henry Ward Baldwin started the Baldwin Laboratories, sending a small insecticide business into national fame in less than five years. His family still resides in Saegertown. In fact, McGills, Hunters, Saegers, and many other prominent names from the area still live on.

A book titled *Around Saegertown* would be at a great loss if it were not to include the surrounding areas. These places include Blooming Valley, Woodcock, and Little's Corners, as well as the many rural areas in between. One of the most well-known country doctors in the area and living in Little's Corners, Dr. Jacob Russell Mosier has several photographs listed in the book. His office is now on permanent exhibit at the Baldwin-Reynolds House Museum in Meadville, completely intact to its 1938 rustic charm. Cheese factories from some of these areas are mentioned as well as Granges, given that at one time Crawford County had over 70, with membership running in the six and seven thousands. The area has a grand history, if one digs enough for it to shine through.

One

Of Town and Country

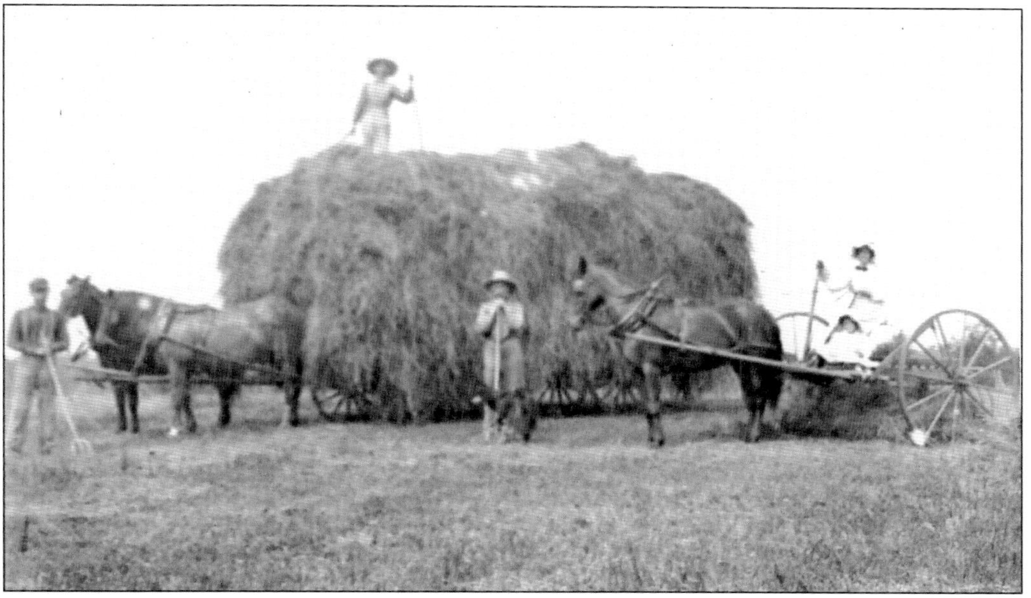

Agriculture has been a staple in Crawford County since its founding. It was the largest industry for the majority of the county's history, having more cheese factories and shipping more milk than any other county in the state for many years. Although the people in this photograph cannot be identified, scenes such as this were commonplace throughout the 19th century in the Saegertown area, the location of this photograph.

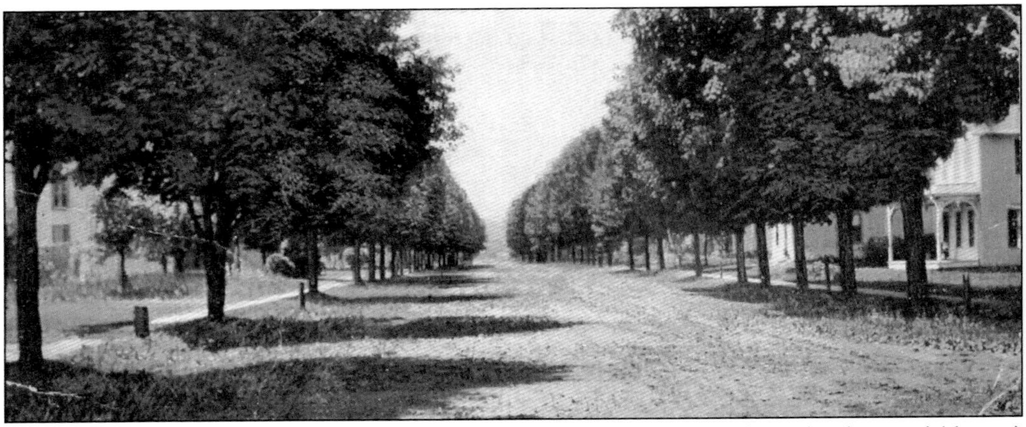

As shown in 1913, Euclid Avenue has changed relatively little to this day. The dirt road (shown) has been paved and some of the buildings have been replaced, but this tree-lined landscape has helped Saegertown gain the title of "Tree City USA." Josiah Kerns, builder of the Saegertown Inn, built and lived in the first house on the right, now restored to its mid-1800s appearance.

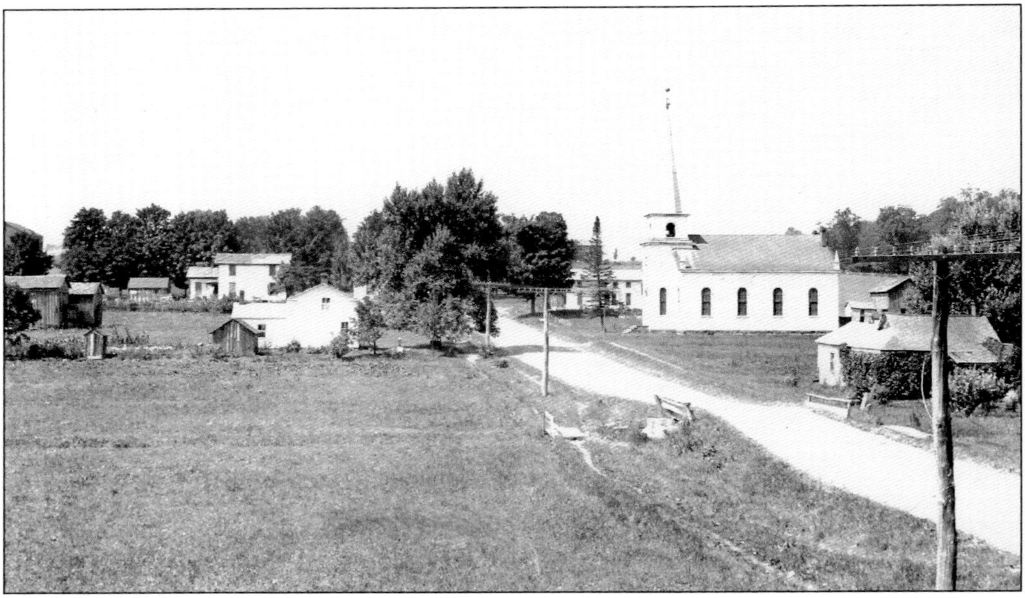

First settled by Seth Nichols in 1829, Blooming Valley was named for the massive amount of flowers found growing here when it was settled. It was not until 1845, however, that the community began to grow and settle with 20 lots parceled out and sold by former farmer Jeremiah Smith. The borough was incorporated in 1867 and grew rapidly throughout the latter part of the 19th and early 20th centuries. It is shown here in 1913.

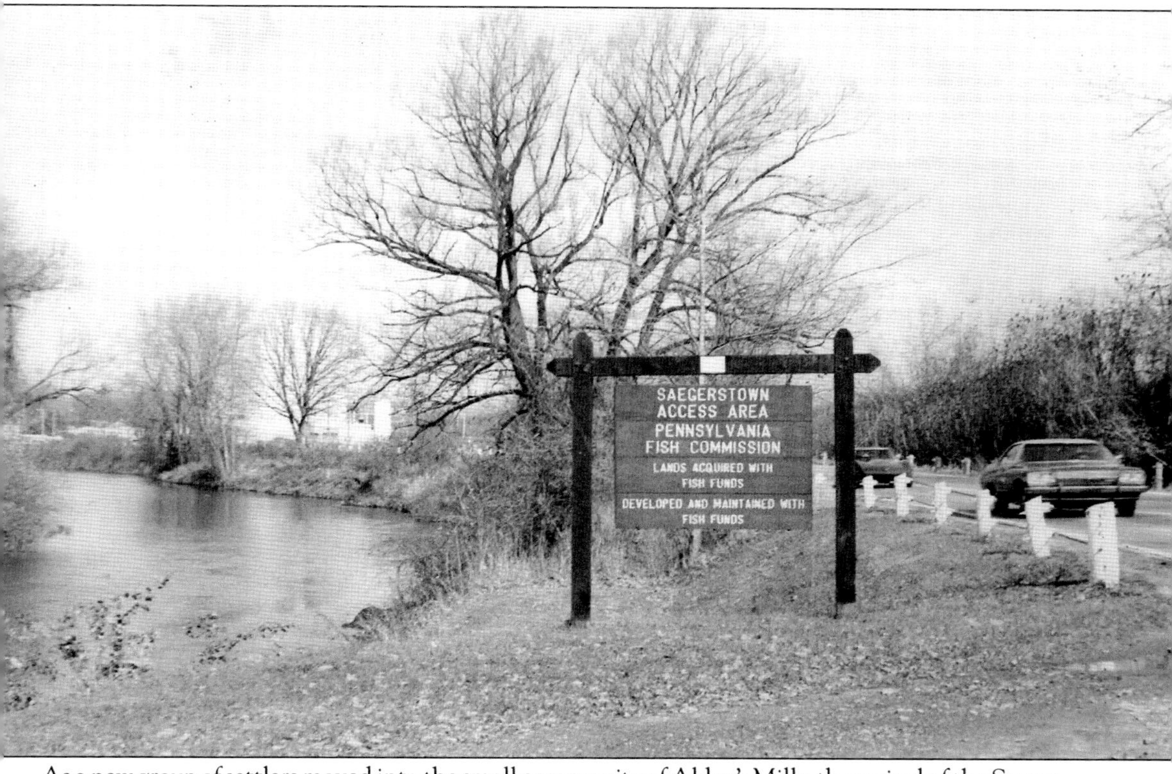

As a new group of settlers moved into the small community of Alden's Mills, the arrival of the Saeger family brought the name Saeger's Town. It eventually became one word, and due to confusion in writing and pronunciation, the people of Saegertown voted to drop the *s*. Some lasting impressions took hold, however, and this mid-1900s sign remained with the original spelling.

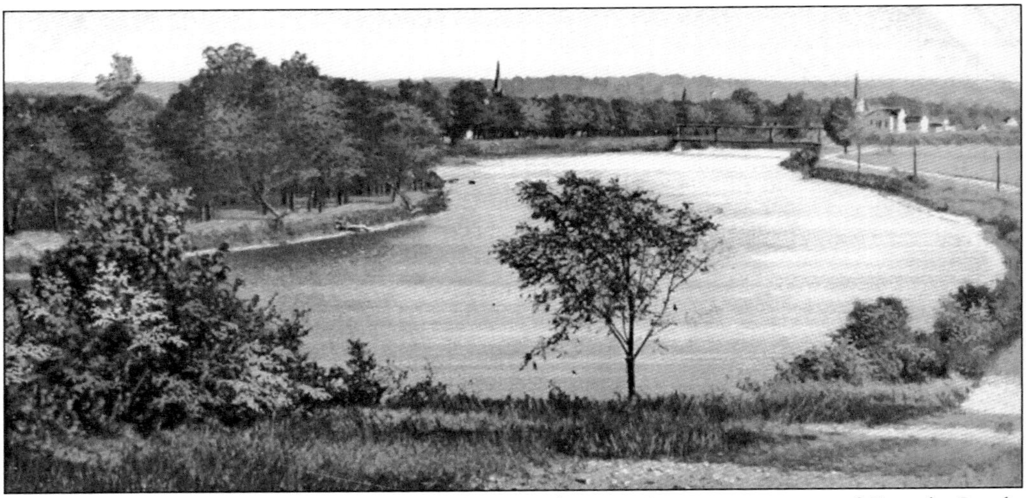

Any book about Saegertown would be lacking without at least one picture of French Creek. In this body of water, an unimaginable amount of history has taken place, including George Washington's travel, economic boom due to water-powered industry, and the growth of the entertainment industry in Saegertown with elegant inns and an exotic animal park. It is a historical monument in its own right—one that cannot be ignored and should not be forgotten.

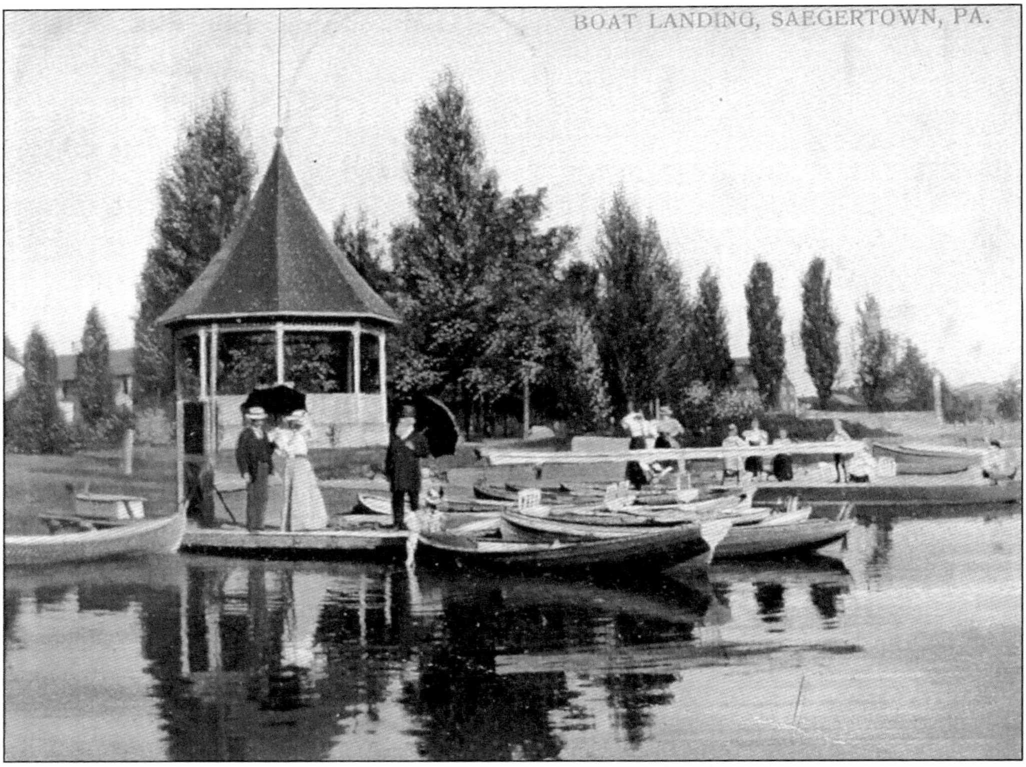

Scenes such as this were commonplace during Saegertown's heyday of inns and tourism. The boat landing seen here was located near the Saegertown Inn and frequented by its guests.

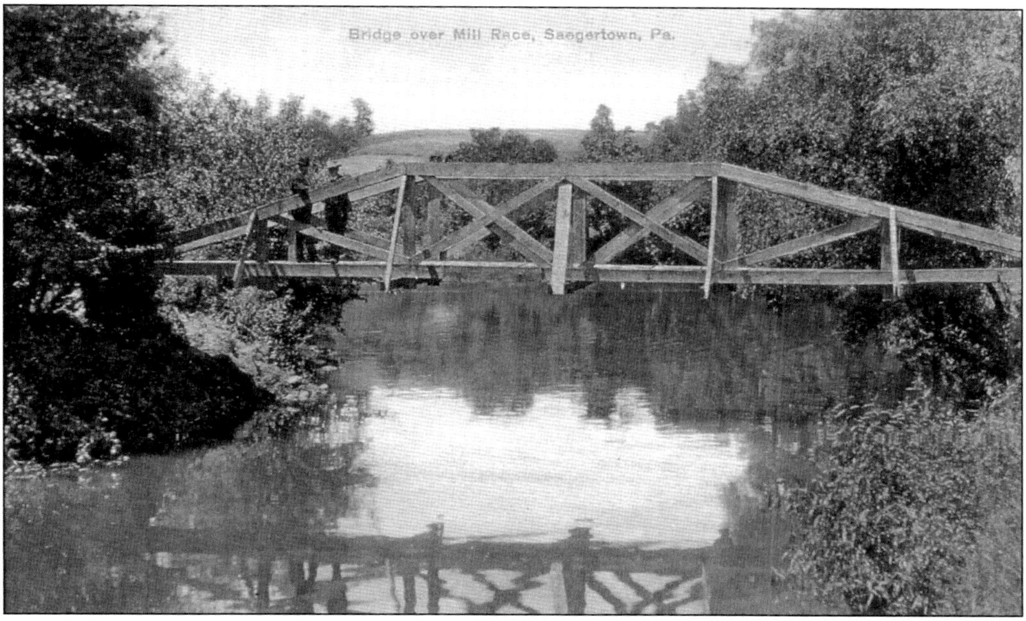

French Creek has many millraces used by mills of all different types in the Saegertown area for waterpower. A bridge over one of these races is shown here.

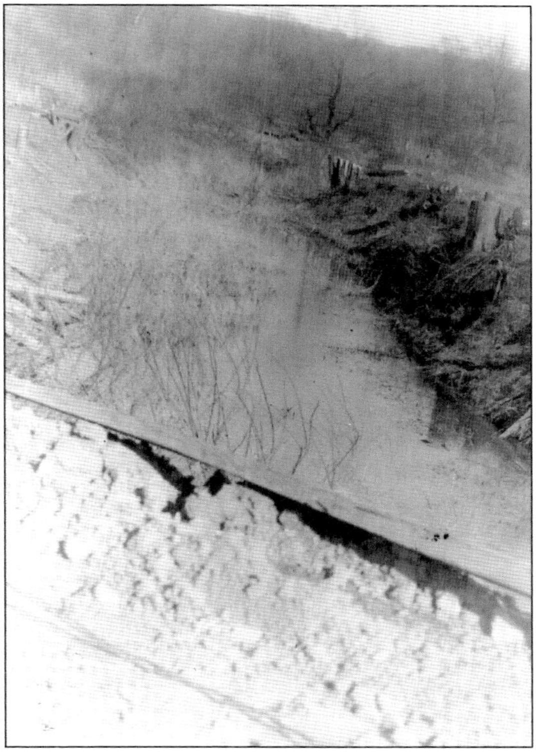

Cussewago Creek, like French Creek, served its local millers with a steady water supply. As of 1876, local businesses taking advantage of the Cussewago included Porter Beebe's handle-turning factory, A. DeForrest's gristmill, and Ed Snyder's bark mill and tannery.

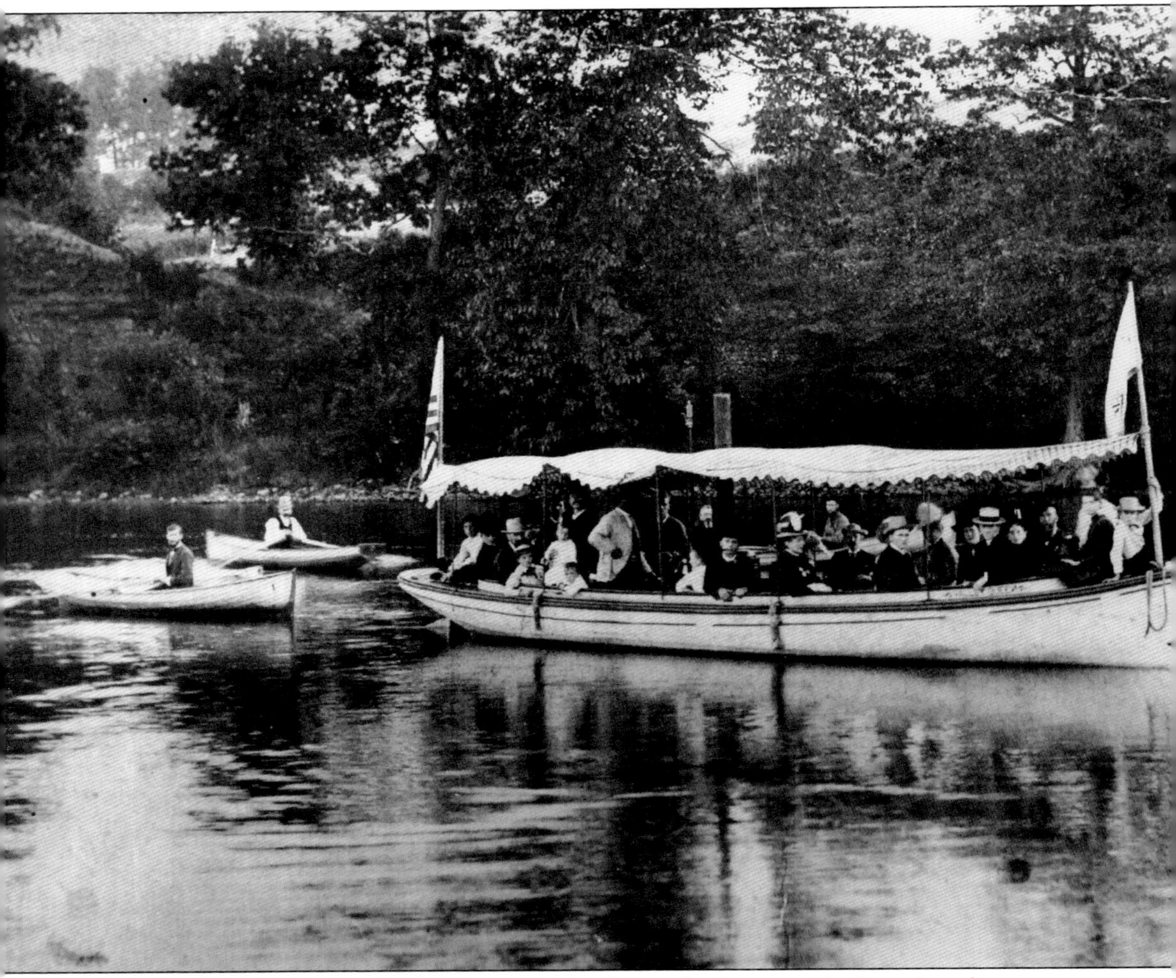

The *Valley Queen* was the first steam-powered boat built to satisfy the mineral water craze in Saegertown during the late 1800s. Capt. Pitt Davis gave residents and visitors rides on French Creek. The fate of the *Valley Queen* was sealed, however, when the popularity of Saegertown's hotels, inns, and healing mineral springs faded just after the beginning of the 20th century.

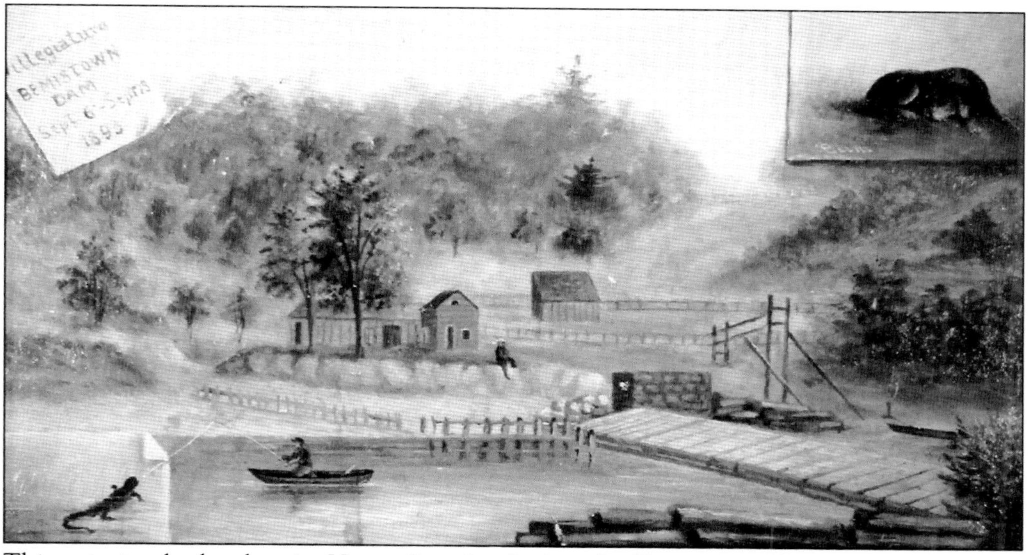

This painting by local artist Henry Satorius depicts the Bemustown Dam in 1893. In 1830, Dr. Daniel Bemus erected a saw- and gristmill between Saegertown and Meadville using waterpower from a dam he built sometime earlier. From here, he floated pine lumber down to Pittsburgh on boats built on-site. An oil mill was placed here soon after and operated for years until a new structure was built to house the facility between 1834 and 1835. It burned, however, on June 13, 1835, before it could be utilized.

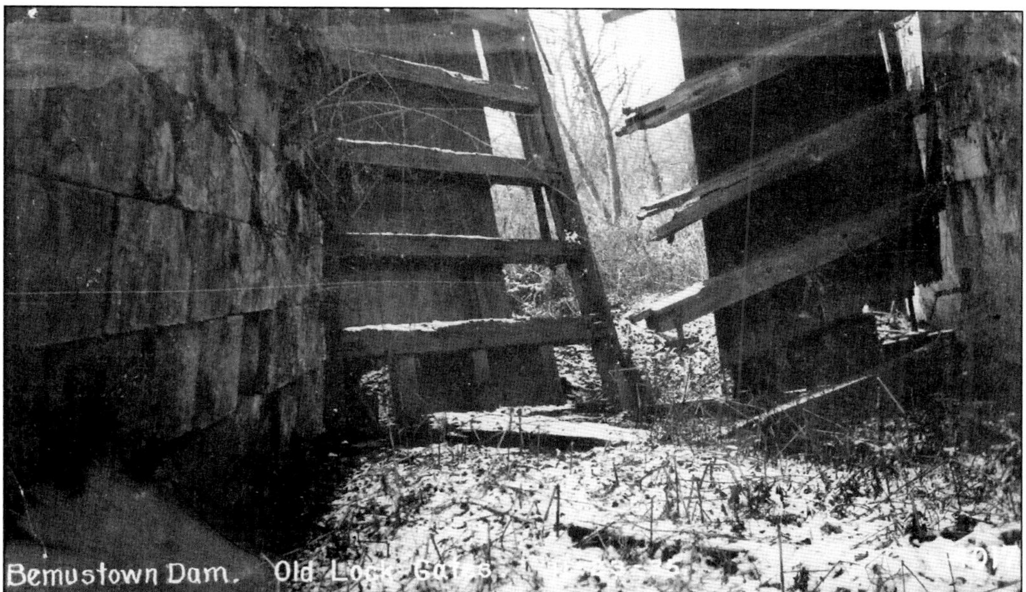

Bemus's saw- and gristmill was destroyed by fire in 1856, and when the feeder to the Beaver and Erie Canal was constructed, it was fed through the dam, turned into public property after the mill's demise. Some of the old lock gates from the dam are shown here.

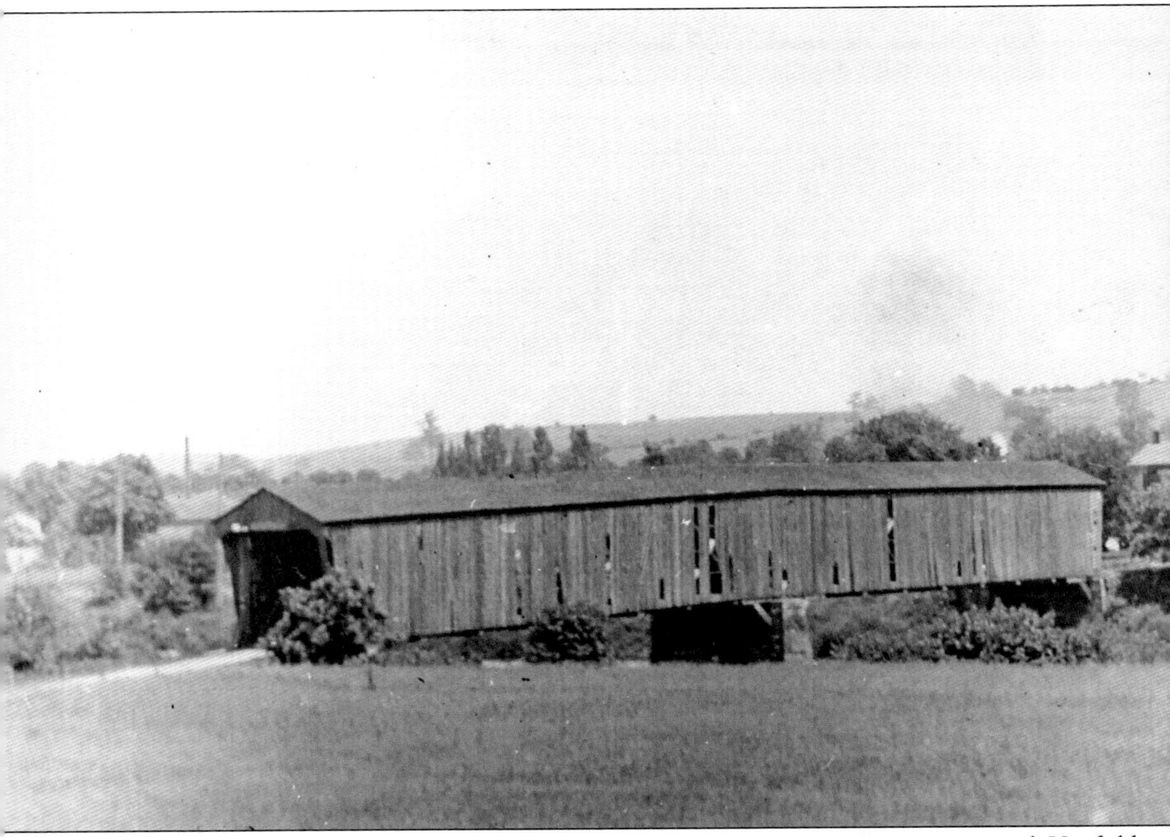

A covered bridge was built during the 19th century to connect Saegertown and Hayfield Township, creating South Street (the short road including the bridge that now connects Main Street and Jordan Drive). In 1902, the bridge was split in half by a house swept off its foundation during one of Saegertown's infamous floods.

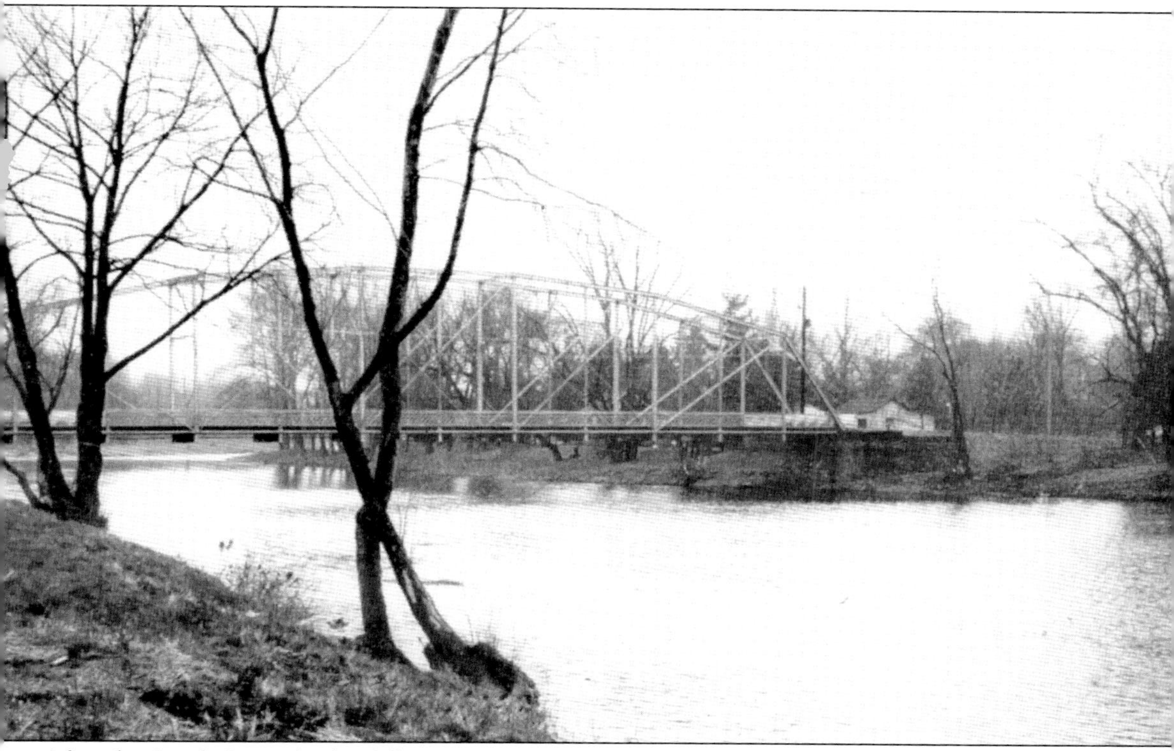

After the South Street bridge fell in 1902, an iron bridge was built in its place. The bridge has been impassible on several occasions, notably the flood of 1913. On March 6 of that year, the bridge had water up to the base of the handrails.

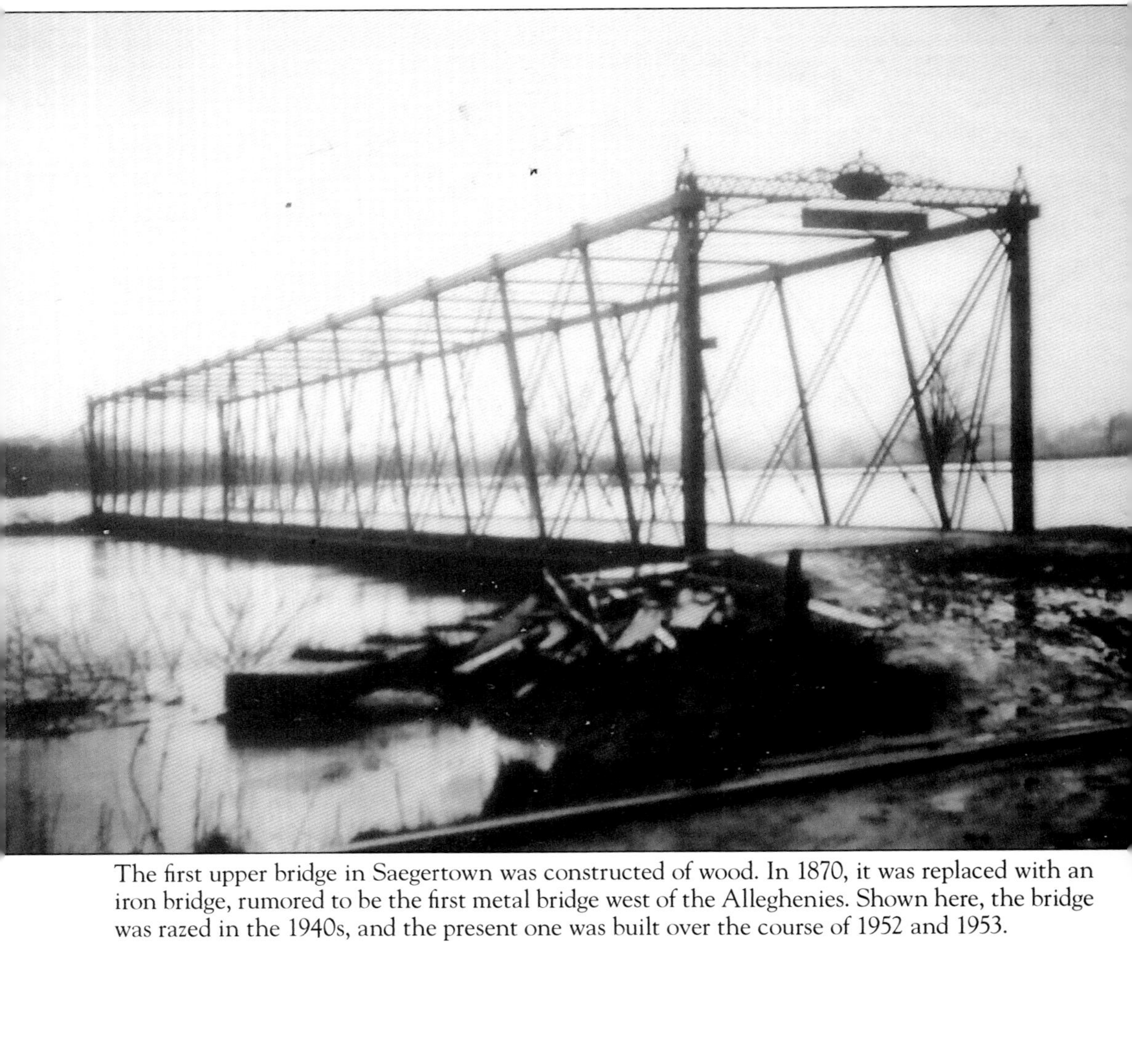

The first upper bridge in Saegertown was constructed of wood. In 1870, it was replaced with an iron bridge, rumored to be the first metal bridge west of the Alleghenies. Shown here, the bridge was razed in the 1940s, and the present one was built over the course of 1952 and 1953.

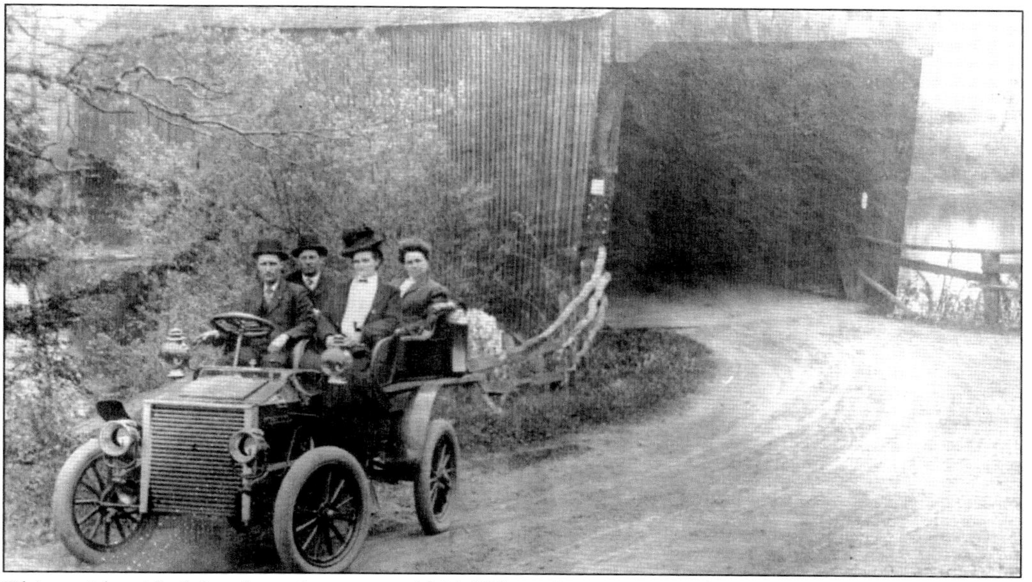

This unidentified family is driving its 1904 White Steamer over the McGuffingtown bridge on May 14, 1908. In the days without modern entertainment, the era of the Sunday drive was in full swing, allowing families to sightsee and spend time together after church. The bridge shown above was torn down a year later and replaced with an iron bridge. That bridge is shown below in 1976.

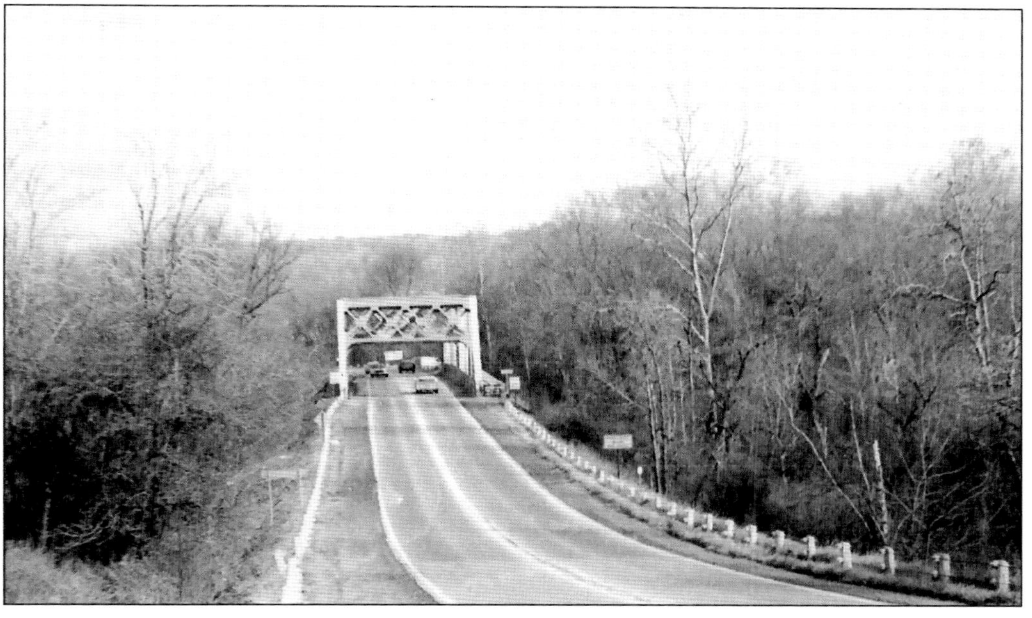

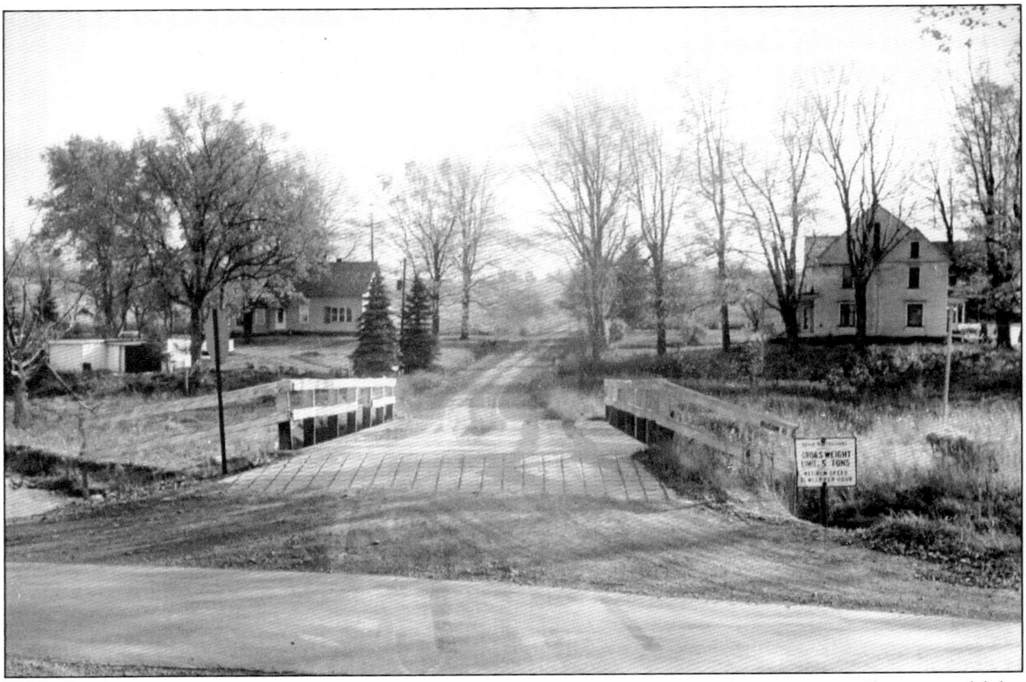

Rural bridges such as these grace creeks and tributaries all over the county. These could be places for local children to go swimming, for fishing from the bridge, or just another scenic place to enjoy when traveling. Miller Bridge is seen above with Stulls Bridge seen below. These metal and concrete bridges were probably once wood, being replaced as horse and buggies faded into cars and trucks. Both shown here were located in the Woodcock Reservoir area.

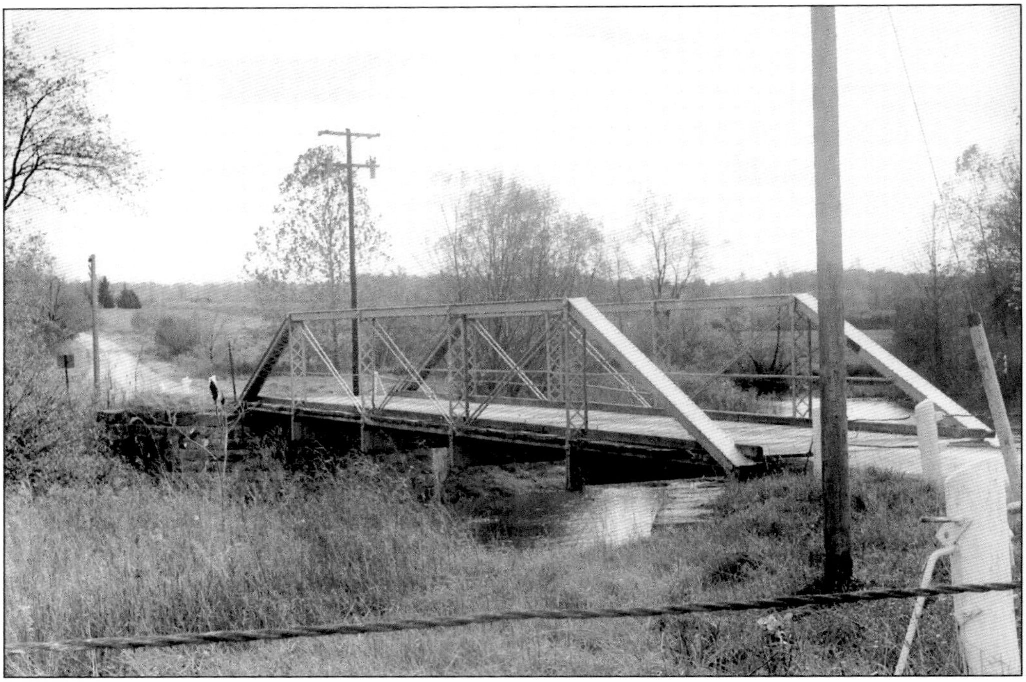

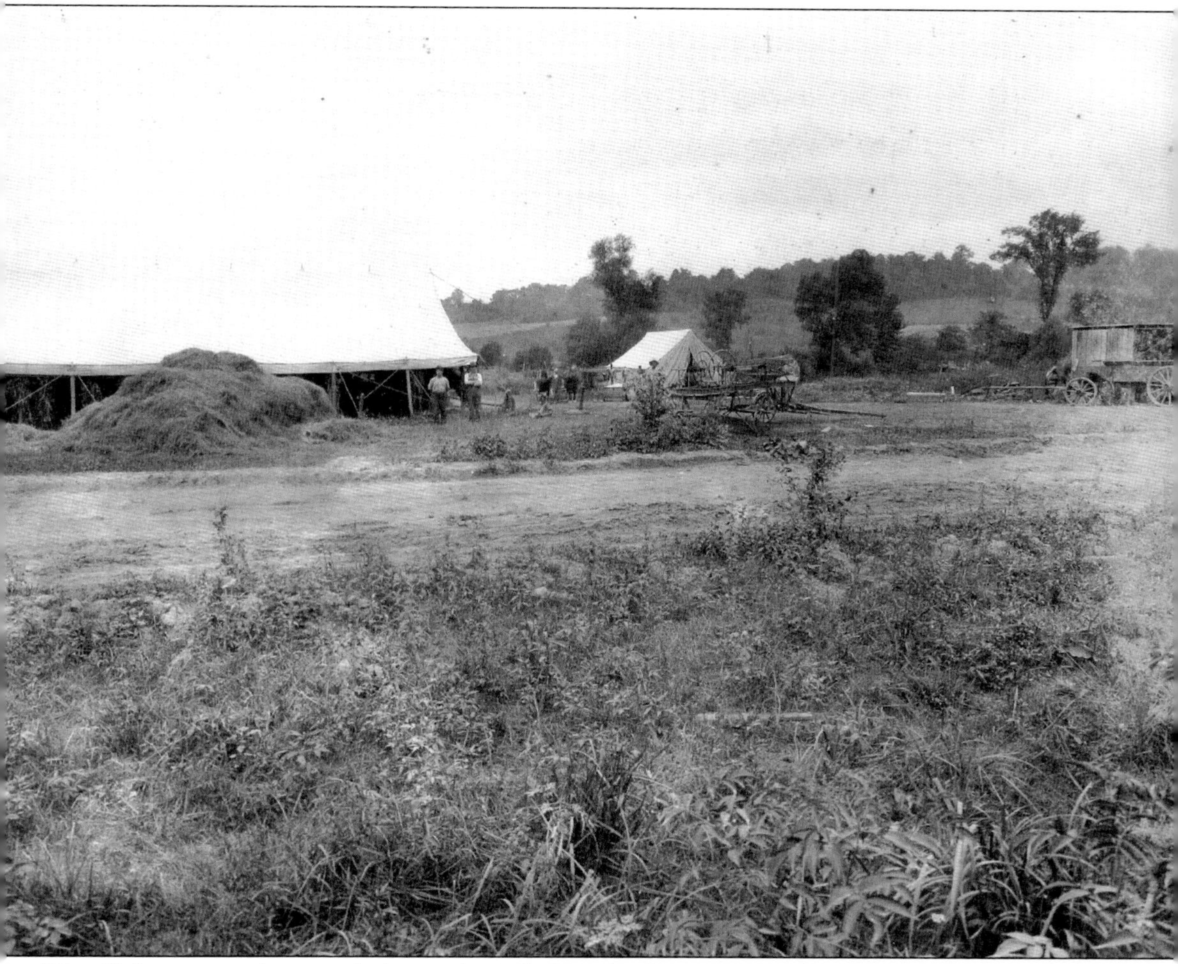

This 19th-century photograph shows what is believed to be some sort of construction team with machinery and tents. The photograph is labeled "Woodcock Bridge."

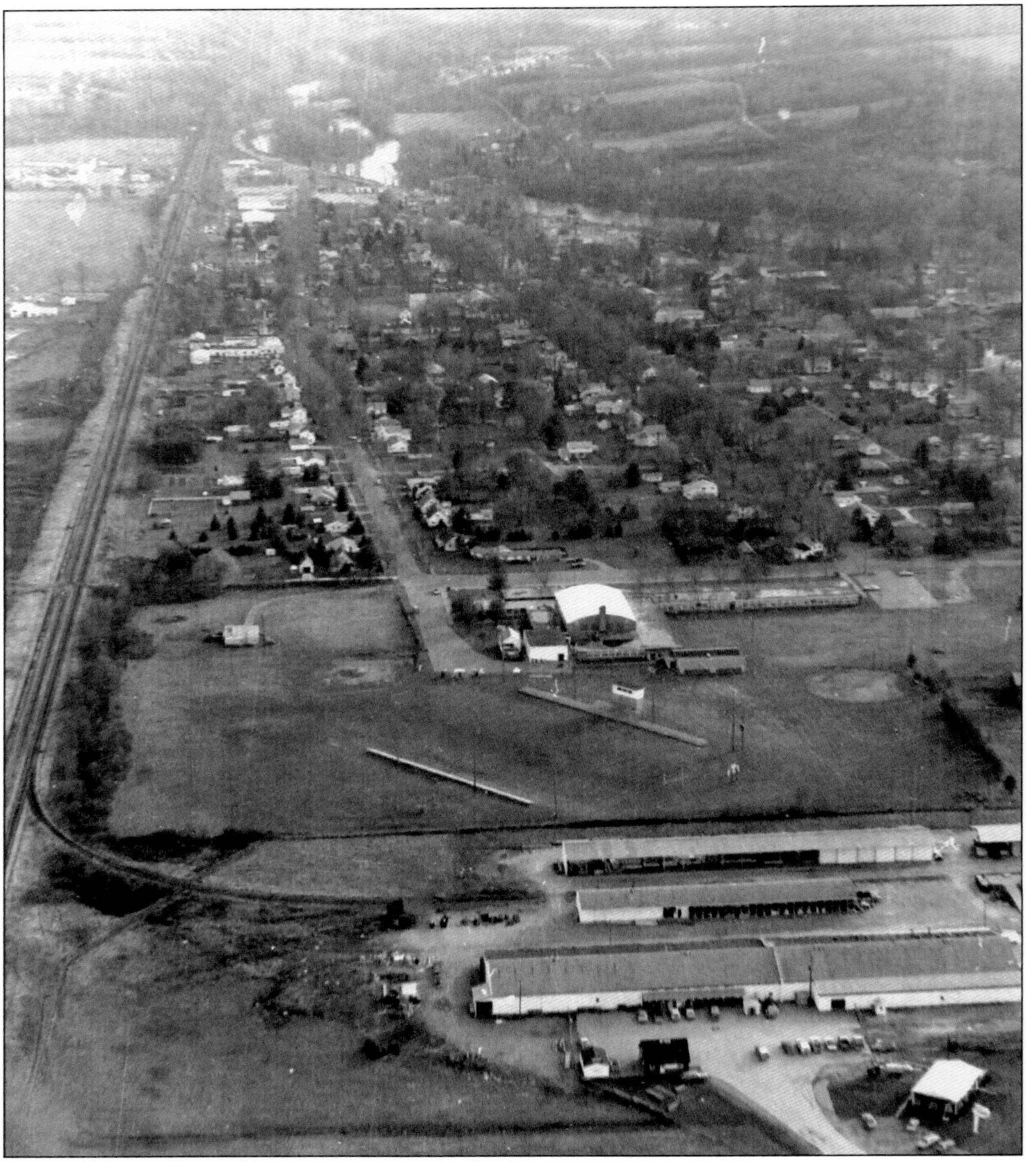

Saegertown is shown here by aerial view in 1976. Looking south, Saegertown Middle School can be seen with its surrounding sports fields and the railroad tracks on the left-hand side. A winding French Creek can be seen in the background. Grant Street, running to the south starting at the school, is parallel to the railroad tracks.

Two

Neighbors, Faces, and Places

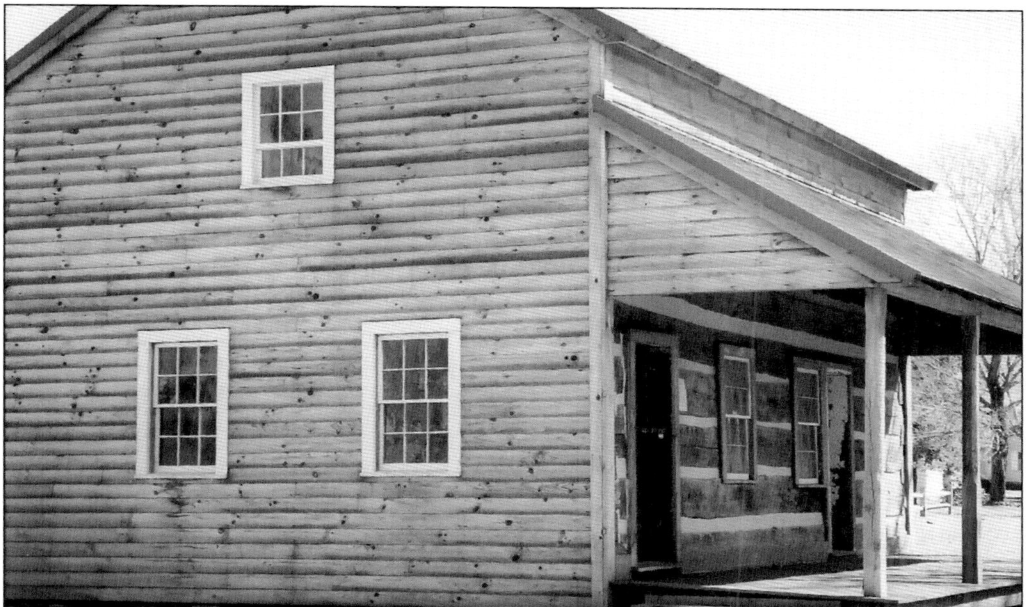

Patrick McGill and his brother Arthur sailed to the Untied States in 1770, docking at Baltimore Harbor. Settling in southeastern Pennsylvania for a time, they ventured to the area now known as Saegertown in the fall of 1792. Patrick and his family built this log cabin in 1802, making it the oldest house currently standing in Crawford County. It has been a constant dwelling on Main Street, being used through the time it was rehabilitated to its former glory. This contemporary photograph shows the house with clapboard siding as it had in the mid-1800s. This was a necessity to preserve the original logs as seen on the front porch.

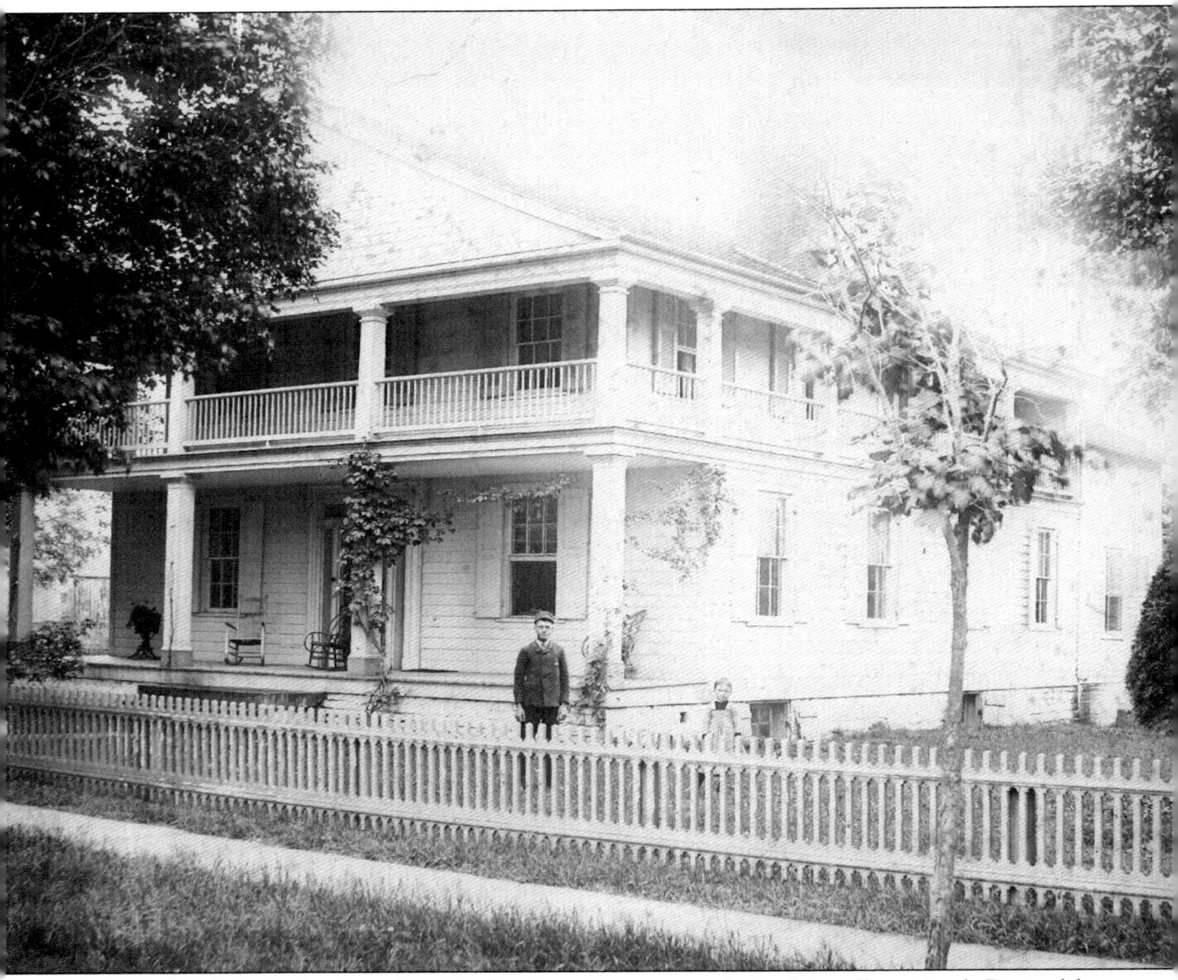

Edward Saeger, the first elected official in Saegertown, built this yellow Greek Revival house that stands as a local landmark in Saegertown in 1842. He left the house to his daughter Abigail and her husband, Dr. Henry Smith, when he became elderly. He lived with the family until his death. Both Henry and his son Rodney received patients in the home (Rodney became a doctor as well) and used part of the house as an office and pharmacy. The Saeger lineage remained in the house until the early 1960s when the last of the Smiths passed away.

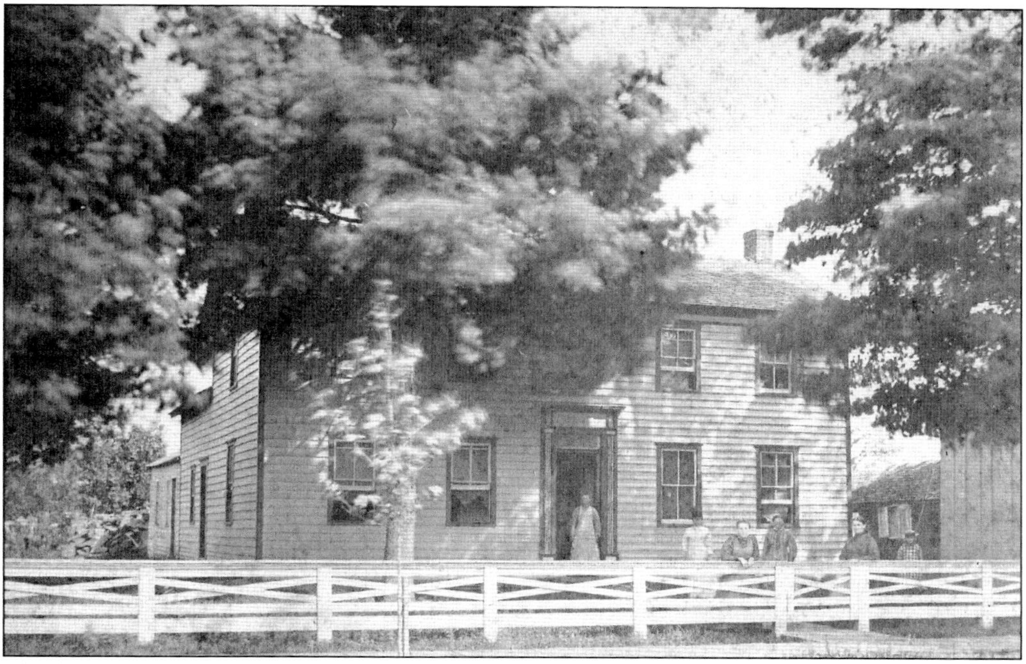

The house shown here is believed to have been built by Wilson Hunter during the mid-1800s, around the time he set up shop as the local undertaker and furniture manufacturer in Saegertown. The house is located on Euclid Avenue.

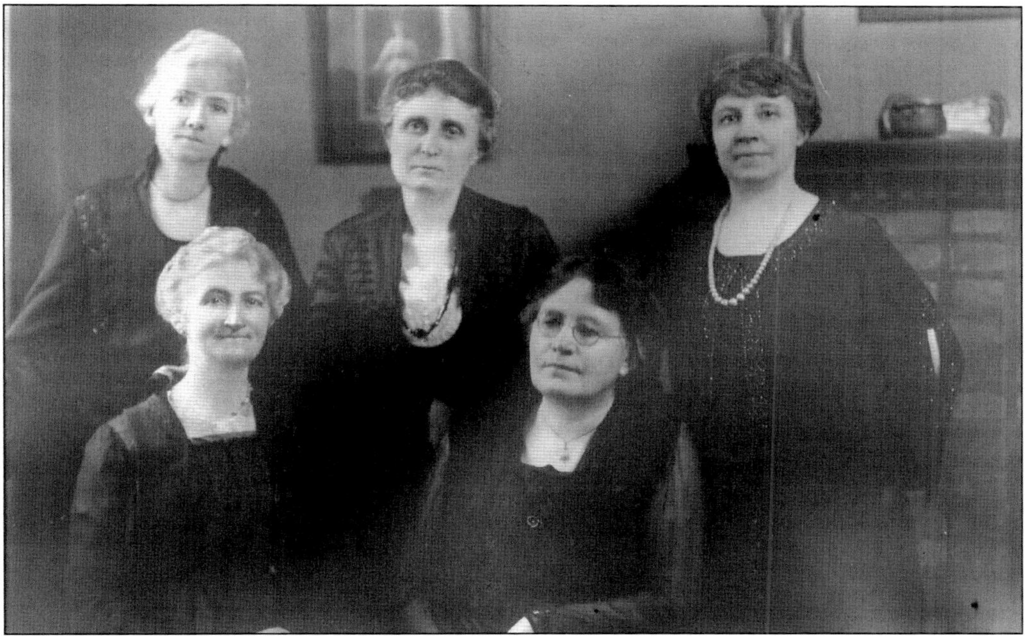

This photograph, taken in the early 1900s, shows five prominent first cousins in Saegertown. Shown from left to right are (first row) Lizzie McGill Mook and Ann Beck Saeger; (second row) Annie McGill Patterson, Mae Floyd Saeger, and Mildred Floyd Davis (wife of Pitt Davis, captain of the *Valley Queen*).

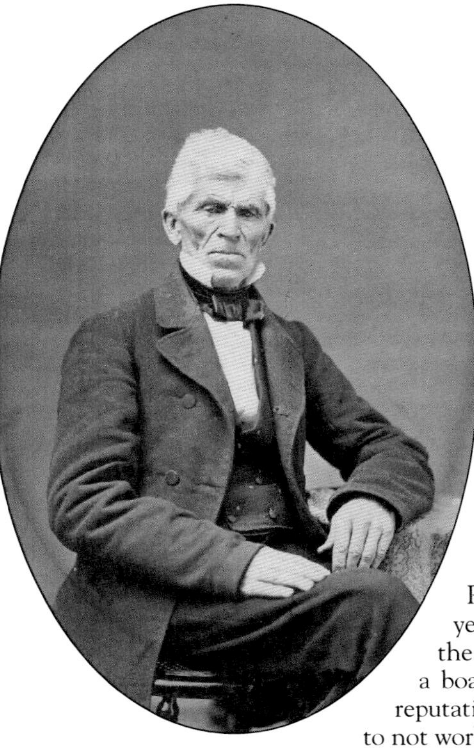

Joseph Dickson and Mary Frazier Dickson were married at the home of her parents on August 13, 1818, by Rev. Timothy Alden. She had "a fair face and pleasing ways," according to a family history read on Joseph Dickson's birthday. They began housekeeping in a house near the mill that Joseph helped his father build in 1815. In his lifetime, he also built one of the first bridges in the area in 1819 and a dam opposite his mill. In 1838, he sold his waterpower business and moved to Meadville, leaving for Pittsburgh and the lumber business the following year and returning less than a year afterward. When the Erie and Pittsburgh Canal opened, he bought a boat and went into the carrying trade. Having the reputation of an honest man, he was one of the few known to not work his men or mules on Sundays.

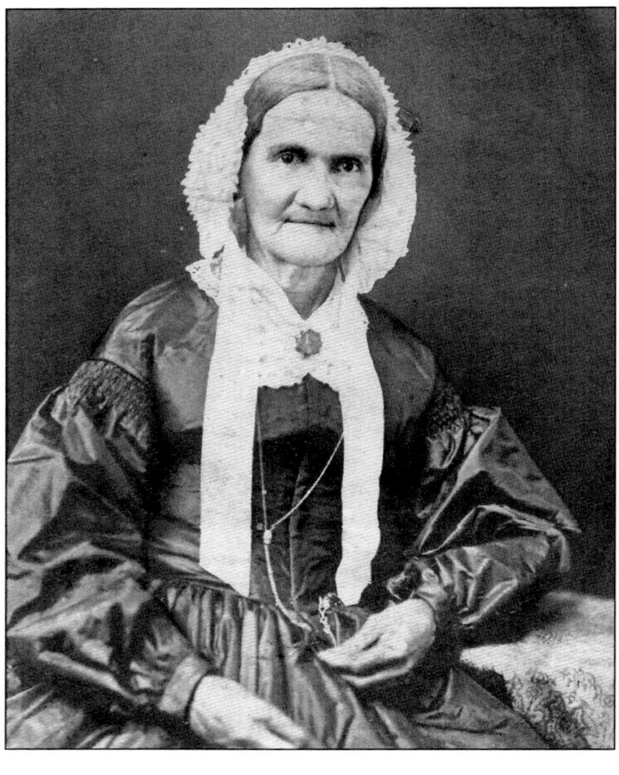

Joseph Dickson's father was an early settler in Crawford County in the area where Woodcock Lake is today. The Dicksons lived in the house shown and owned and operated both a sawmill and a gristmill for many years across the street from their home. Among their regular customers, abolitionist John Brown traded flour and ground feed for tanned hides from his tannery in New Richmond Township.

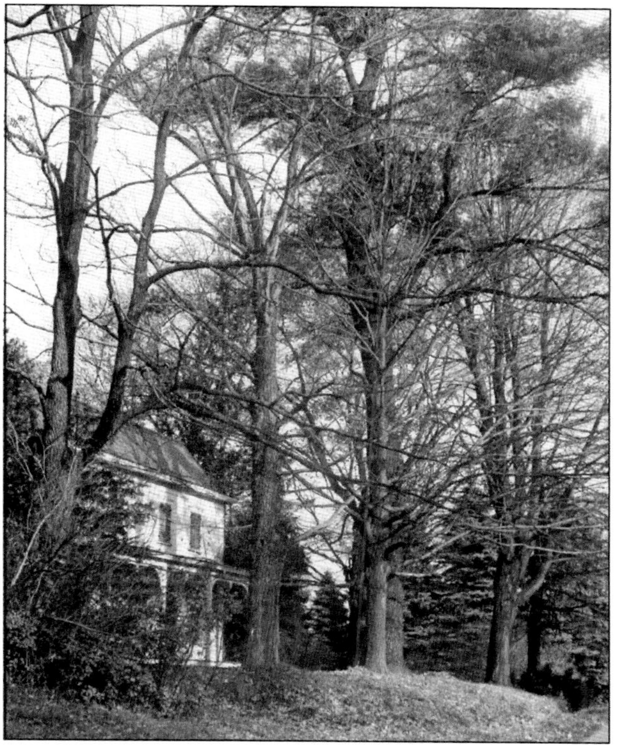

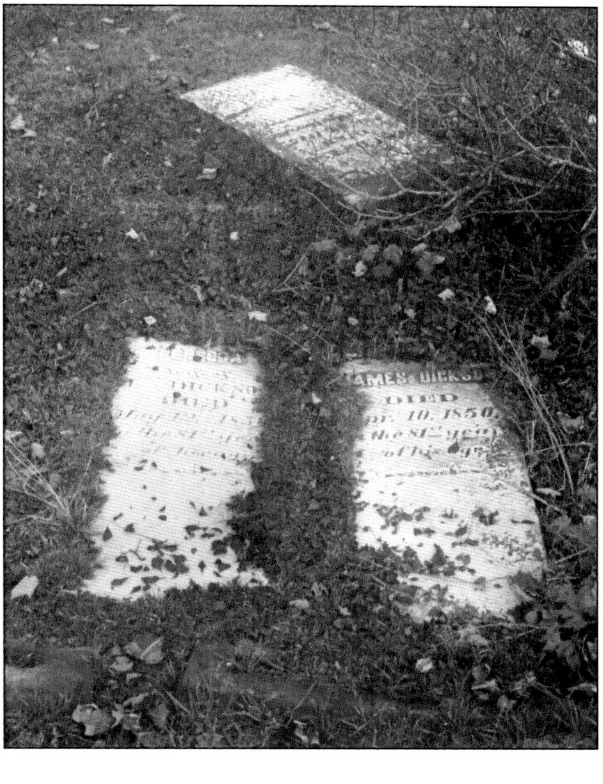

The Dickson family cemetery is shown here. James and Rebecca Dickson both passed away in the 1850s. The cemetery was evicted and moved before Woodcock Dam was finished and the lake was filled.

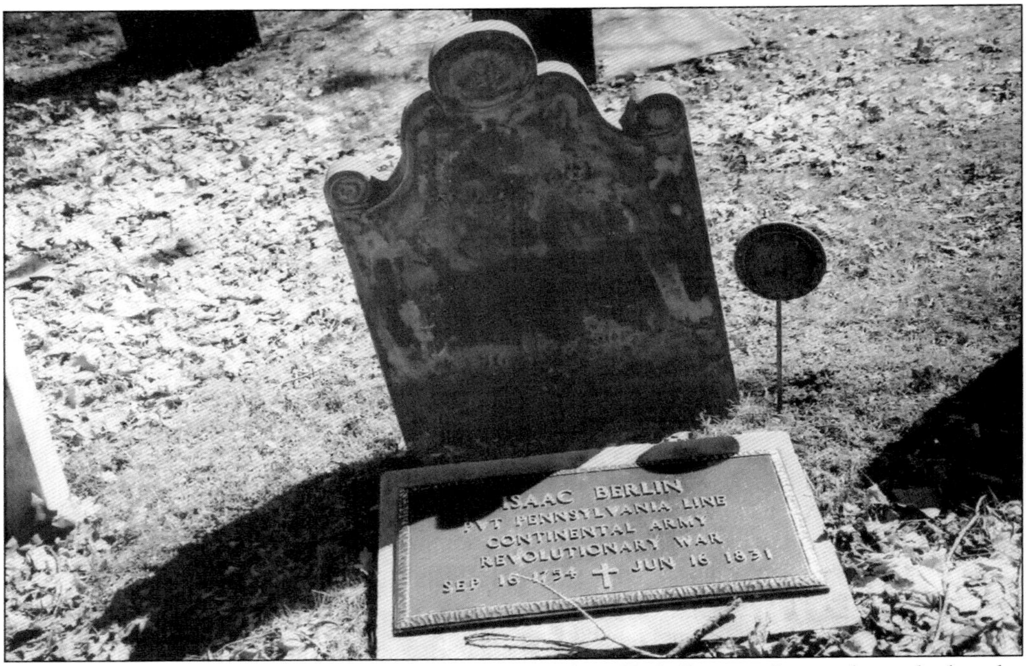

Isaac Berlin was a transplant in the Peiffertown area from York County during the early decades of the 19th century. He was a rifle maker and a very good one; it was a trade that could not have taken place in Crawford County at a better time. Berlin manufactured rifles during the period between 1810 and 1815, and many were used in the local militia during the War of 1812, which his son Israel fought in. A few still survive in the hands of county residents.

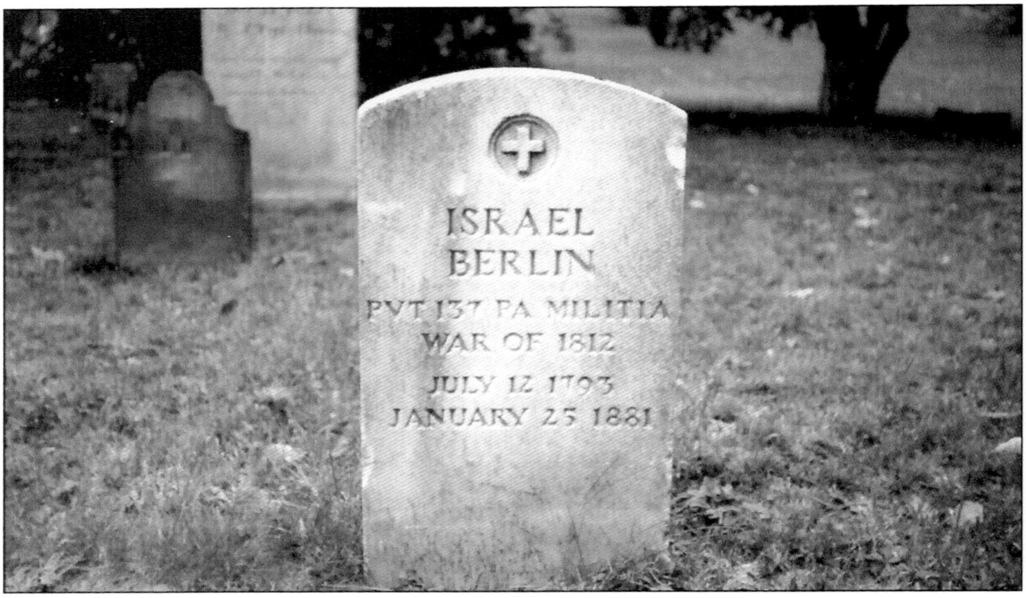

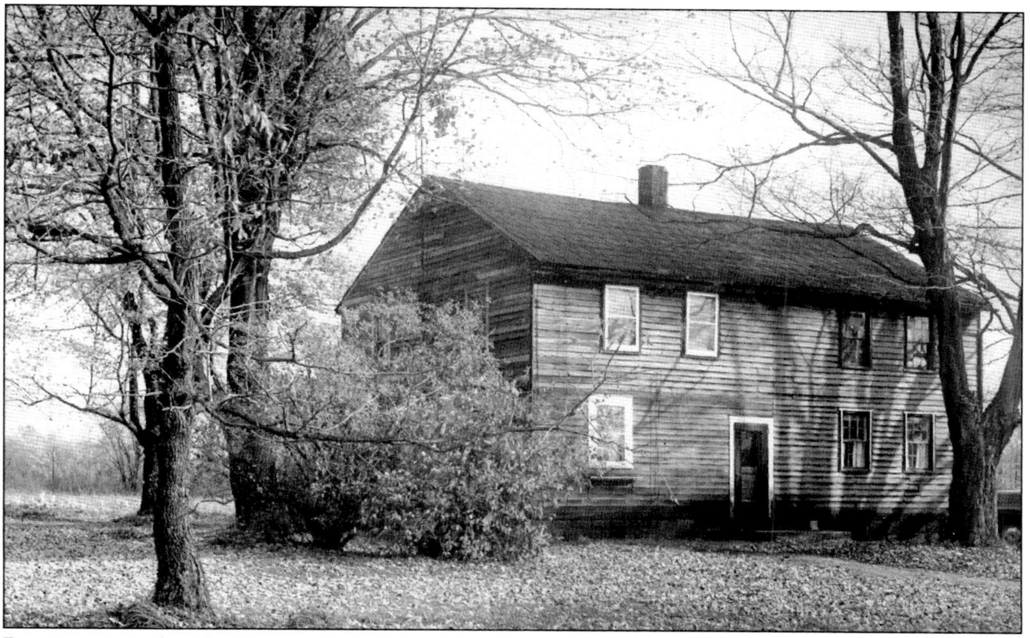

Born in Woodcock Township on November 2, 1806, Samuel B. Long was elected Crawford County sheriff in 1845. He established a post office at his home on December 29, 1869, making him the first postmaster in that area. His daughter Mrs. O. H. P. Dickson held the position until rural free delivery was introduced on May 31, 1901.

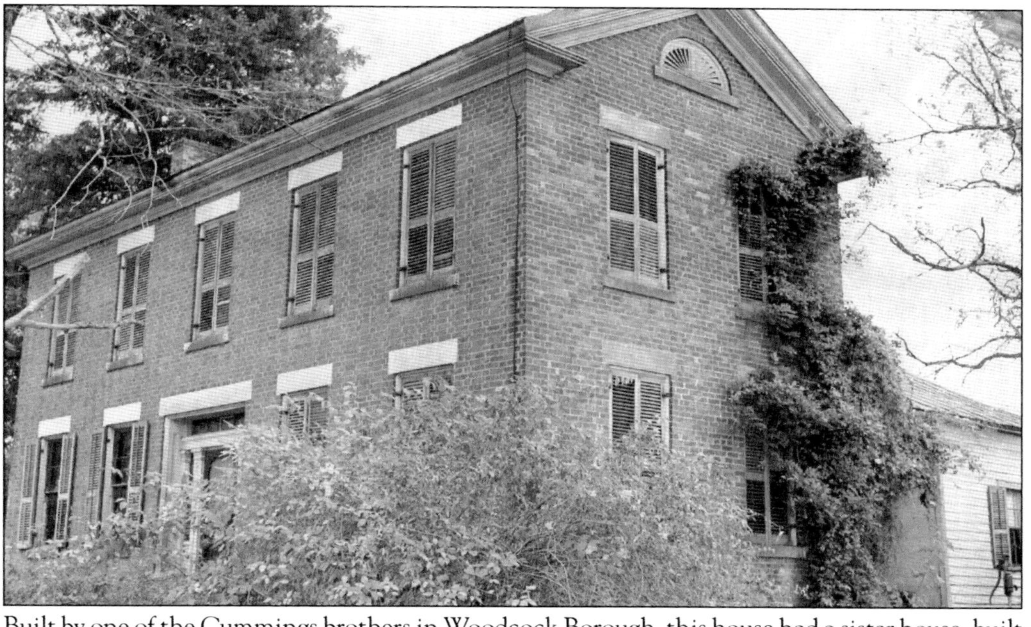

Built by one of the Cummings brothers in Woodcock Borough, this house had a sister house, built by the other brother, across the street exactly identical in appearance. The Cummings family was involved in cheese making in Woodcock, among other things, and was quite profitable at its endeavors. The house shown had an eight-seat brick outhouse built behind it complete with a stove for warmth in the winter months.

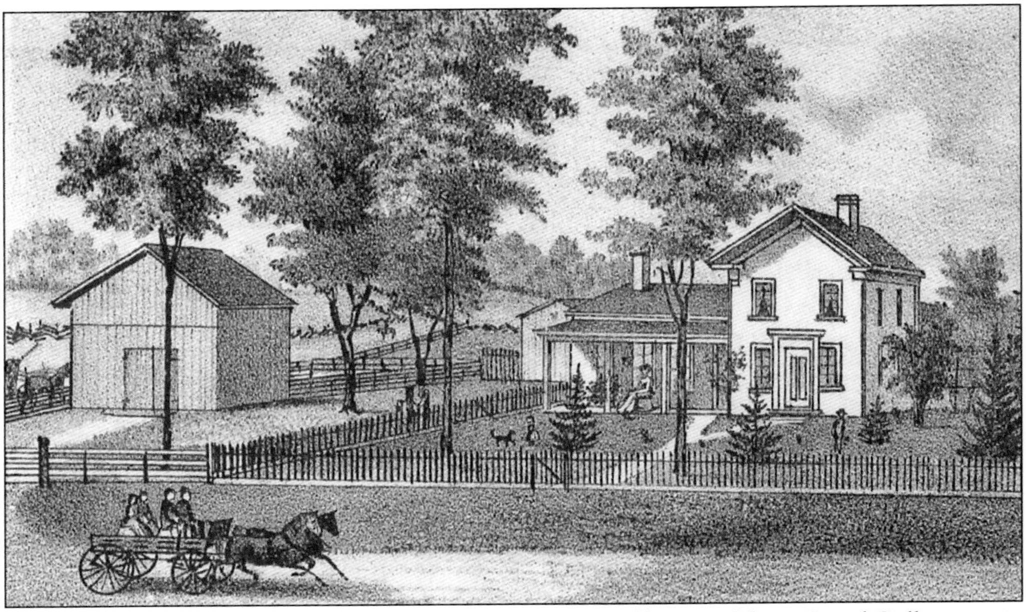

Alonzo Drake bought this farm as well as the Blooming Valley Hotel from David Culbertson in 1866 upon the retirement of Culbertson and his wife. When Blooming Valley was incorporated into a borough in 1867, Drake became one of the first council officers. Little else is found on Drake, although he was known to be farming the same area as of when this lithograph was commissioned in 1876.

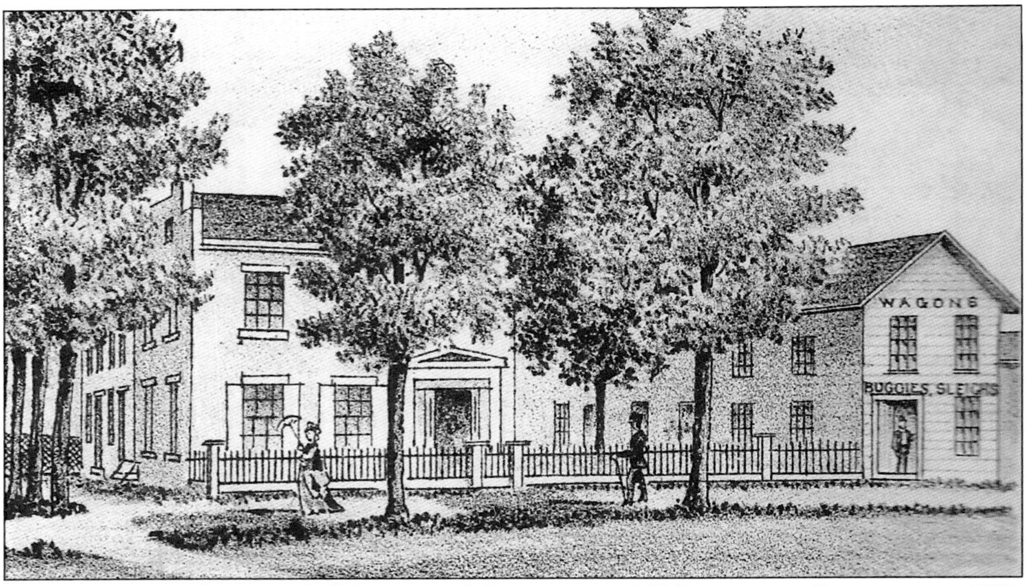

B. G. David moved to Crawford County with his parents in 1825, moving to Saegertown in 1832. He started his career as a miller with his father before learning the wagon making trade from local man Cyrus Townsend and practicing under this apprenticeship in both Meadville and Pittsburgh. He returned to Saegertown in 1842 and took up this trade. A vocal advocate of the temperance movement, David was elected to the Pennsylvania legislature in 1849 and as county commissioner in 1865. Under his term as commissioner, the Crawford County Courthouse was built.

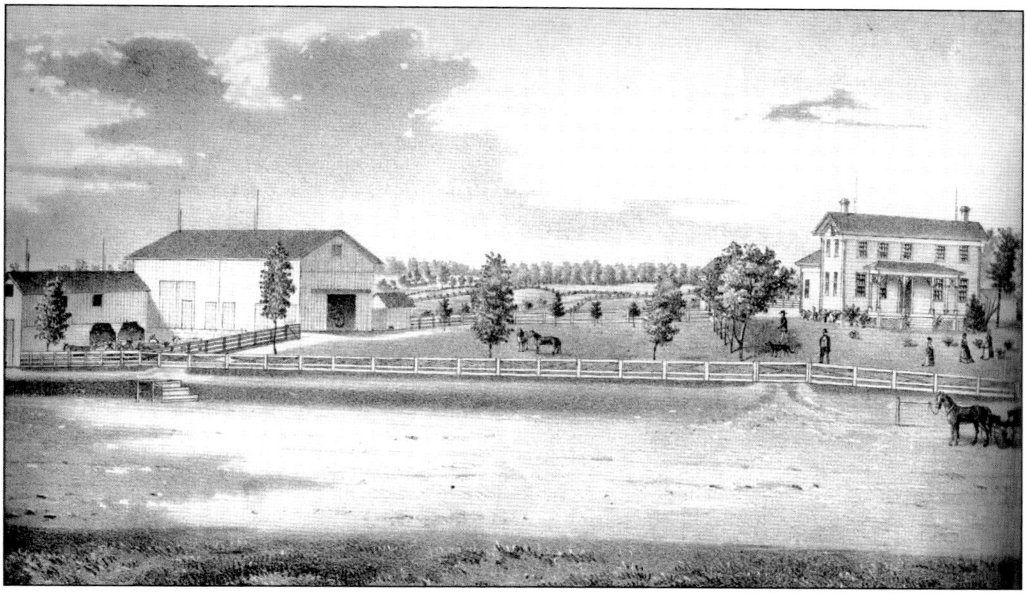

Levi Peters was born in what later became Hayfield Township on January 16, 1821. He married Eliza Lienhart on January 16, 1842, having seven children through this marriage. He was supervisor and school director of Hayfield Township at one time.

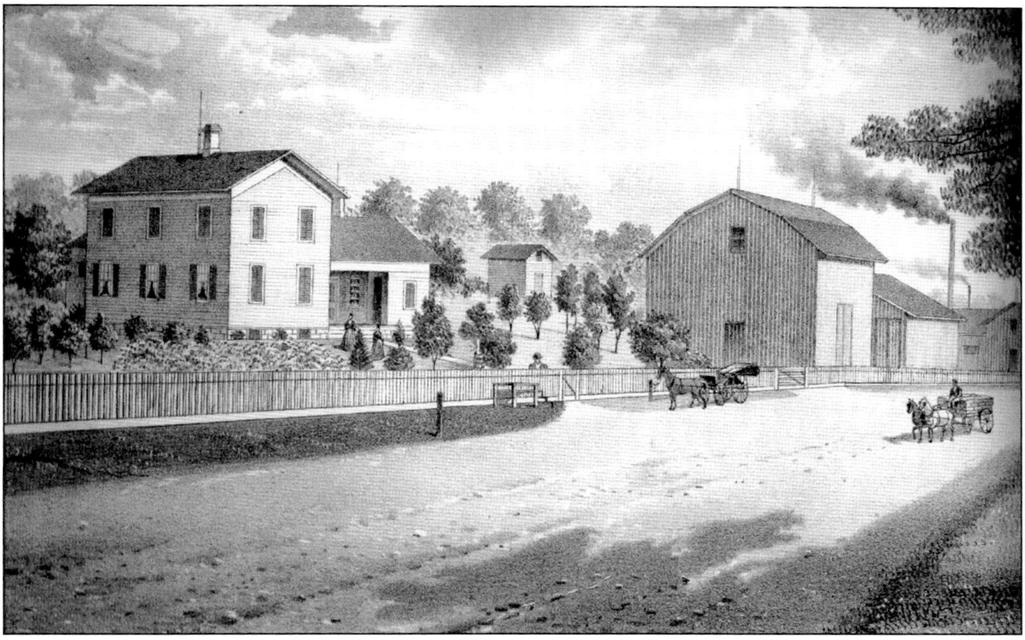

William V. Morse came to Crawford County in 1837, moving several times and eventually settling in Hayfield Township, not far from Little's Corners. He built a sawmill in 1858 for the manufacture of lumber and shingles. Morse was married twice, first to Margaret Brown Matthews in 1838 and then to Caroline McKelvey on June 16, 1854.

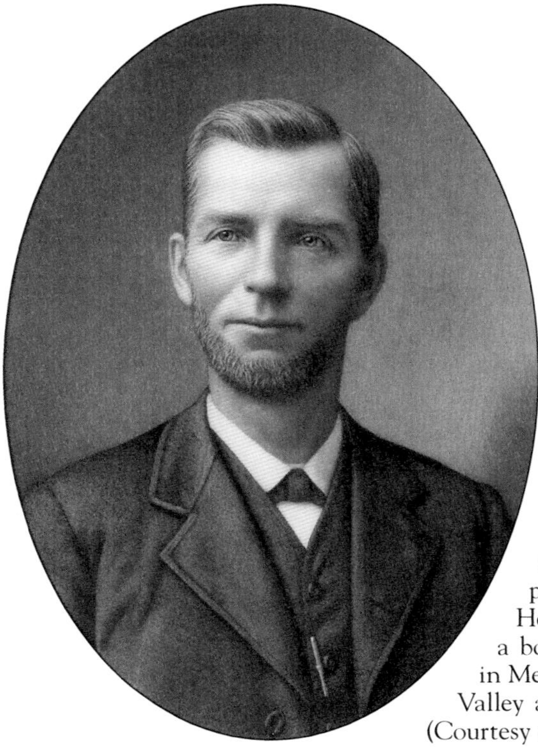

Francis C. Waid was born on April 23, 1833. His wife, Eliza C. Masiker, was slightly older, being born on April 13, 1832. Francis was Blooming Valley's first teacher. He was also a farmer and autobiographer. He wrote three books on his life called his first, second, and third "Souvenir." According to the postscript in his final memoir, Francis passed away at age 59 on February 20, 1892. He met his fate while kneeling down preparing a box of his latest book to distribute to friends in Meadville. Documenting much of the Blooming Valley area to paper, he was an author to the end. (Courtesy of Francis C. Waid's Third Souvenir.)

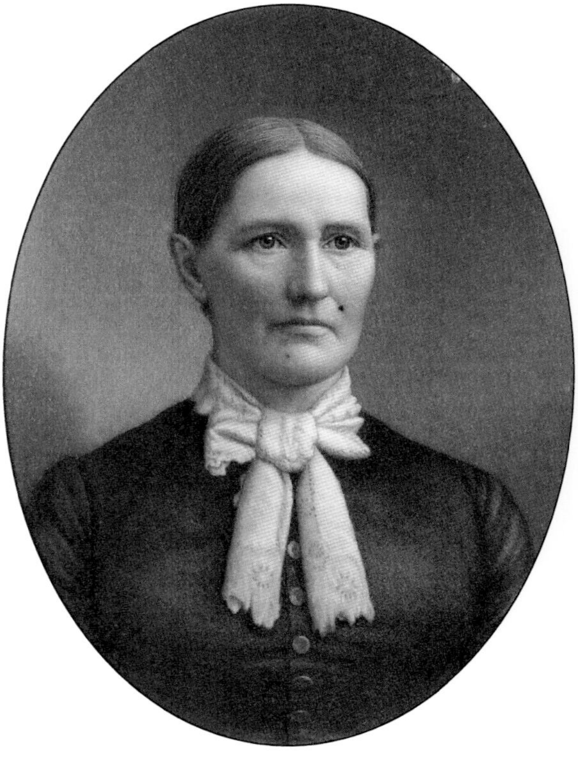

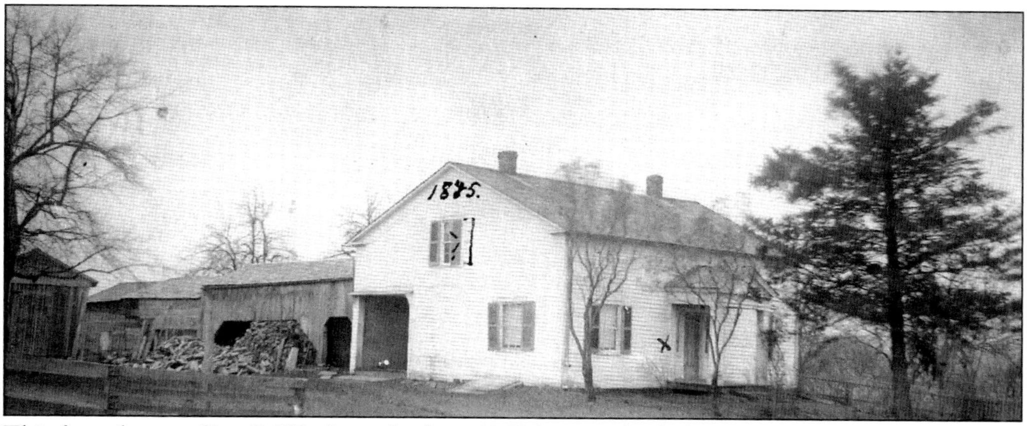

This farm, home of Ira C. Waid, was built in 1845. Ira was the father of Francis C. Waid. Francis's son Guinnip Waid lived in his grandfather's house after his death. This photograph was taken on April 15, 1886.

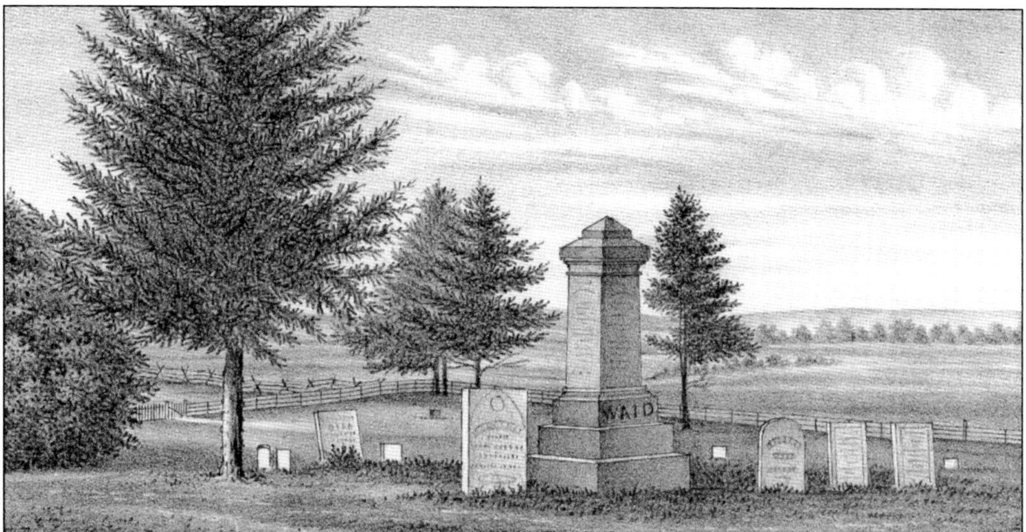

The tall monument pictured, erected on August 13, 1884, and a twin monument put in place on December 11, 1888, were a tribute to Eliza C. Waid and many others in the Waid family. This image of the Waid lot, although created for Francis C. Waid's Third Souvenir, is a different, unpublished version of the one seen in the volume.

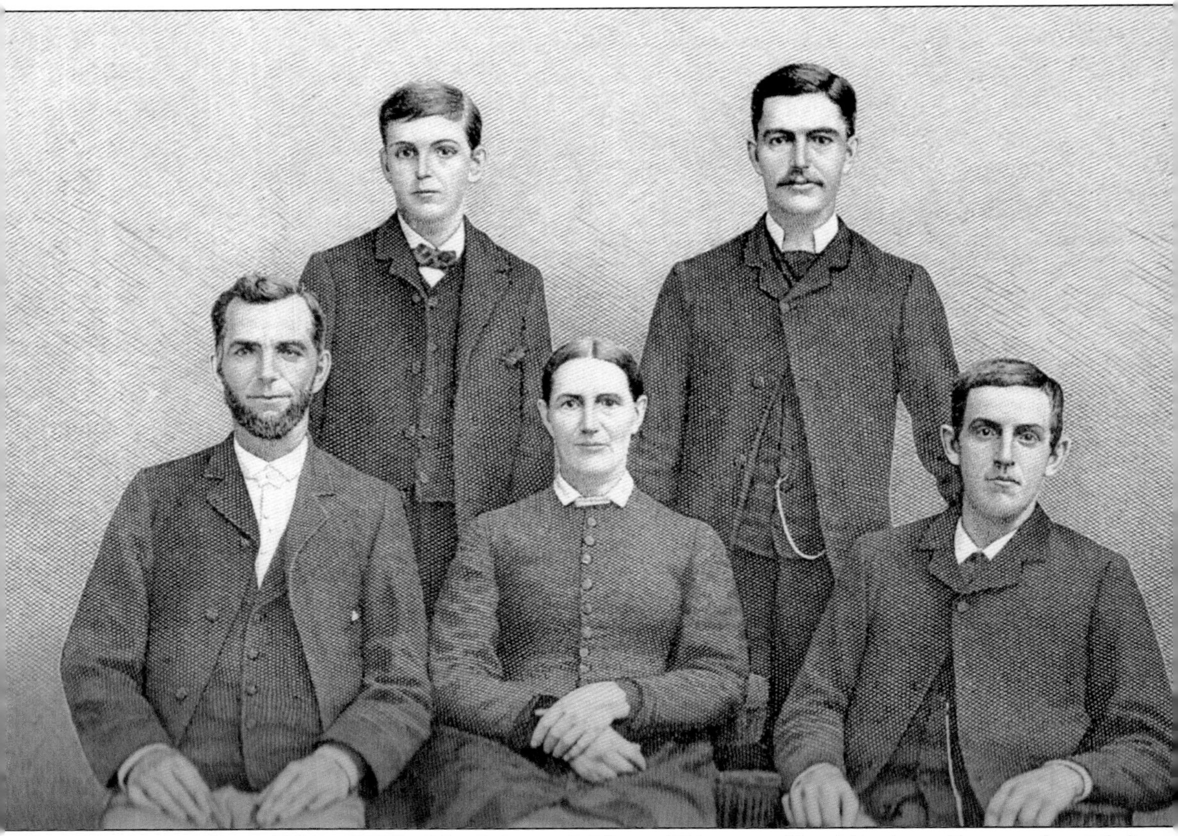

Francis C. and Eliza C. Waid had three children. Oldest son Franklin (standing on the right) was born on January 5, 1855. Their second child, Guinnip, who is sitting next to his mother, was born on September 22, 1859, and their youngest child, Fred, was born on March 6, 1868. (Courtesy of Francis C. Waid's Third Souvenir.)

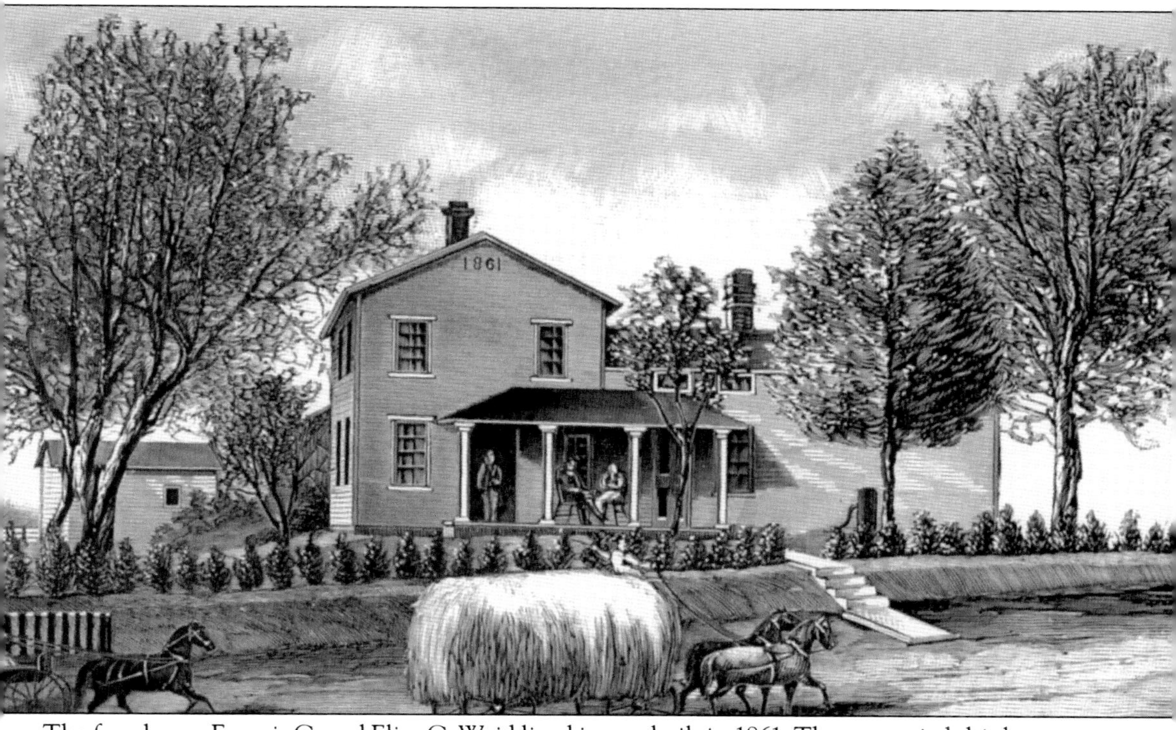

The farmhouse Francis C. and Eliza C. Waid lived in was built in 1861. They occupied this home until 1889. (Courtesy of Francis C. Waid's Third Souvenir.)

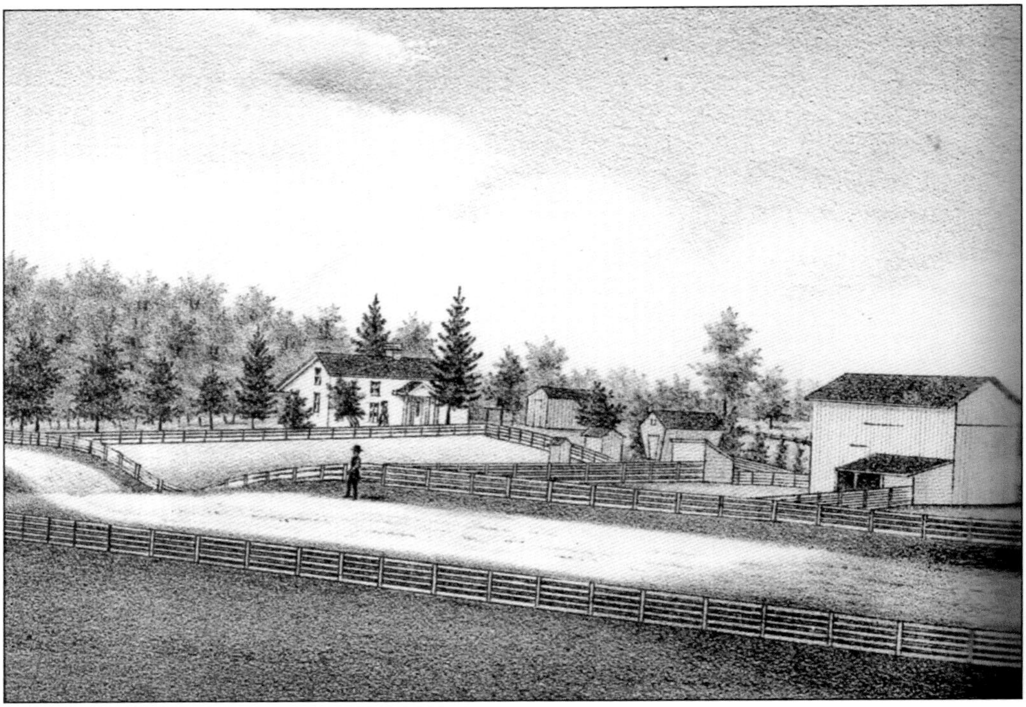

Jacob Brookhouser's farm was located at the top of the hill going into Saegertown; the hill still holds his name to this day. He and his wife were some of the earliest members of the Methodist congregation started in Saegertown in 1839. He lived here in Hayfield Township until his death on September 26, 1884, at 81 years.

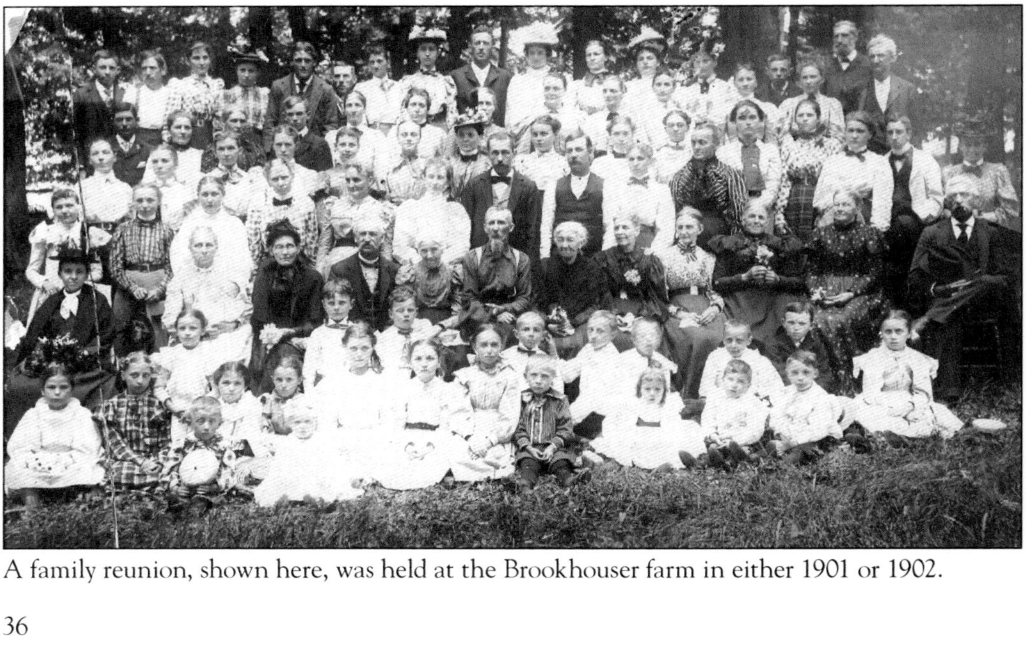

A family reunion, shown here, was held at the Brookhouser farm in either 1901 or 1902.

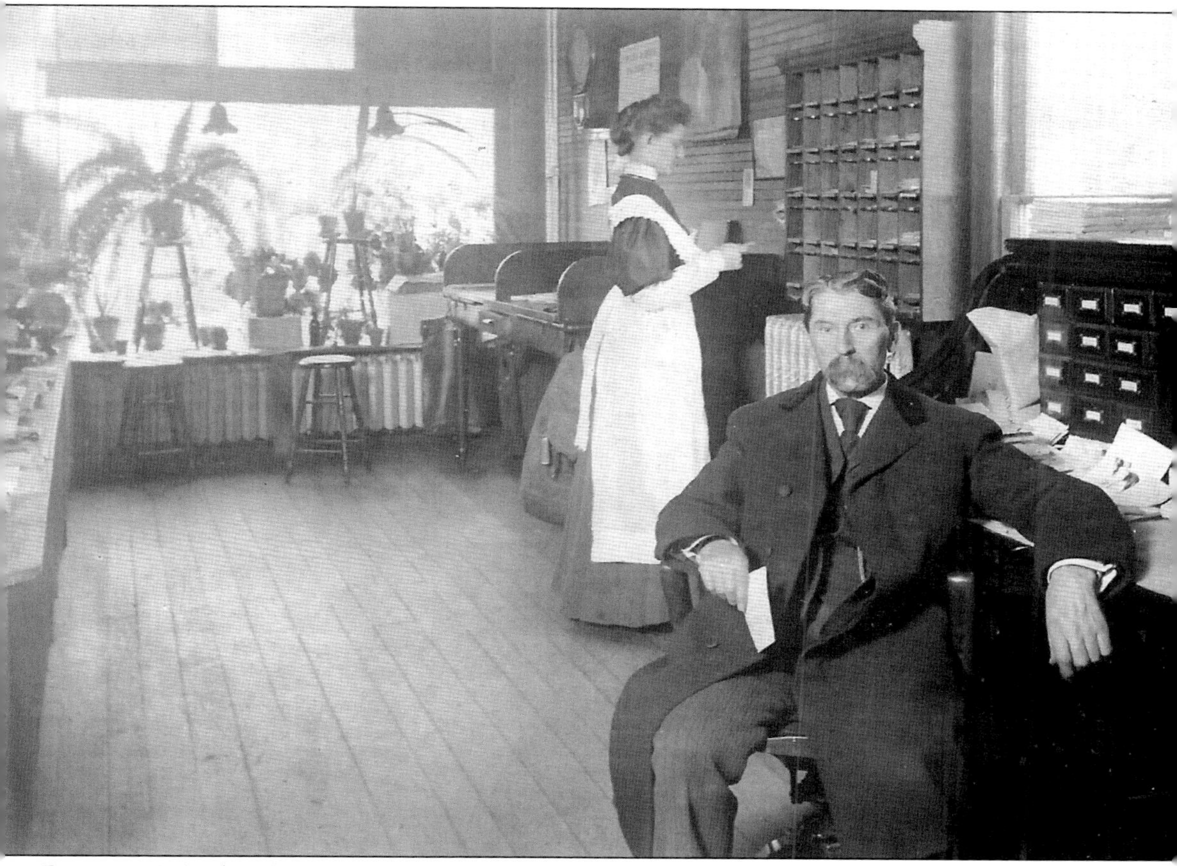

Between 1883, when Saegertown was chartered with an official post office, and when the *Tribune Republican* published its sesquicentennial edition of the newspaper in 1938, 10 postmasters had held the office. The first postmaster, Absalom Mook, held the job for over 27 years, before the post office was officially chartered. The postmasters were, in order, Absalom Mook, Charles E. Hunter, W. F. Moyer, W. H. Sigendall, Oliver Saeger, W. E. Wade, John C. Minich, Preston L. Peters, Adah E. Pettis (shown here with his wife), and Belle Luce.

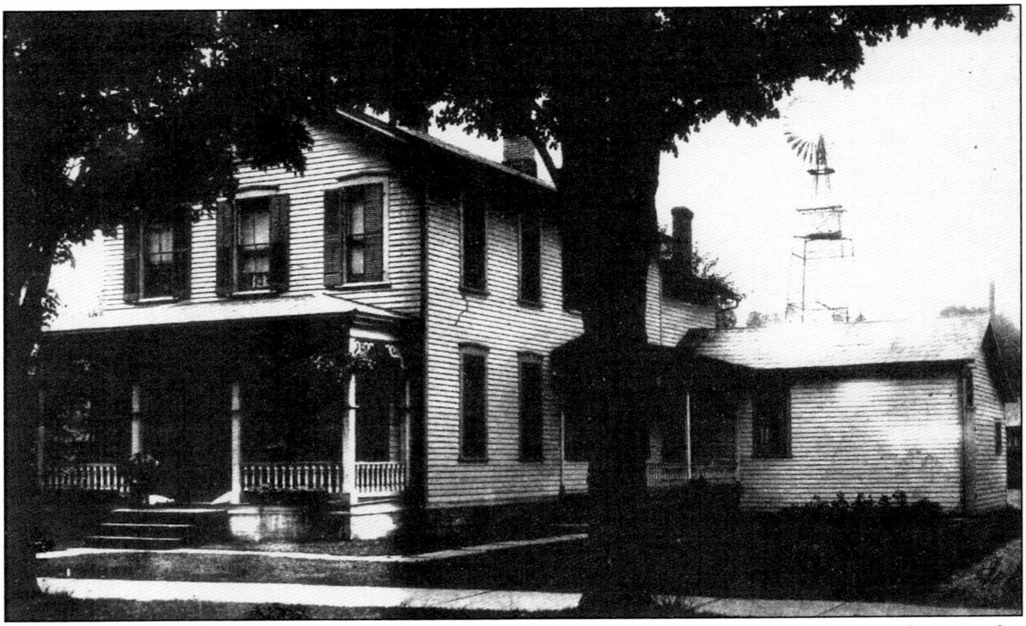

Built in 1872 for storekeepers Oliver and Amos Saeger, this house is located next door to the Saeger General Store. It remained under the Saeger name until 1902 when the Patterson family (cousins of the Saegers, McGills, and many other local notables) purchased and moved into the building. The Pattersons were close relatives of Alice M. Bentley.

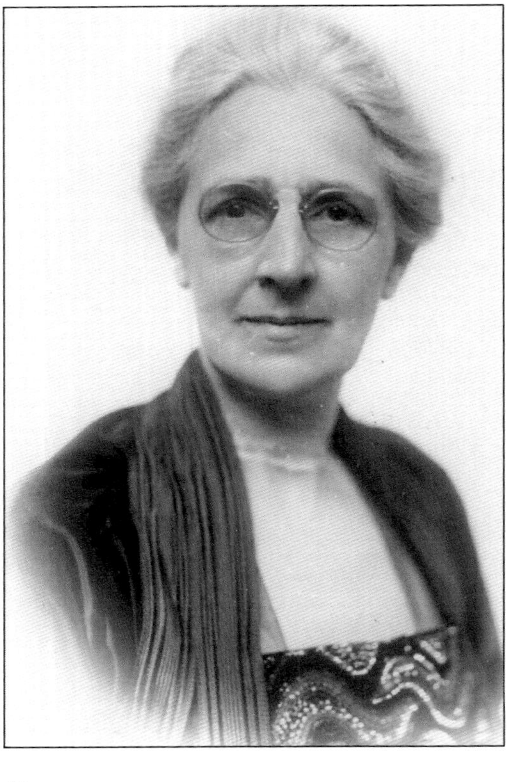

Onetime Saegertown resident Alice M. Bentley was one of three women to be elected to the Pennsylvania General Assembly in 1922. She spent her youth as a schoolteacher for over 20 years, spending another two decades as a representative of Mutual Life Insurance. According to her obituary, she was the first woman to preside over the Pennsylvania State House of Representatives and the first female chairperson of the House Education Committee, retiring in 1929.

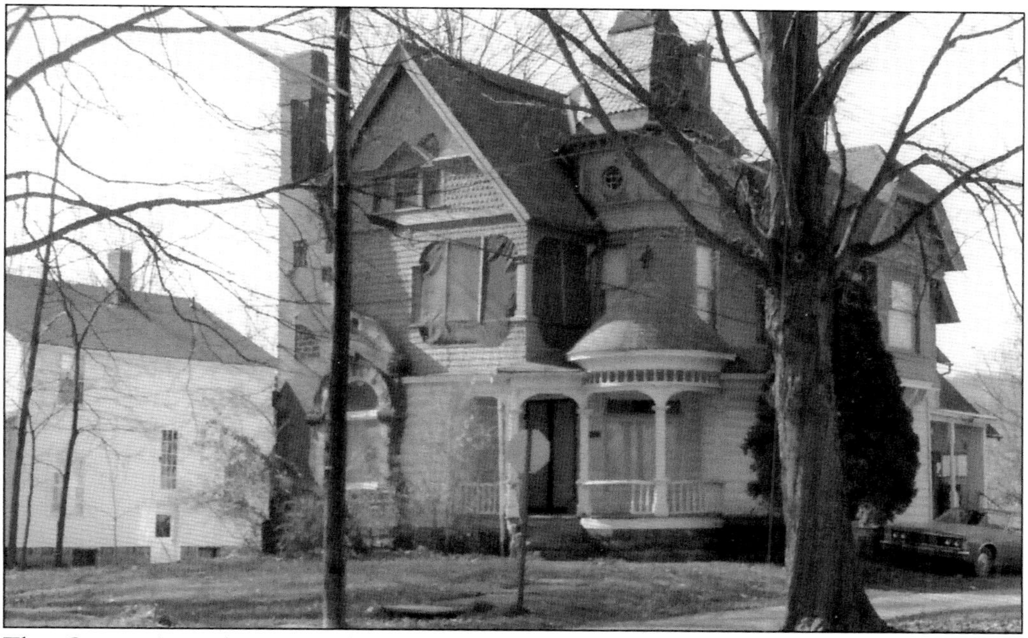

This Queen Anne house was built by Frank Roueche, the brother of Meadville hardware business owner George Roueche, in the 1890s. W. W. Deichman, a Saegertown banker, lived here later. The plans for the house could be ordered and the house built independently or by a kit sent by rail.

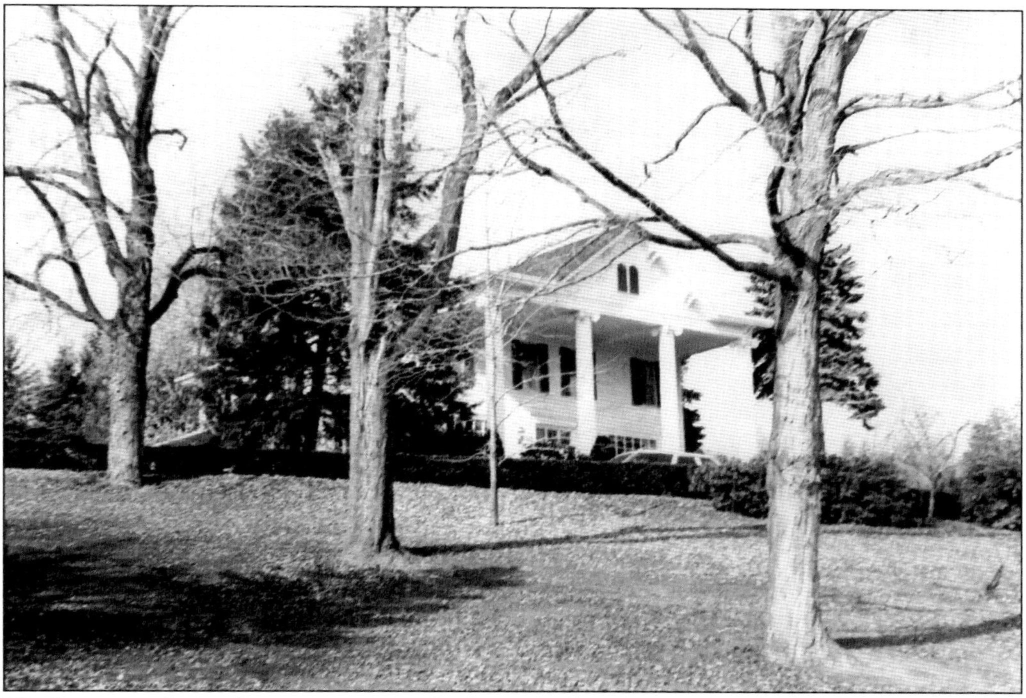

The location of a pig farm at one time, this house is shown in 1976 as the home of the Chalmer Jordan family.

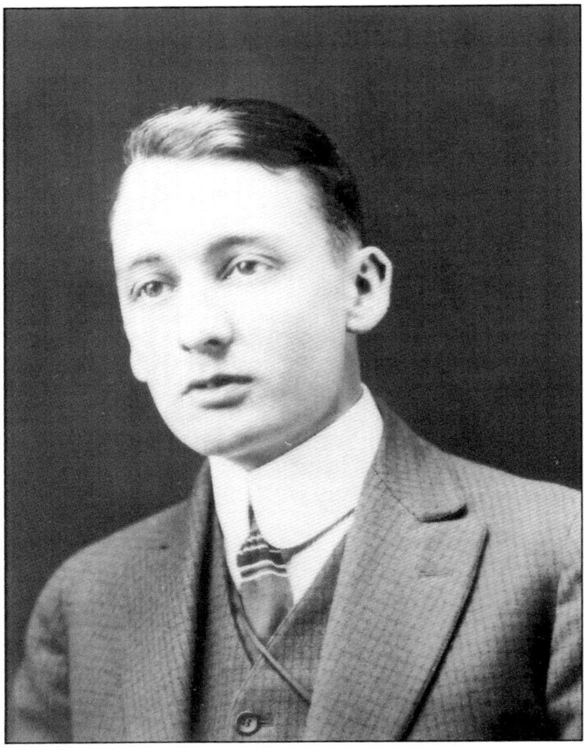

Henry Ward Baldwin was born on February 17, 1889, in Punxsutawney. He moved to Saegertown in 1922, already having experience in the insecticide business. He married Marie Hunter not long after arriving. The daughter of D. J. Hunter, her father often grew vegetables and weeds in his garden for use at Baldwin's laboratory where insecticides were tested. (Courtesy of Lea Baldwin.)

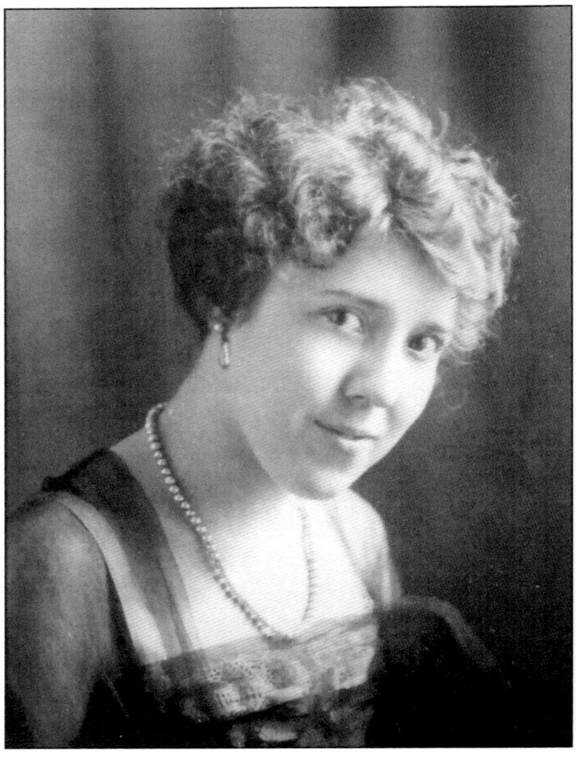

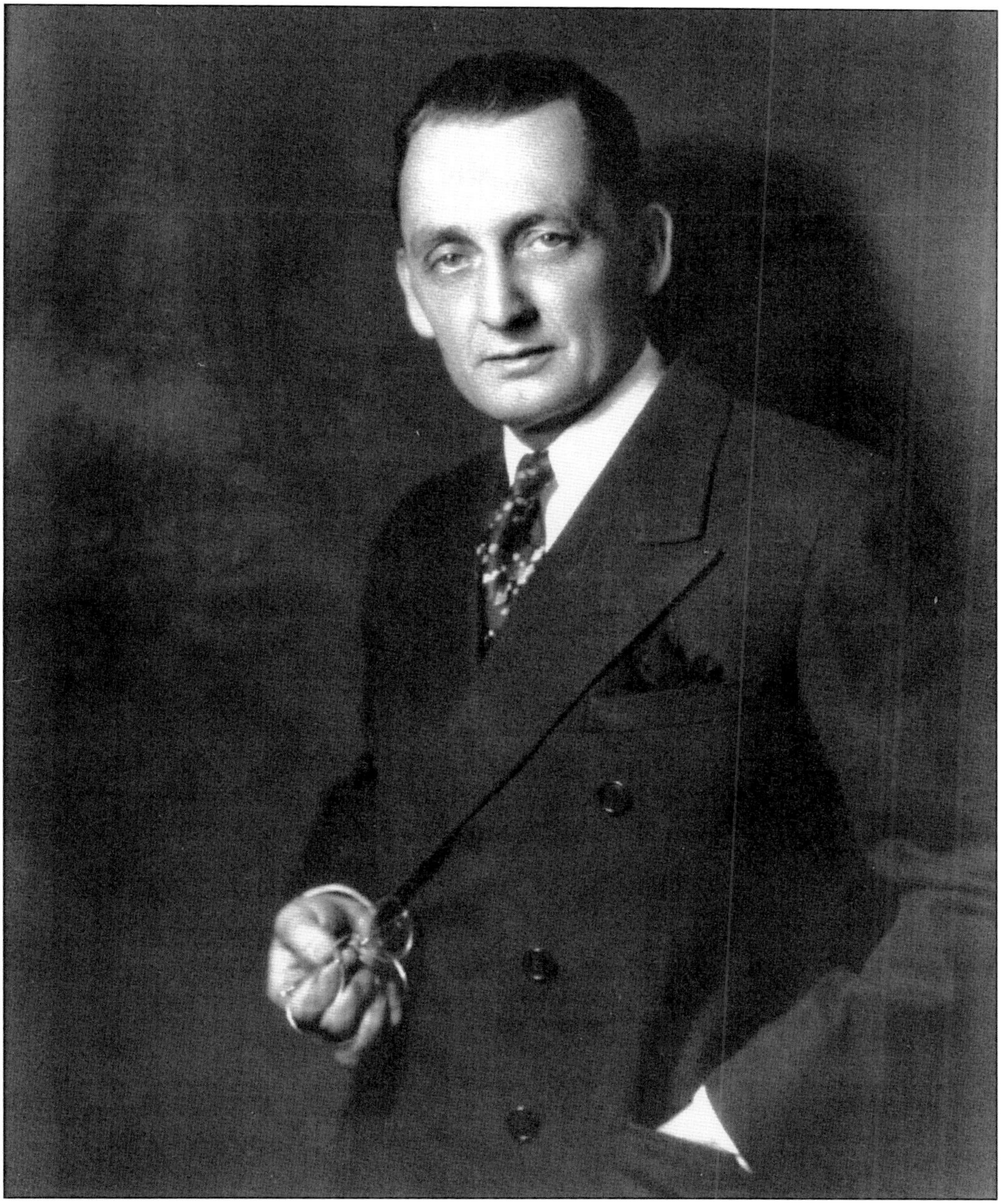

Baldwin elevated his insecticide business from an amateur effort to a nationally recognized company in roughly five years. Upon retirement from business, he and his wife continued to live in the area, where at least some of his children still reside. (Courtesy of Lea Baldwin.)

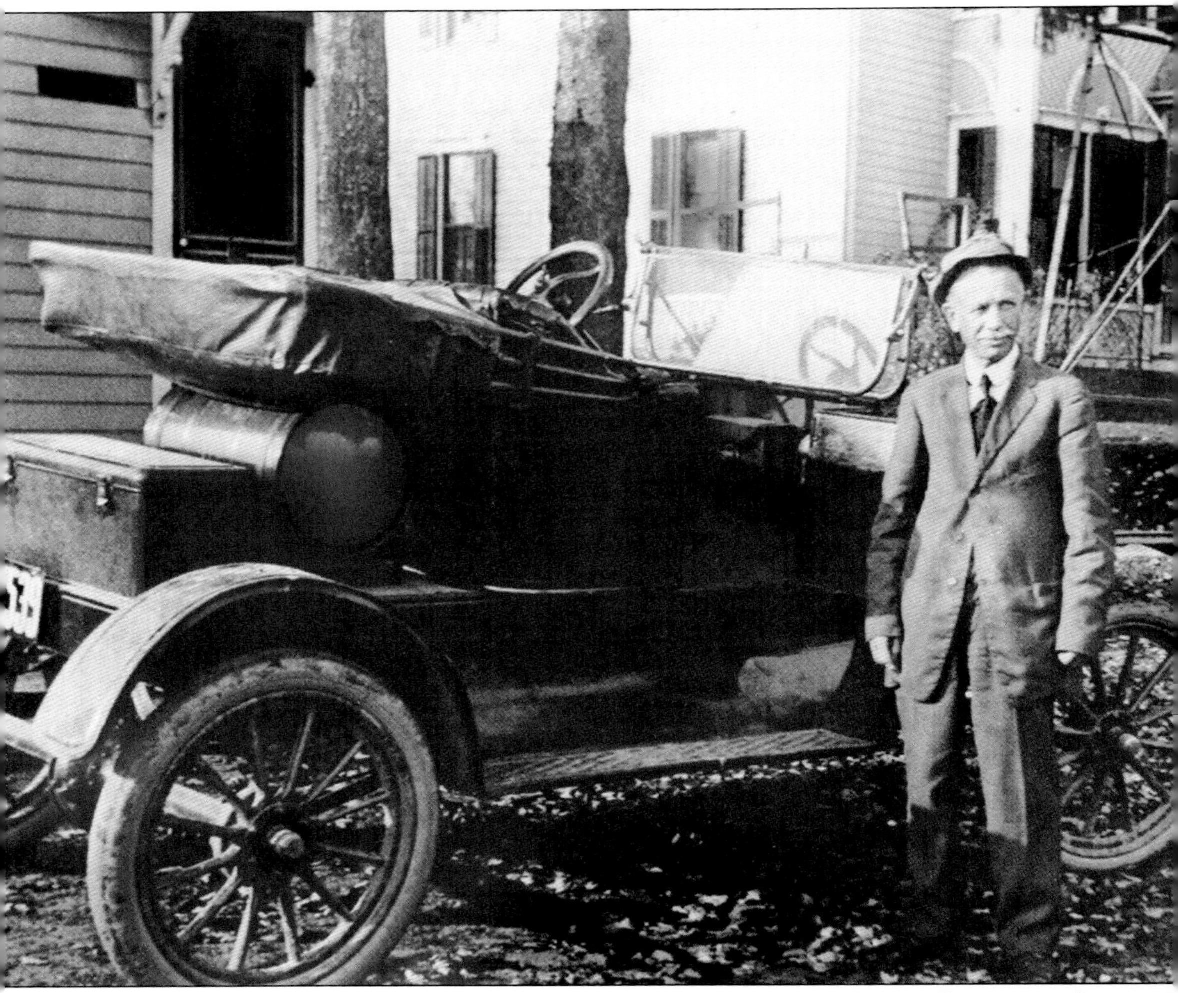

A rural legend in the eyes of those who visited his office, Dr. Jacob Russell Mosier is shown in front of the Ford Model T he sped (quite literally) to and from house calls with. Practicing medicine from 1883 through 1938 in Little's Corners, he was known for his terrible driving ability, a huge heart, and, of all things, the stuffed porcupine in his waiting room. His office is now on permanent exhibit at the Baldwin-Reynolds House Museum in Meadville and is completely intact to its 1938 appearance.

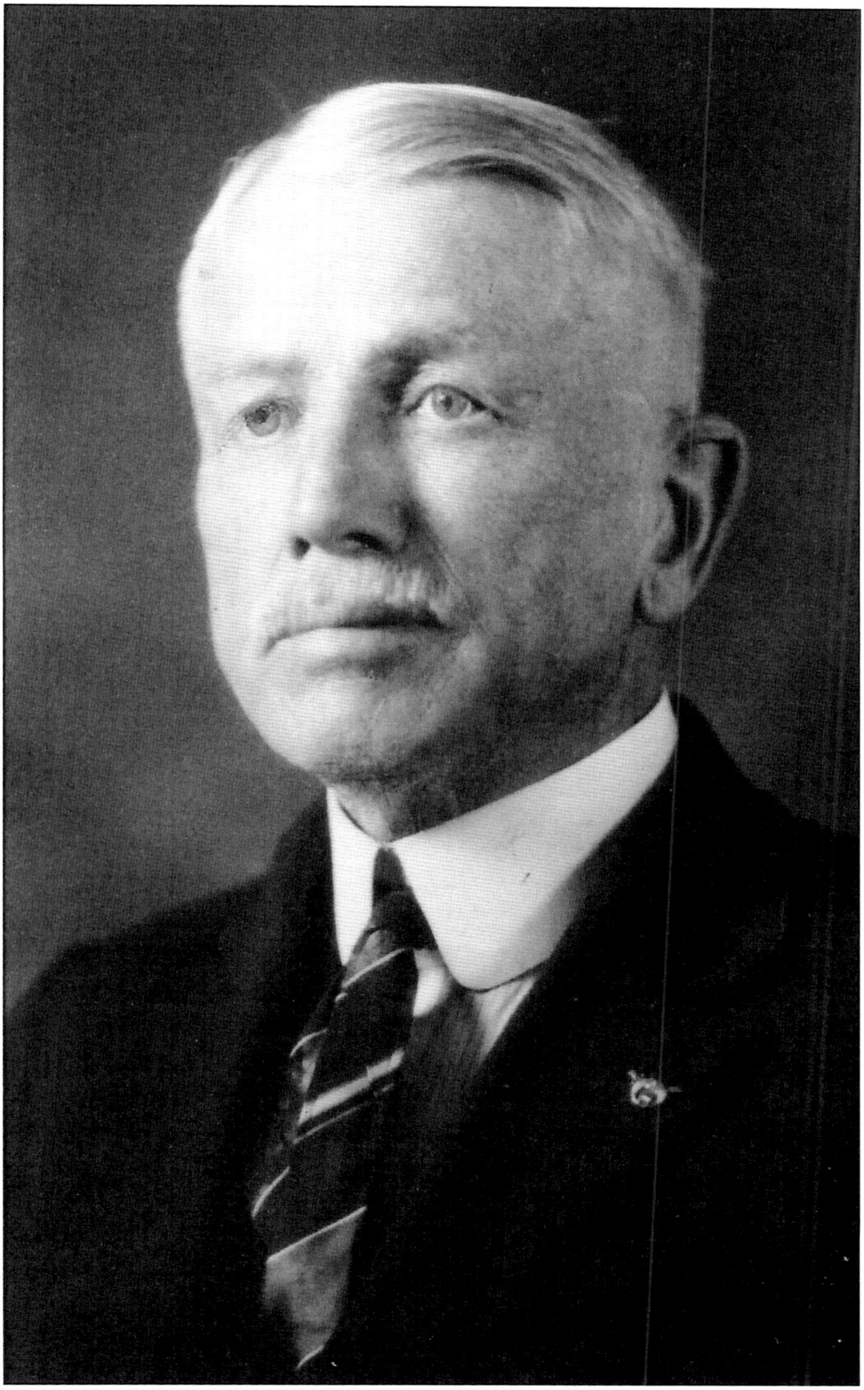

Jacob Russell Mosier married Alice A. Boyd on July 22, 1875. They had two healthy sons and a daughter who died at birth. Mosier became a doctor in 1883 and established his first practice in Rundelltown where he grew up. In 1884, he bought Dr. Munson Boyd's practice and office in Little's Corners.

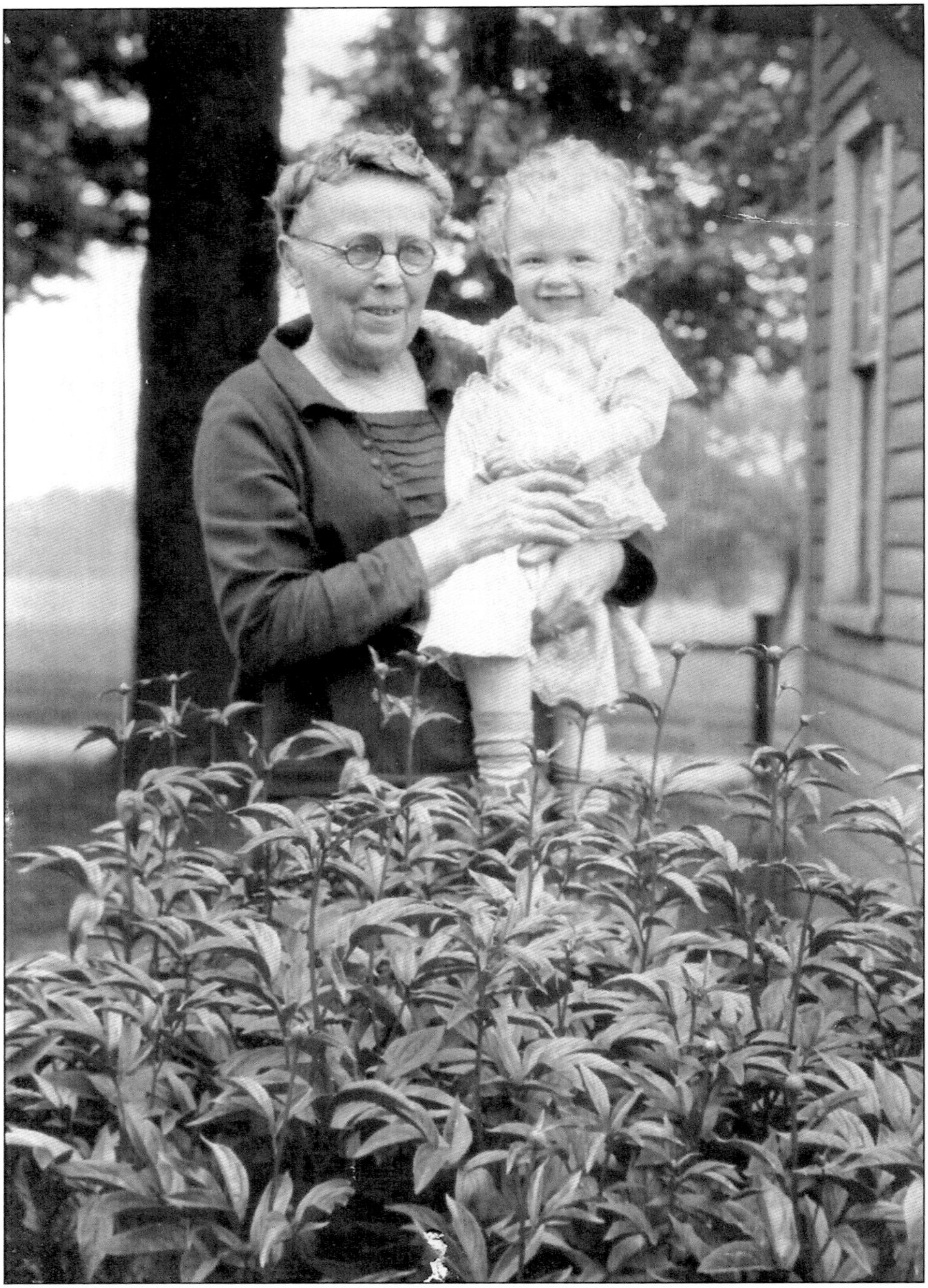

Seen here with a child, Alice Mosier was a dressmaker, and her income helped greatly in putting Jacob Russell Mosier through school and later buying drugs for his practice. Early in his career he received more trade items than cash. Of the Mosiers' two sons, only one survived well into adulthood. Ora Mosier died while setting off fireworks during the community Independence Day celebration on July 4, 1929. A firework exploded in his face, and after being rushed to Jacob's office, he could not be saved.

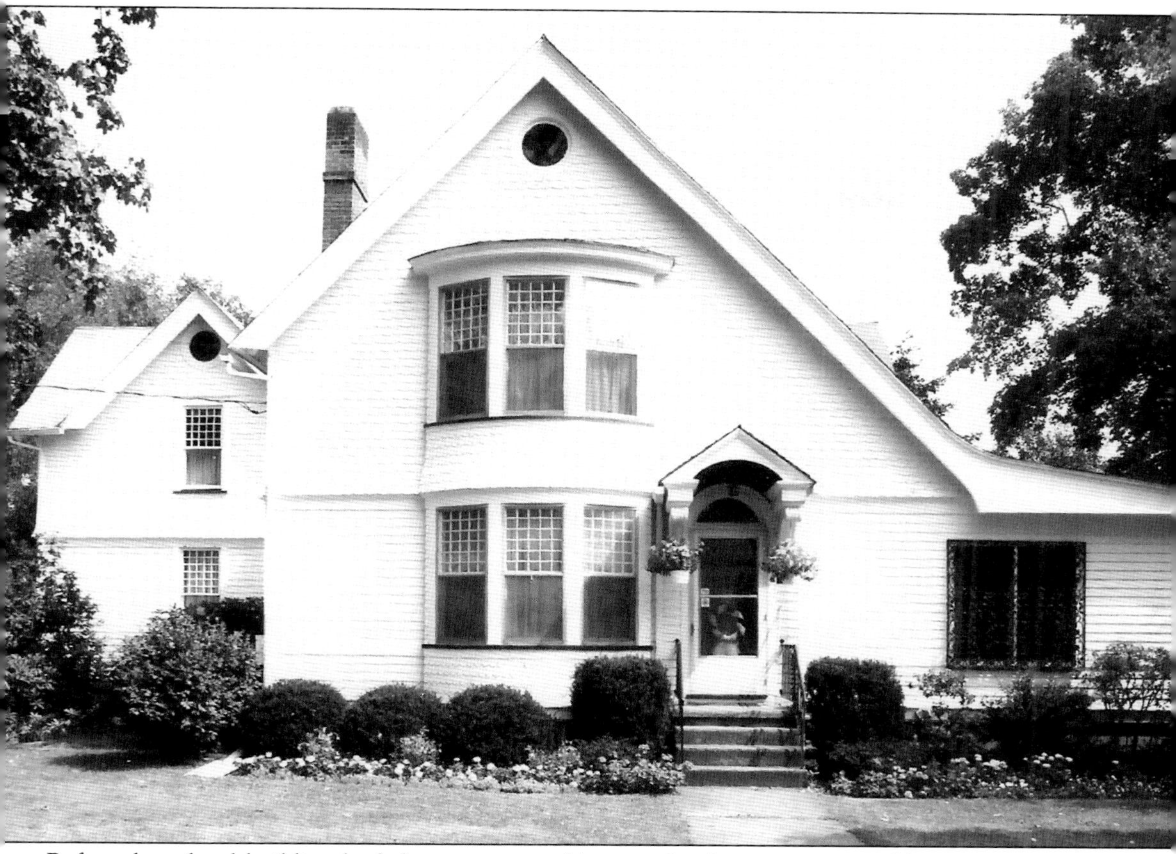

Before the school building had the necessary additions, this house was owned by Saegertown High School. Its home economics department was housed on the first floor with boarding for the school janitor on the second. After the appropriate facilities were added onto the school, Dr. and Mrs. Gerald Brooks purchased the property and lived there for several decades.

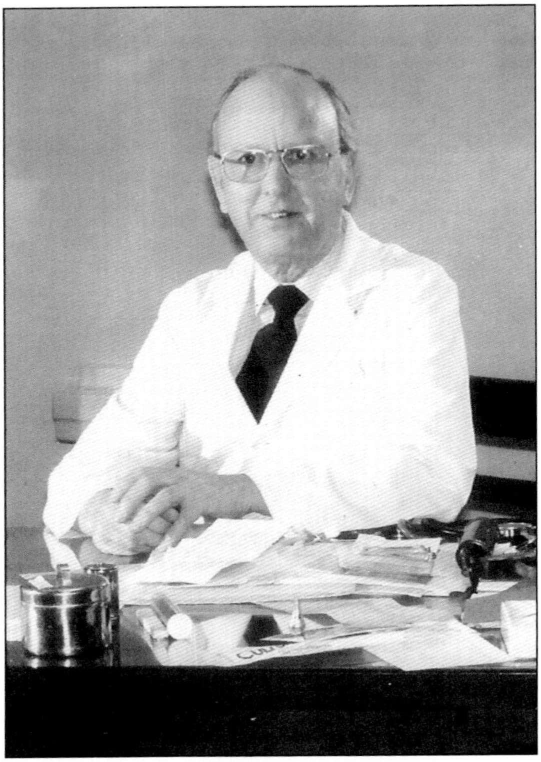

Dr. Gerald Brooks is shown here in his later years of practice.

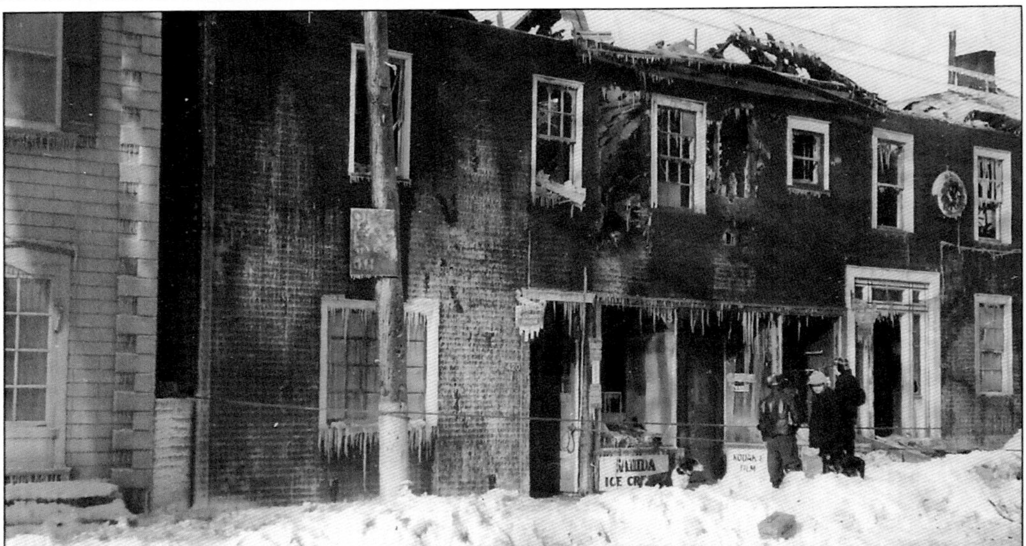

Brooks practiced medicine in this office until December 27, 1950, when it was lost to fire. There were two theories as to the cause of the blaze at the time, one possible cause being Harry Main, the building owner, thawing frozen pipes with a blowtorch and the other being a new furnace installed by Brooks not long before. Brooks continued to practice medicine in Saegertown for several decades after this.

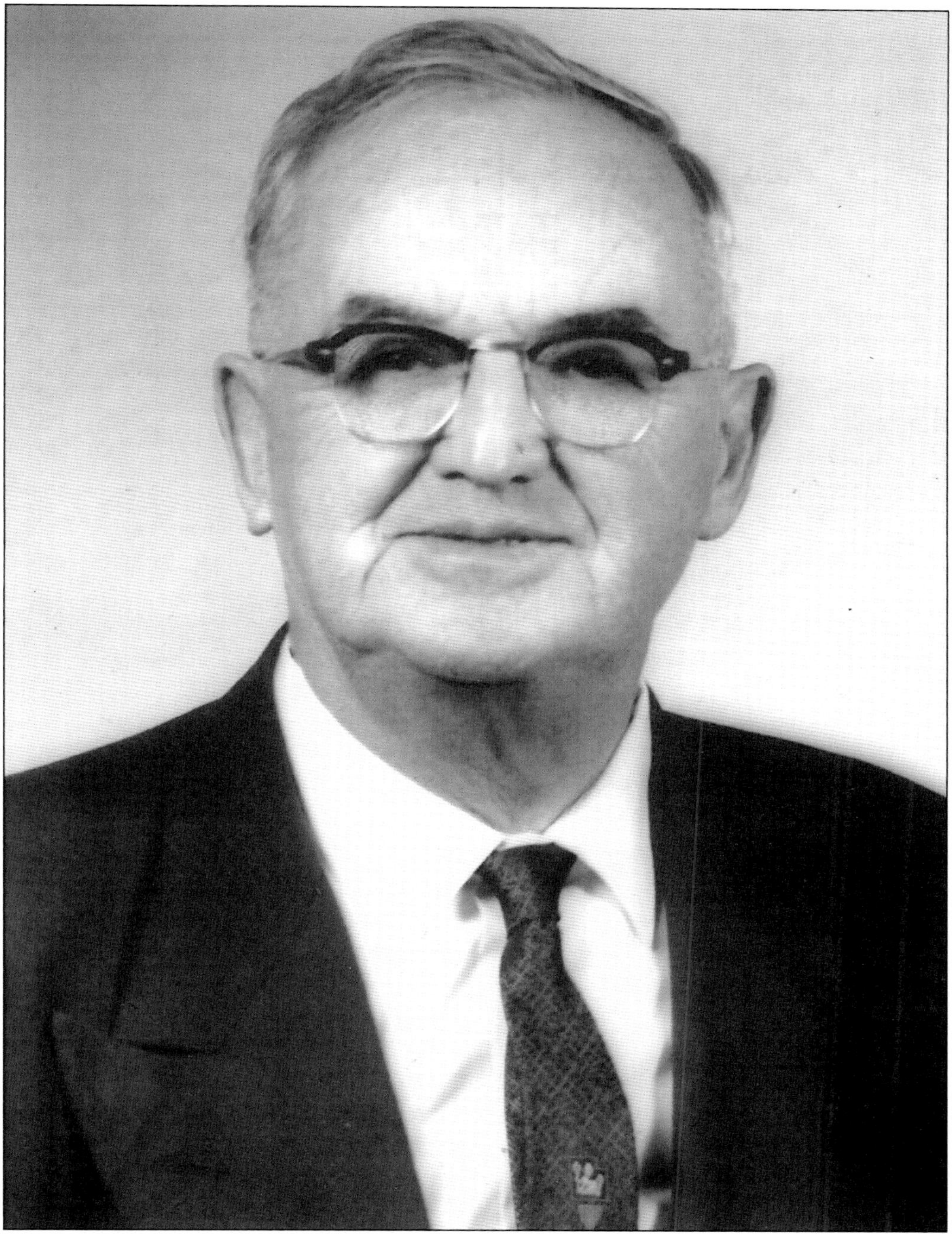

Dr. Kenton Bertram was a well-known chiropractor in Saegertown. He became the borough manager of the Merchants National Bank and Trust Company on Main Street when the Saegertown office was opened on September 20, 1955. He made the first deposit in the new branch that day as a christening of sorts. Bertram remained active in public and business affairs. Years later, Bertram Field, created from land he donated, was named in his honor for his years of community service.

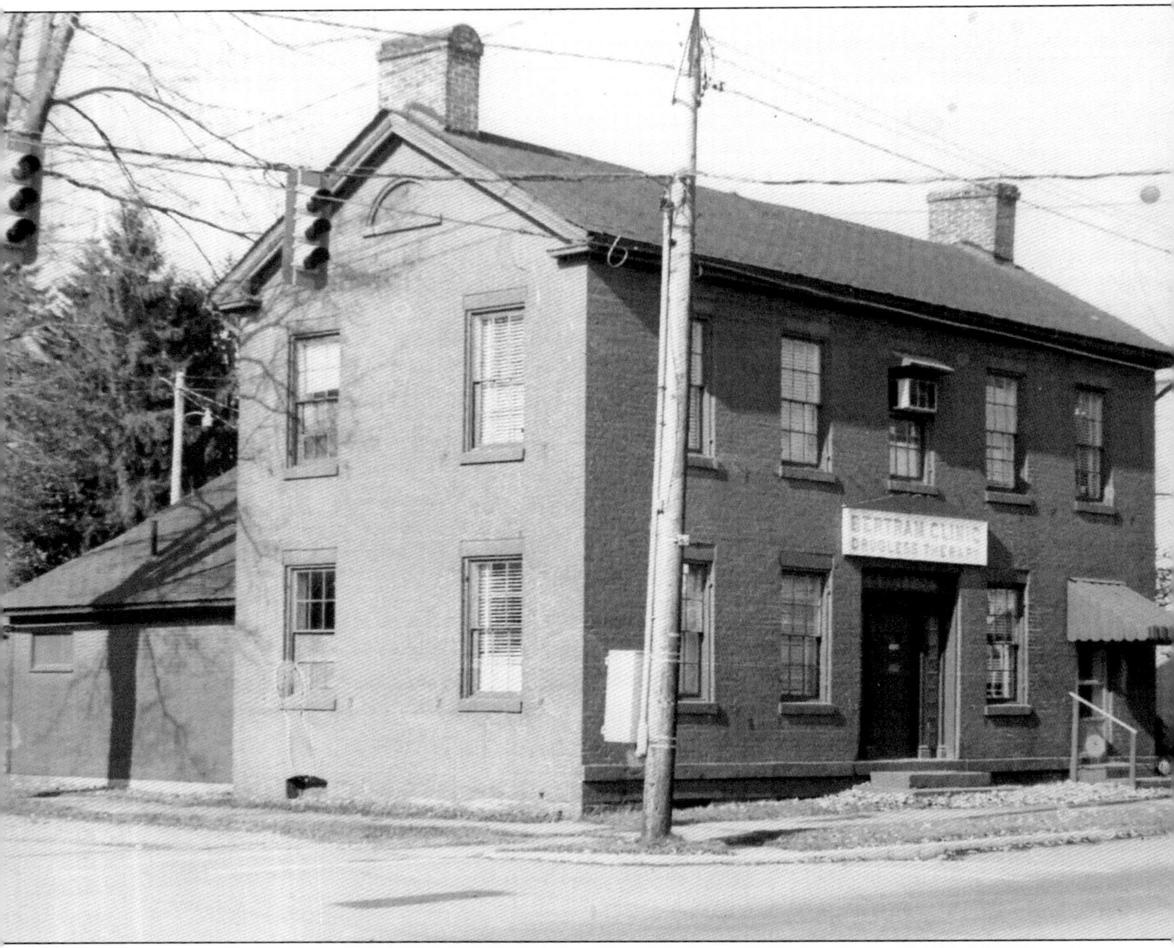

Dr. Abraham Deichman was the first doctor to settle in Saegertown in 1837. The Deichman family quickly became fairly wealthy and was influential in local affairs. Deichman retired in 1874. This building was his residence, and it was later used as Dr. Kenton Bertram's chiropractic clinic in the mid-1900s.

Three

Impacting the Community

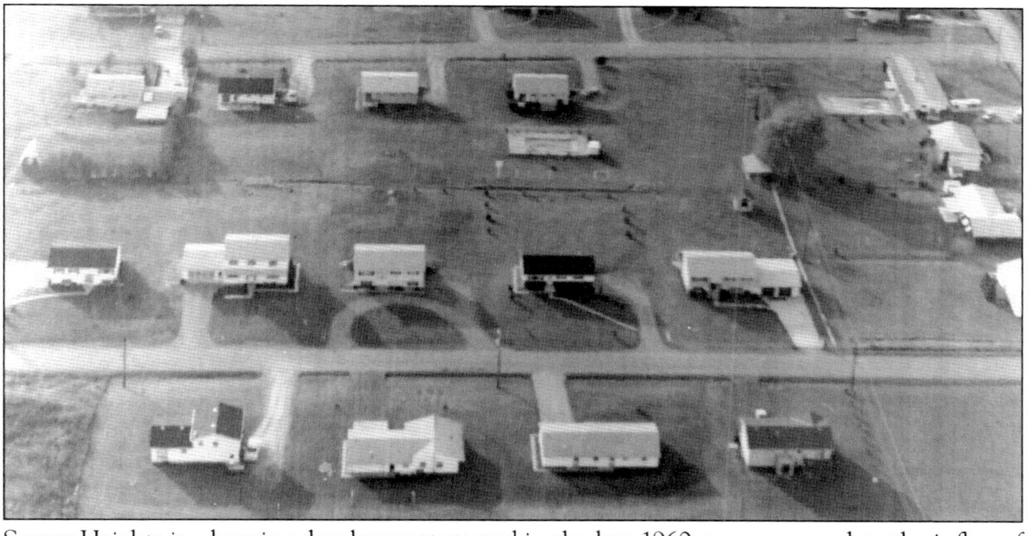

Saeger Heights is a housing development started in the late 1960s to accommodate the influx of new residents to Saegertown. An increase in the tool and die industry brought people from cities such as Pittsburgh looking for work. This aerial photograph was taken in 1976.

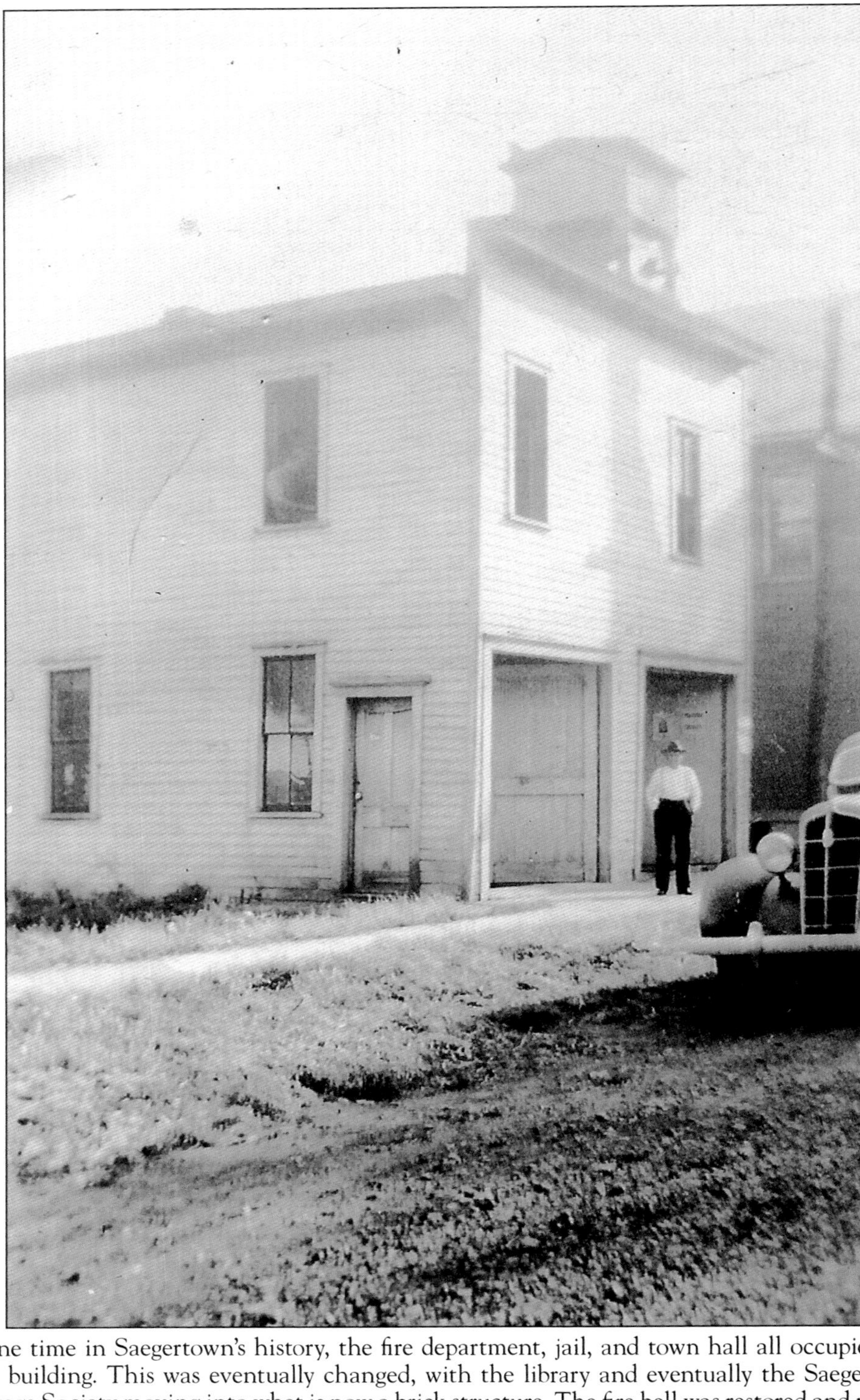

At one time in Saegertown's history, the fire department, jail, and town hall all occupied the same building. This was eventually changed, with the library and eventually the Saegertown Heritage Society moving into what is now a brick structure. The fire bell was restored and moved to its present place outside the current Saegertown Fire Department.

A farmer along Oil Creek at the time of Edwin L. Drake's oil discovery in nearby Titusville, John Benninghoff soon found himself rich and mistrusting of banks after some of his money was stolen on the way to be deposited. He delegated the task of his banking to his close relative, a Dr. Benninghoff, living between Saegertown and Meadville. On January 16, 1868, the perpetrators stole an undisclosed amount of money, reported from around 100,000 to several million. The best estimate of the stolen funds is between $250,000 and $500,000. The robbers were eventually caught, although the money was never recovered. It was known as the largest oil robbery of all time.

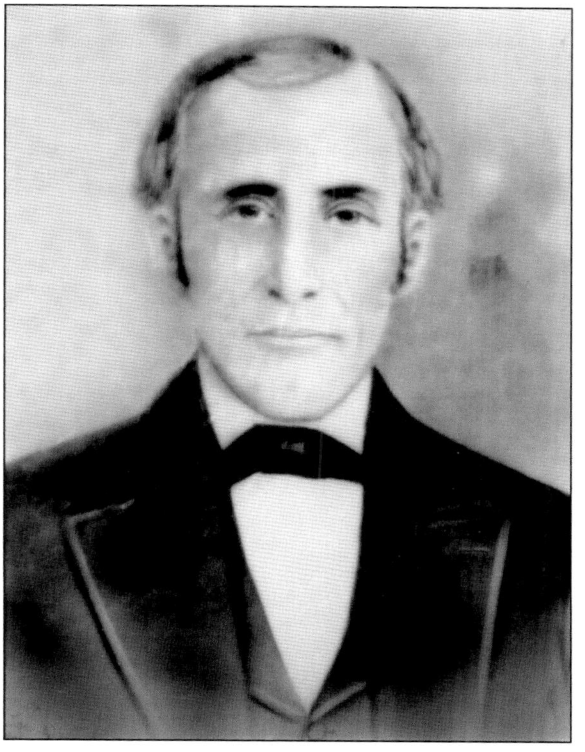

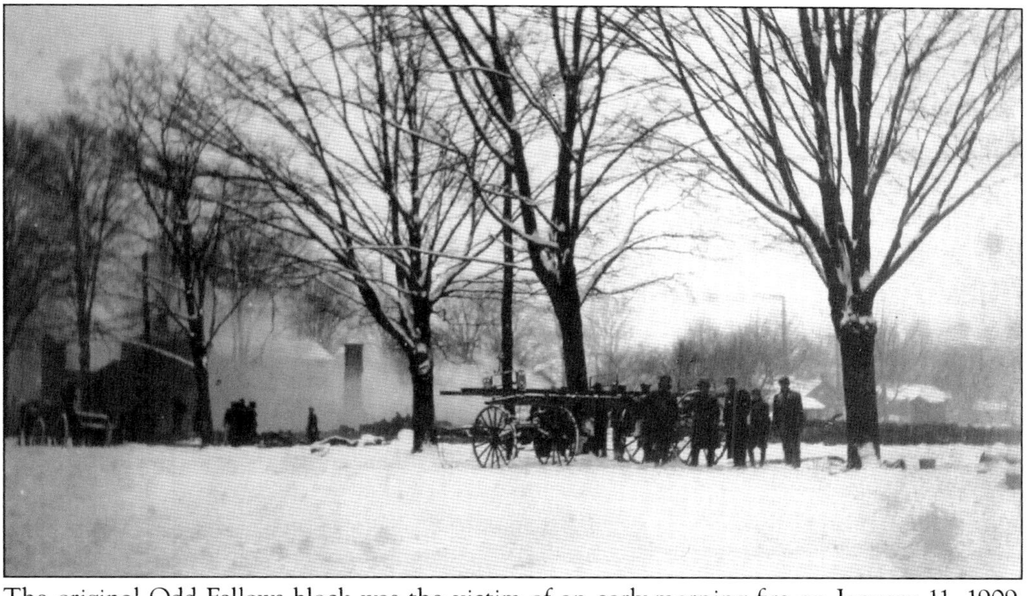

The original Odd Fellows block was the victim of an early-morning fire on January 11, 1909, leveling the wooden structure in half an hour. Saegertown's bucket brigade was called out shortly after 3:00 a.m. with Meadville's fire department and engine on the way by rail. When the train reached Saegertown, however, the railcar carrying the fire engine was not to be found, uncoupling itself halfway back. Two other residences were lost to this fire.

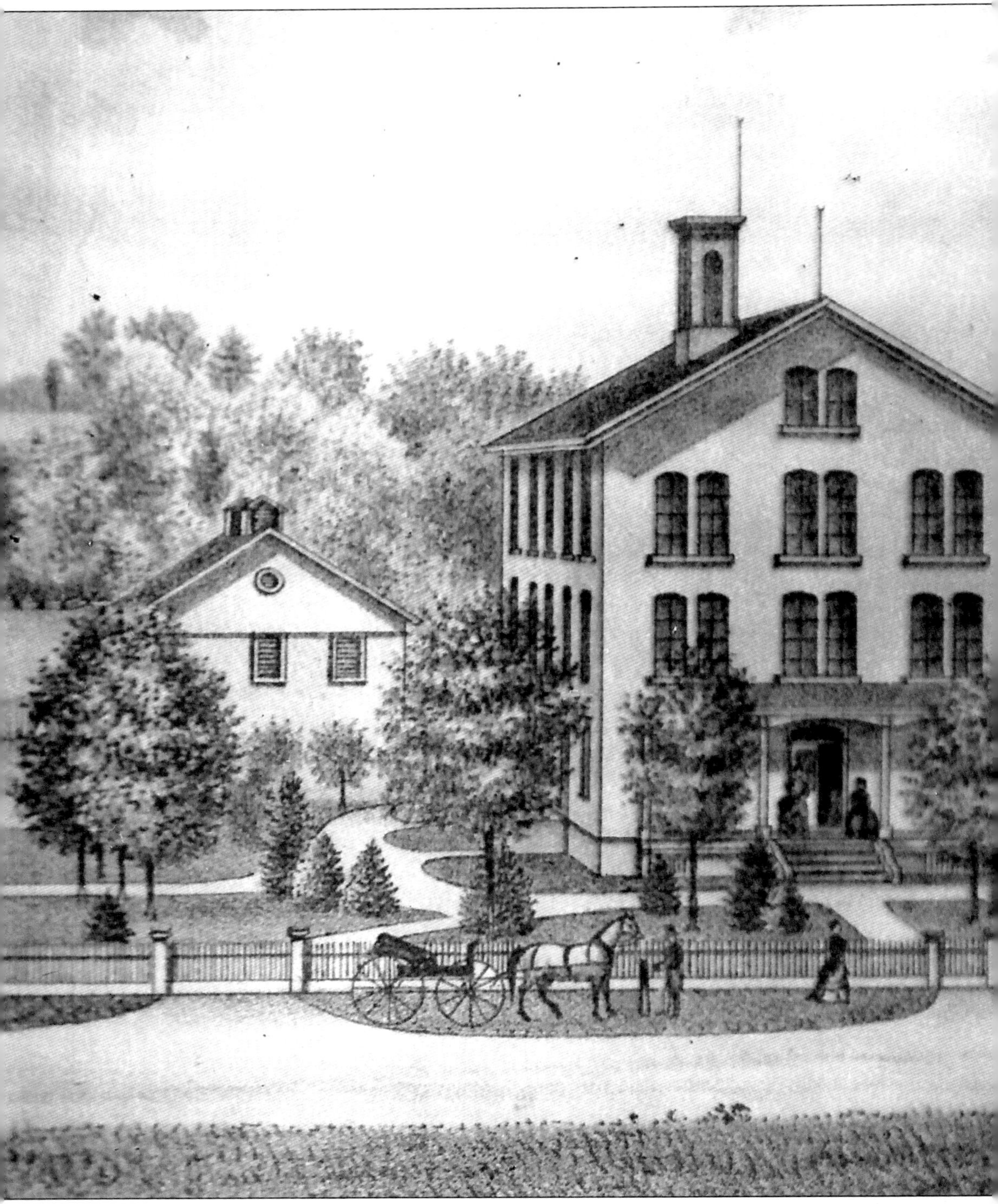

The Crawford County Home, located on 215 acres in Woodcock Township, was once known as the county infirmary or county poorhouse. The original structure was built in 1854 and added onto in 1868 at the cost of $1,000. After this, the addition became the main building, leaving

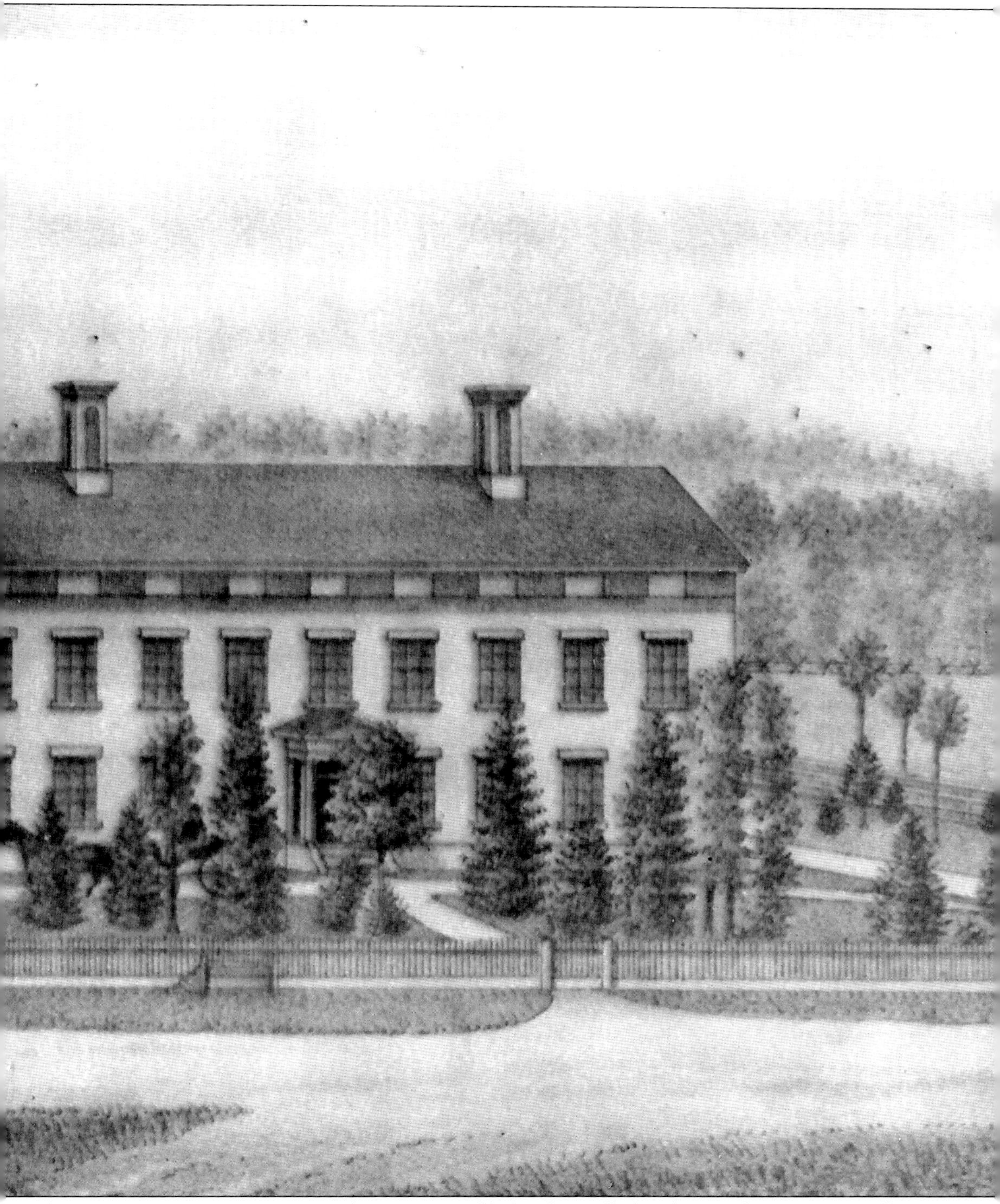

the 1850s section as a wing. It was home to 150 elderly, physically handicapped, or economically disadvantaged residents as of 1876.

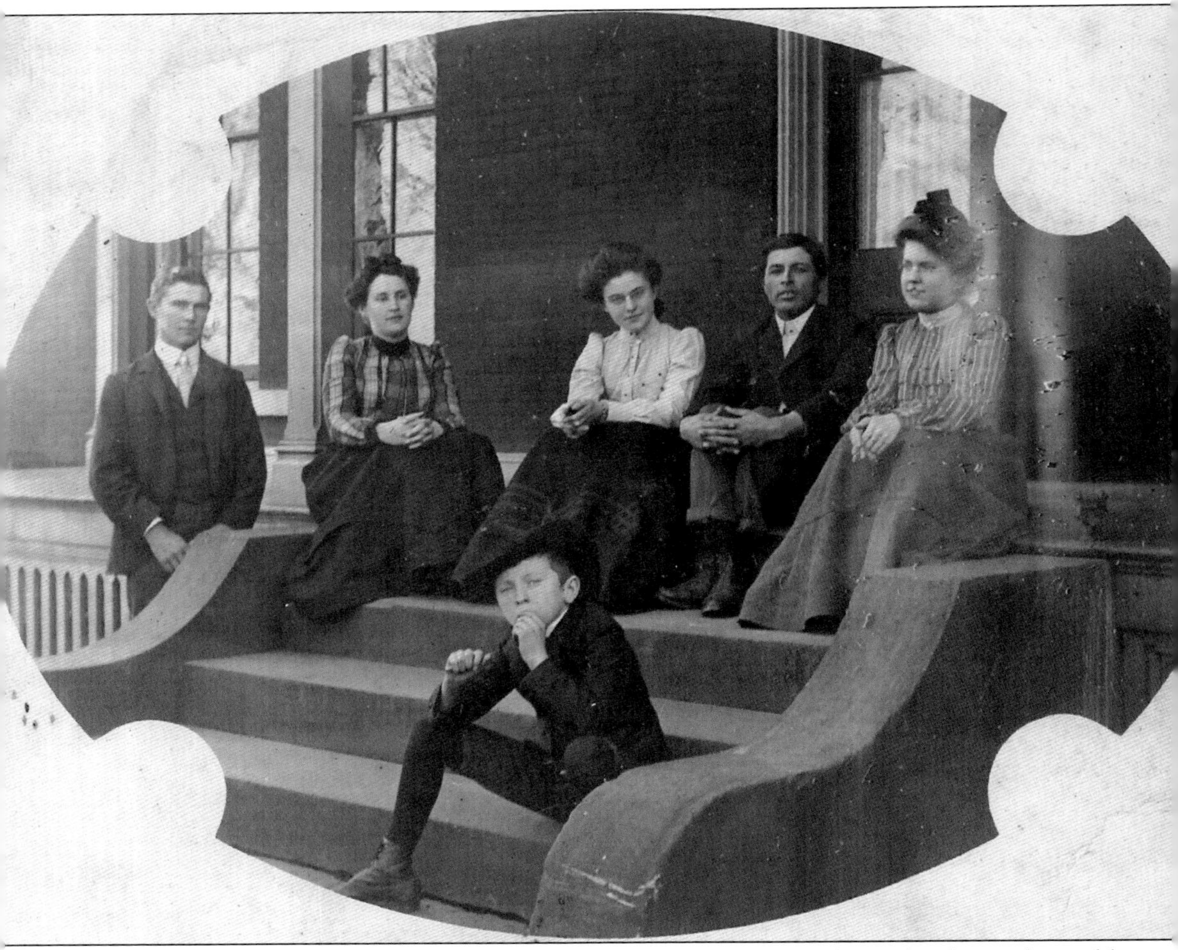

Residents at the Crawford County Infirmary (a few of which are shown here) were housed by gender, the females living in the new building, and the males boarding on the second story of the original structure. A physician was seen once a week, and the residents were given wholesome food, good beds, and comfortable apartments. No provisions were made for the insane.

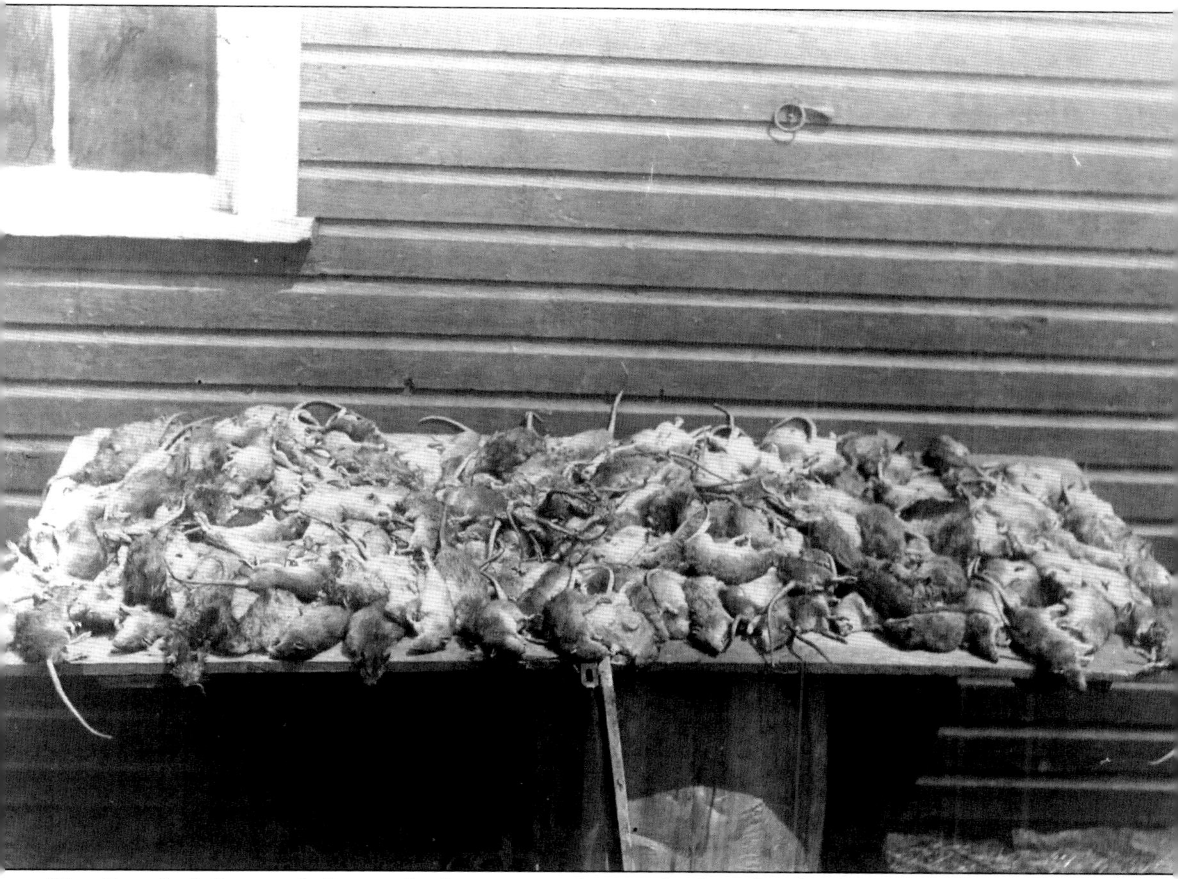

The Crawford County Infirmary had an on-site farm to both make the facility self-sustaining and to provide something for residents to do to pass the time if they so desired. This photograph, taken in 1908, shows the rats killed when replacing an old pigsty on the premises, 165 in total.

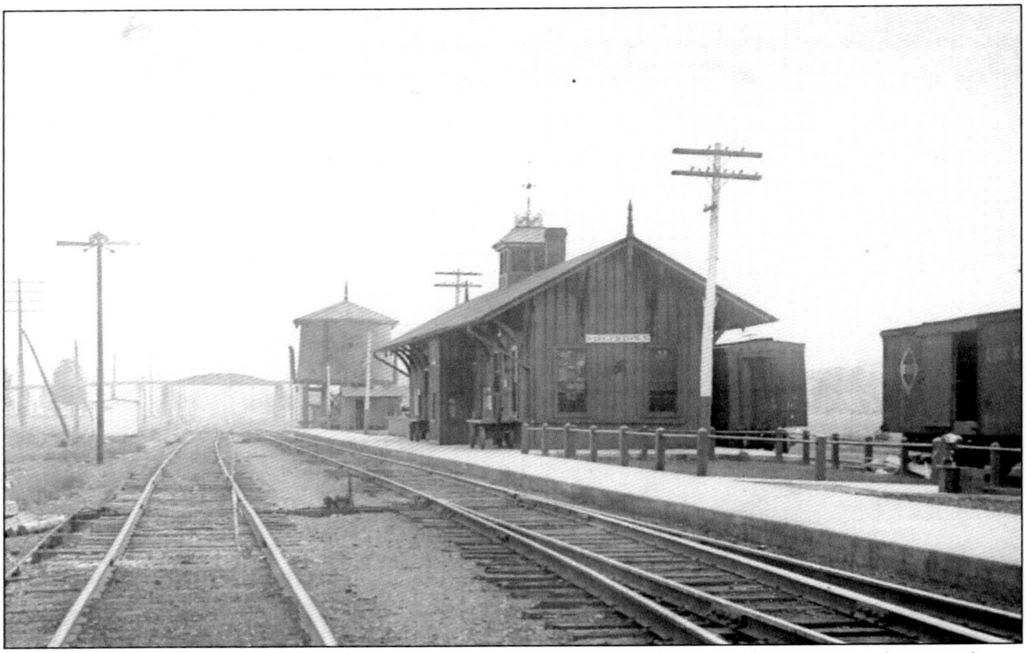

In 1861, the first railroad tracks were laid in Saegertown in the same location as the canal was proposed several years earlier. The first train did not stop here, however, until 1888. Shown here in the early 1900s, the railroad station was built in 1869.

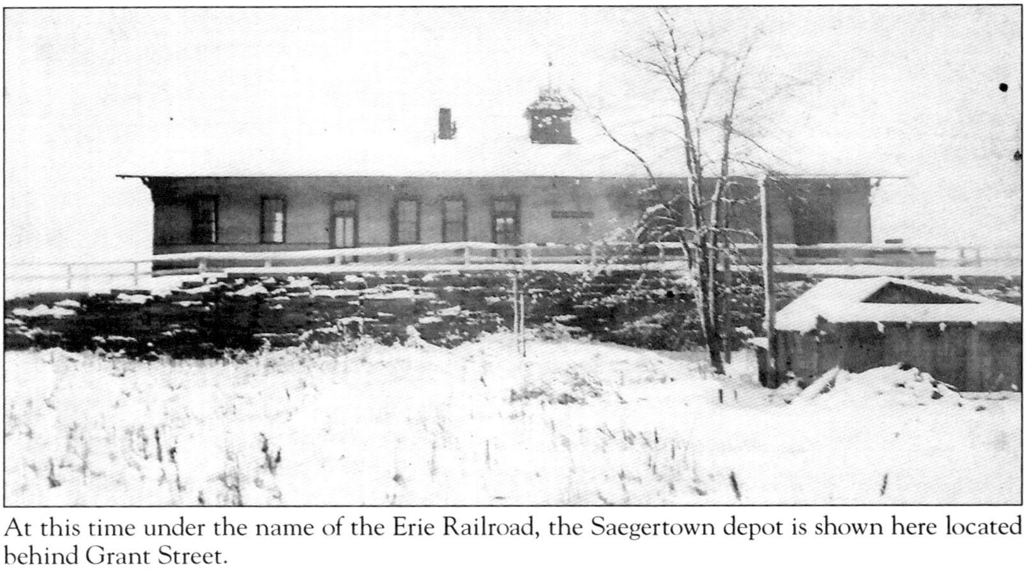

At this time under the name of the Erie Railroad, the Saegertown depot is shown here located behind Grant Street.

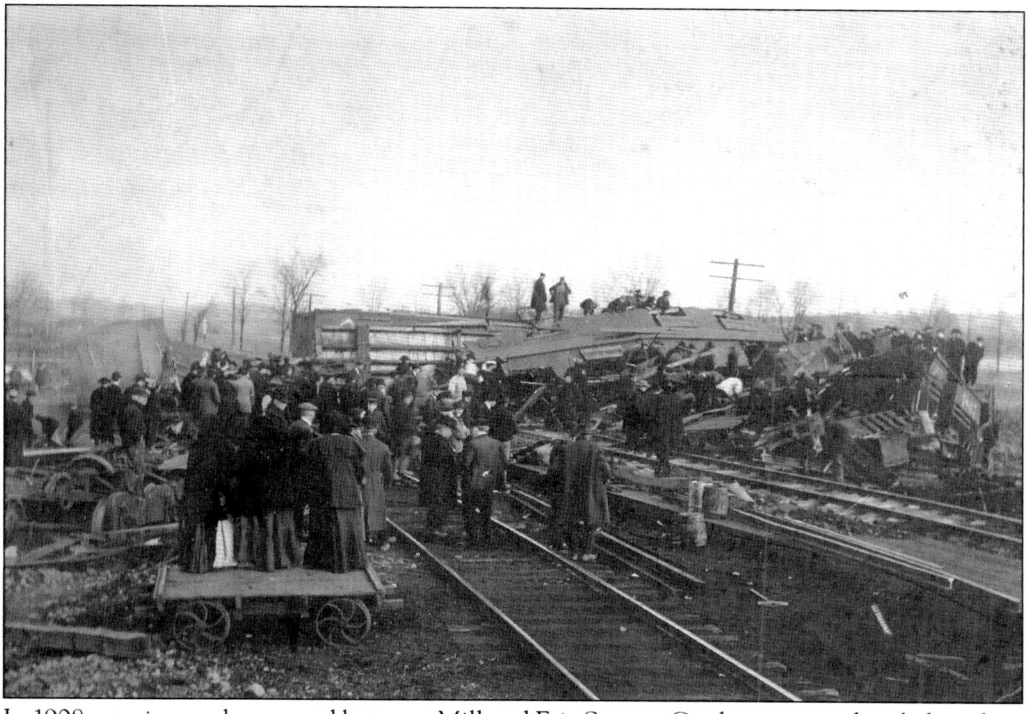

In 1908, a train wreck occurred between Mill and Erie Streets. Cattle cars were derailed on their way to the east, killing several cattle and allowing the rest to stampede through town, causing damage. Only one human was killed in this accident, an illegal rider on the train.

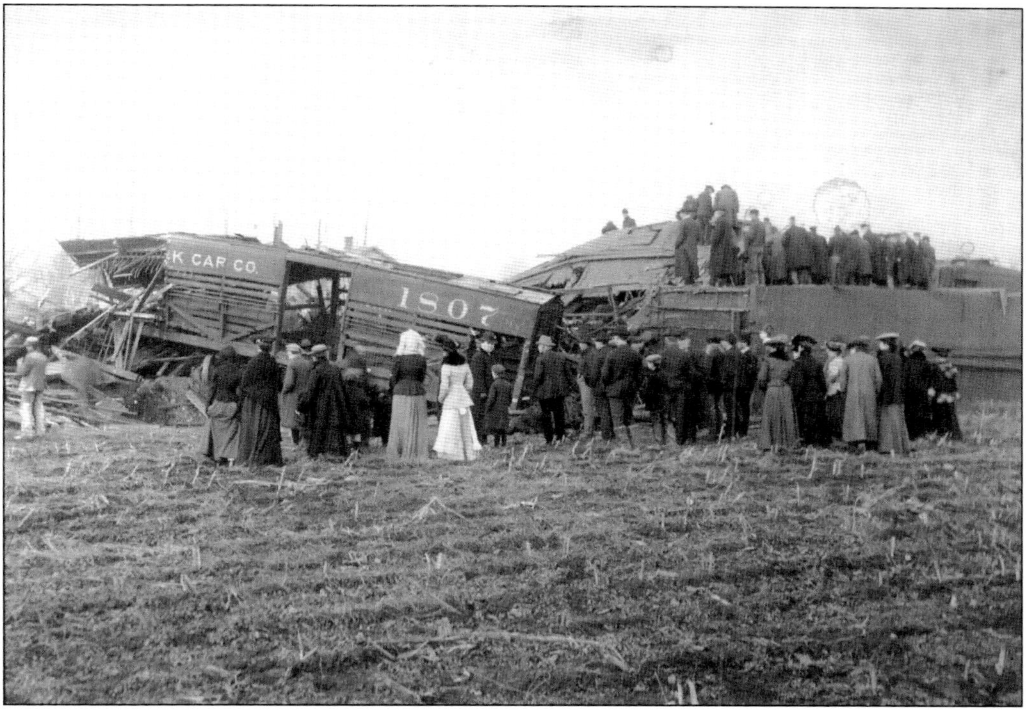

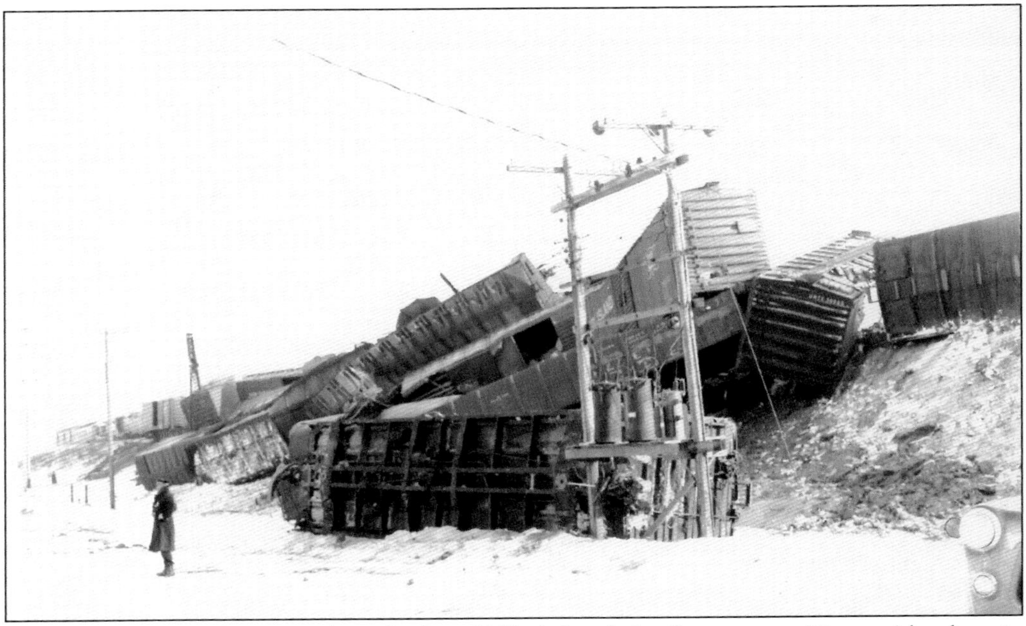

Another train wreck occurred in the late 1950s behind the Saegertown Ginger Ale plant in Saegertown, near the site of the 1908 incident.

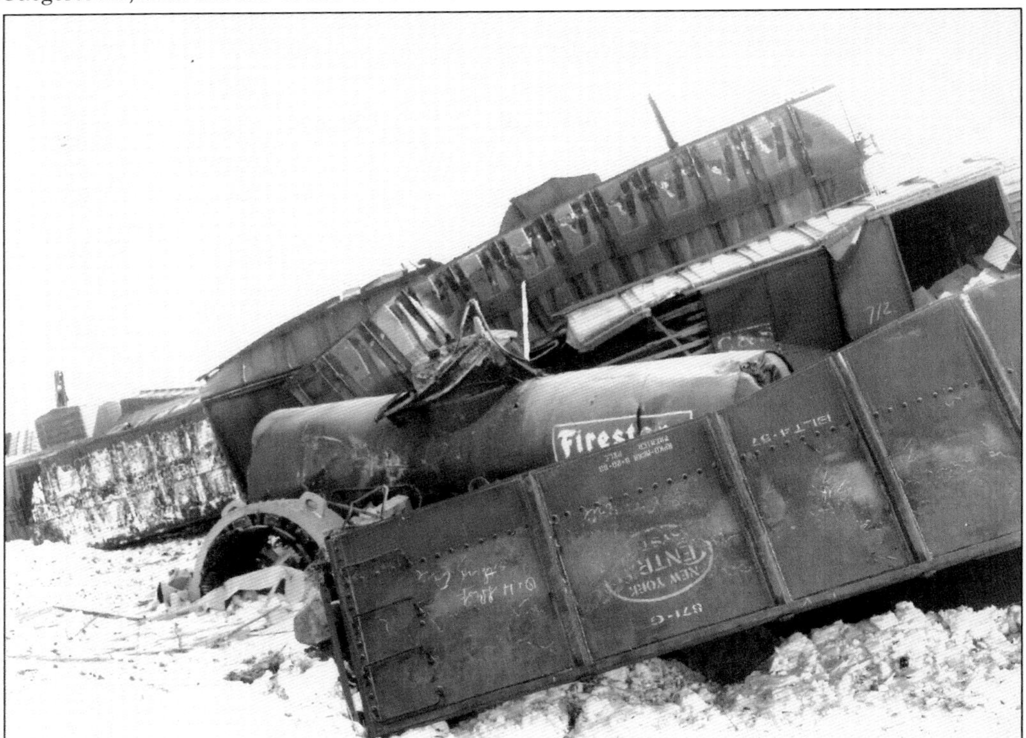

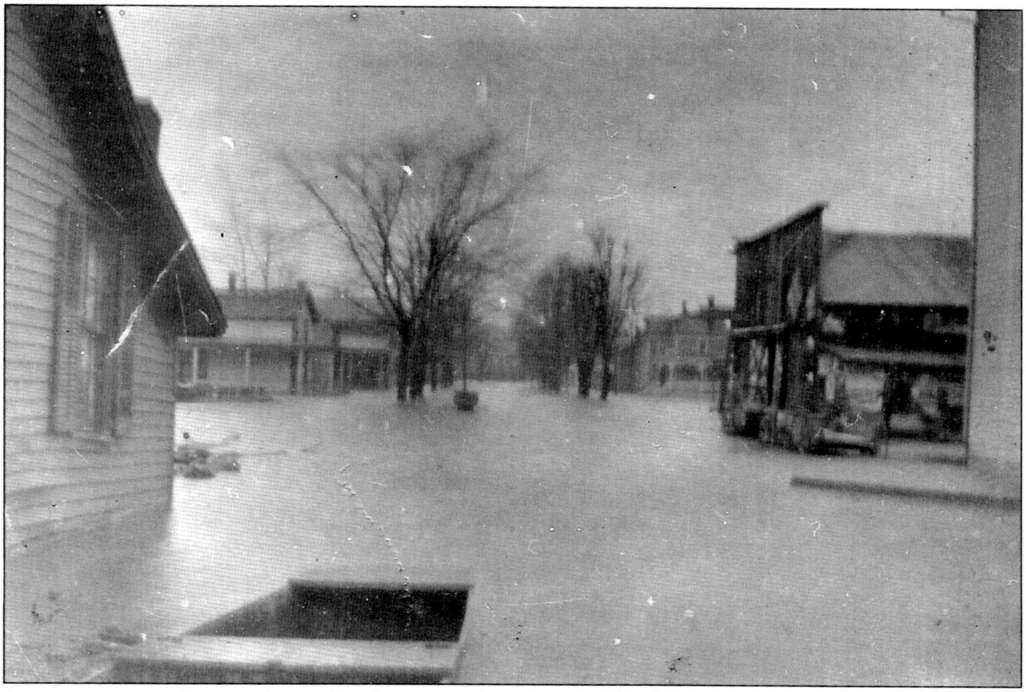

Saegertown was famous for its floods, as seen here. Major floods occurred in Saegertown in 1902, 1913, 1935, and 1947.

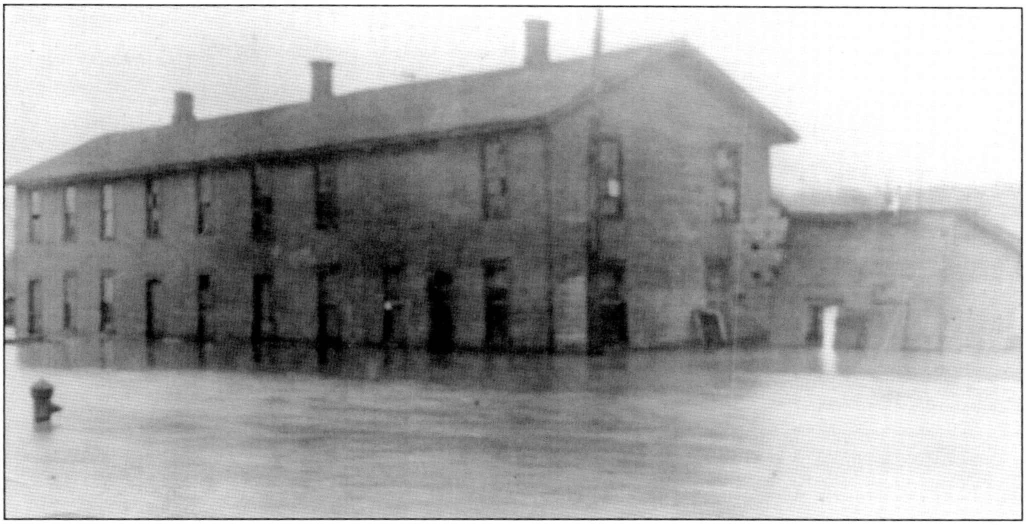

The flood of 1913 did a great deal of damage throughout Saegertown, and Crawford County for that matter. Shown here in 1913, the Saegertown cheese factory has water up to its first floor. The factory was originally owned by Daniel Saeger and was located next to the mills at the end of Mill Street.

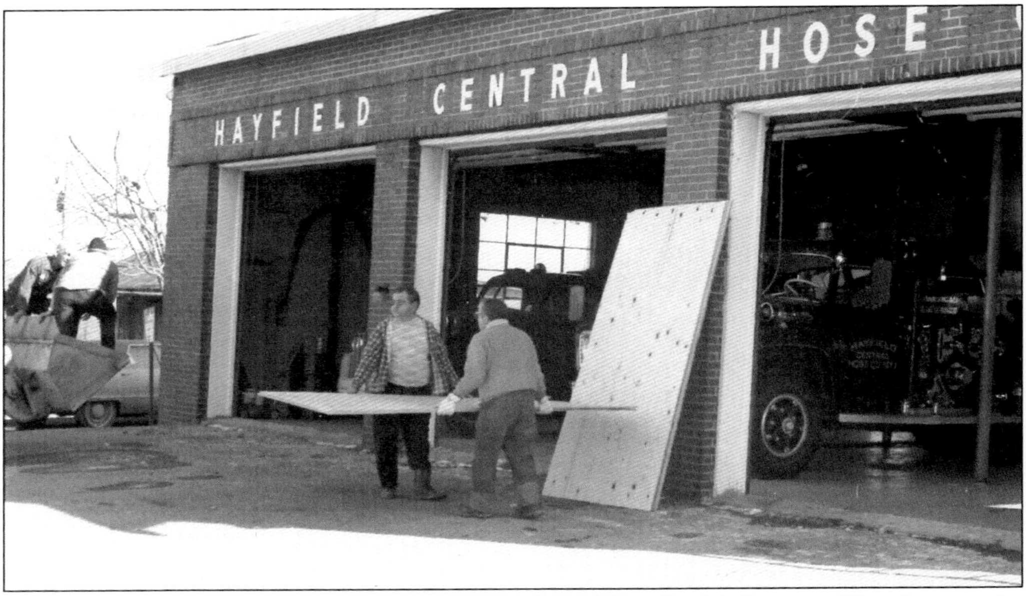

Hayfield Volunteer Fire Department was chartered in 1947 in Little's Corners. The photographs featured here were taken in 1973. This photograph shows, from left to right, Ken Hill, Art Ketchum, Don Patch, and John Daniels. (Courtesy of the Hayfield Volunteer Fire Department.)

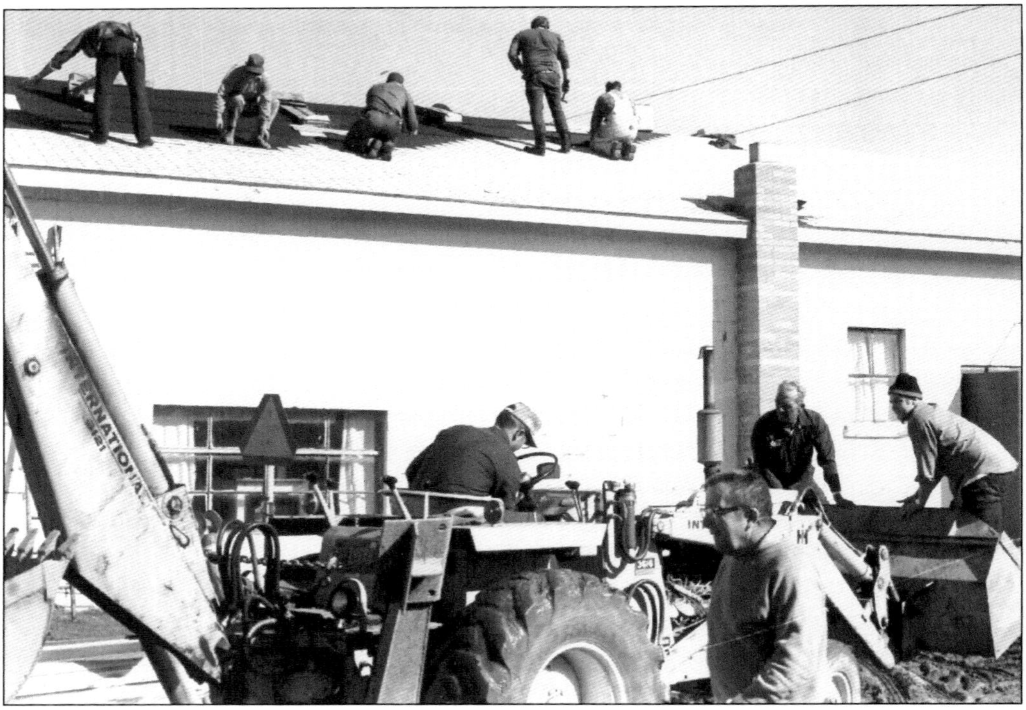

Members of the fire department are seen here working on the new roof. Shown on the roof from left to right are Ron Phelan, Hugh Yokes, Mike Constanovich, John Hanks, and Roger Dillaman. On the ground, Jim Reichel, John Daniels, Ken Hill, and Art Ketchum are working. (Courtesy of the Hayfield Volunteer Fire Department.)

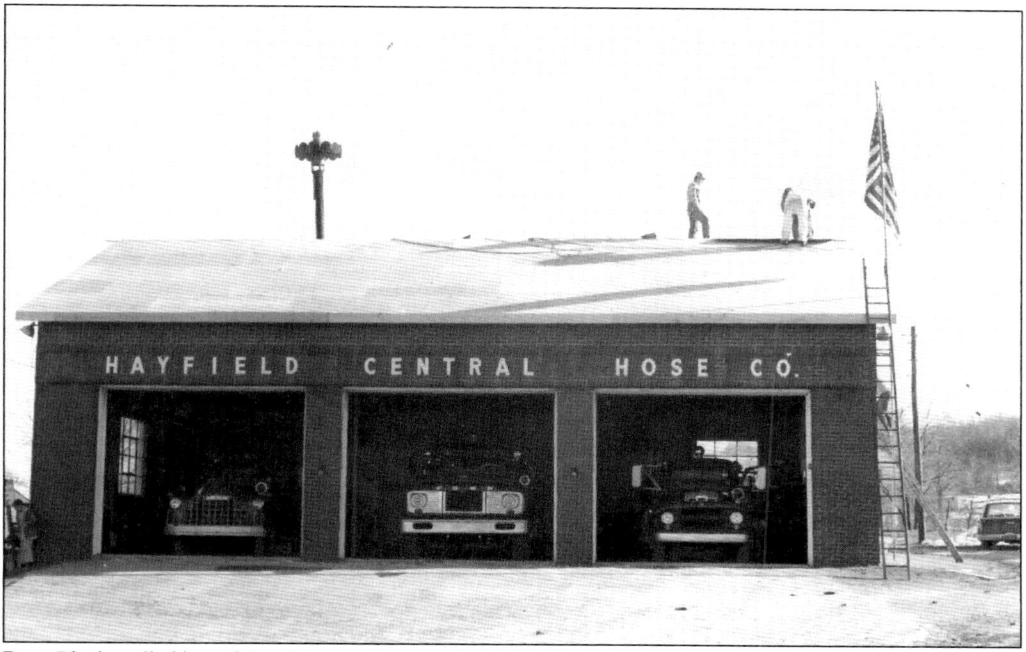

Ron Phelan (left) and Joe Myers are seen here finishing the fire department roof. (Courtesy of the Hayfield Volunteer Fire Department.)

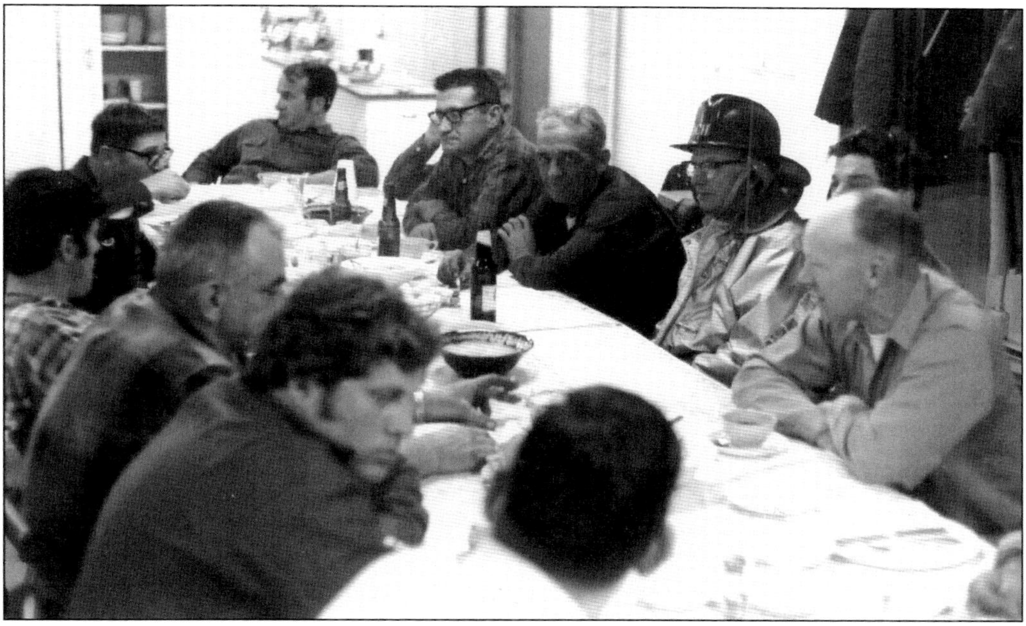

A hard day's work means a good lunch. Sitting around the table clockwise from front right are Tom Eckart, John Hanks, Ed Truchan, Ron Phelan, Jim Reichel, Wayne Brown, Harry Stanford, Ken Hill, Lenon Smith, Mike Constanovich, and Hugh Yokes. Harry Stanford was the owner of Stanford's Garage in Little's Corners. He served in the 8th Air Force during World War II and was a Hayfield Fire Department charter member. (Courtesy of the Hayfield Volunteer Fire Department.)

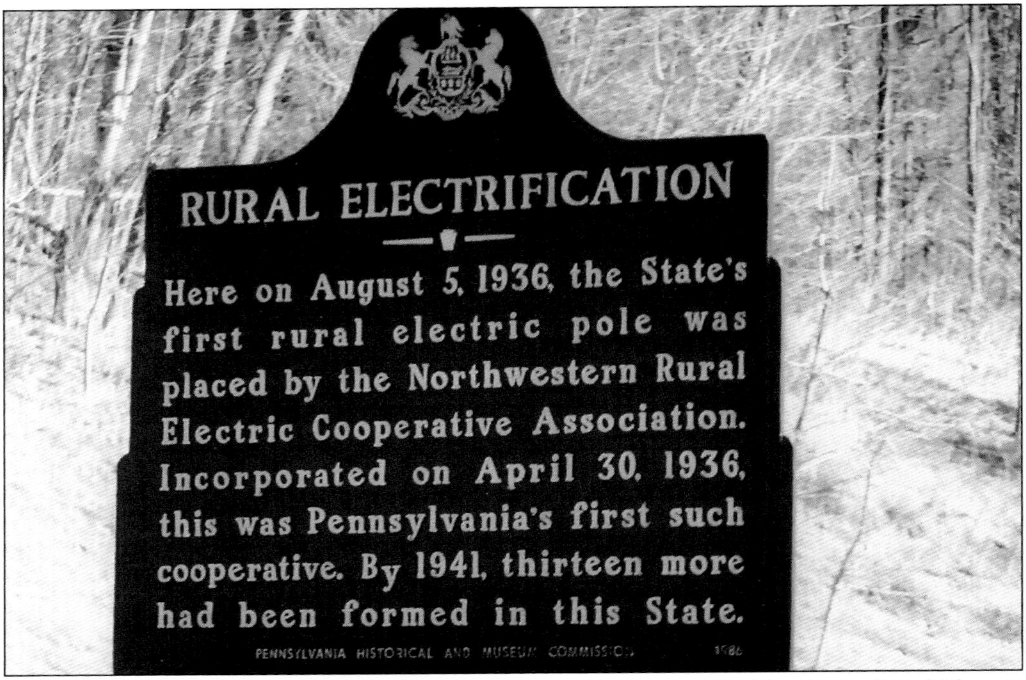

As seen in the sign, Pennsylvania's first electric cooperative was the Northwest Rural Electric Cooperative Association. The first pole was placed near Blooming Valley on State Route 198. This marker was placed in 1986.

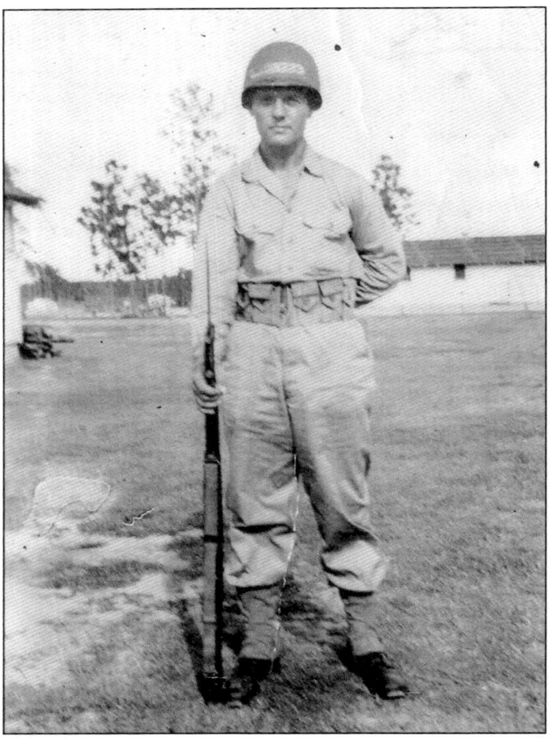

Pfc. Kenneth Hunter was a member of the 10th Mountain Division, serving in Italy during World War II. A pair of his gloves, on display at the Saegertown Heritage Society, has large tears from being torn through when shrapnel punctured his backpack while being worn. The shrapnel never made it completely through the backpack, leaving Hunter uninjured.

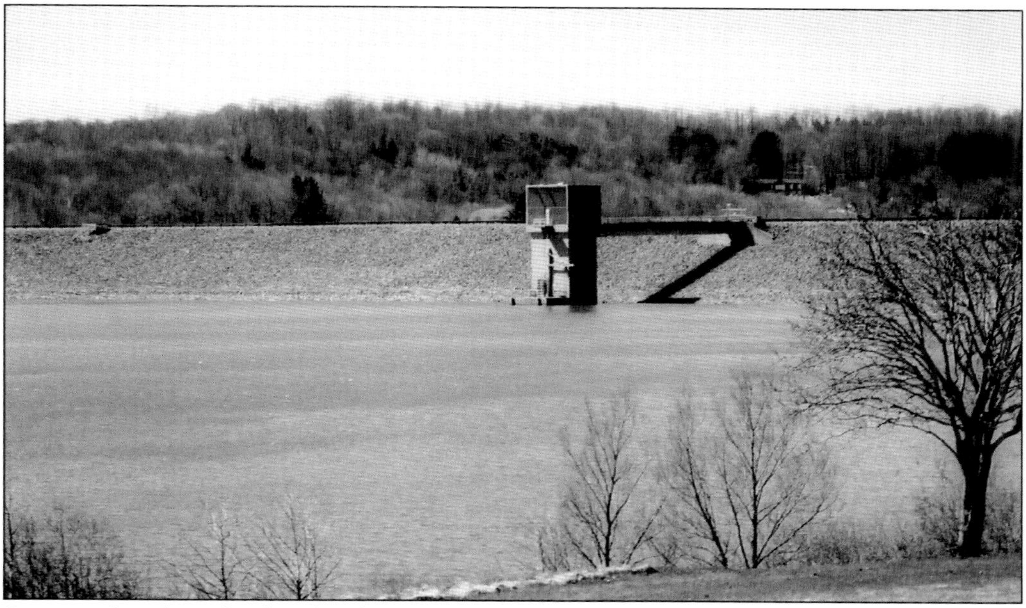

Since its founding, flooding has been a constant problem in the Saegertown area. The Army Corps of Engineers built the Woodcock Dam in 1973 to help with flood control. Millions of dollars were spent on the dam and recreation area associated with it. Woodcock Lake, formed by damming up Woodcock Creek, is 333 acres but varies by season and drought year.

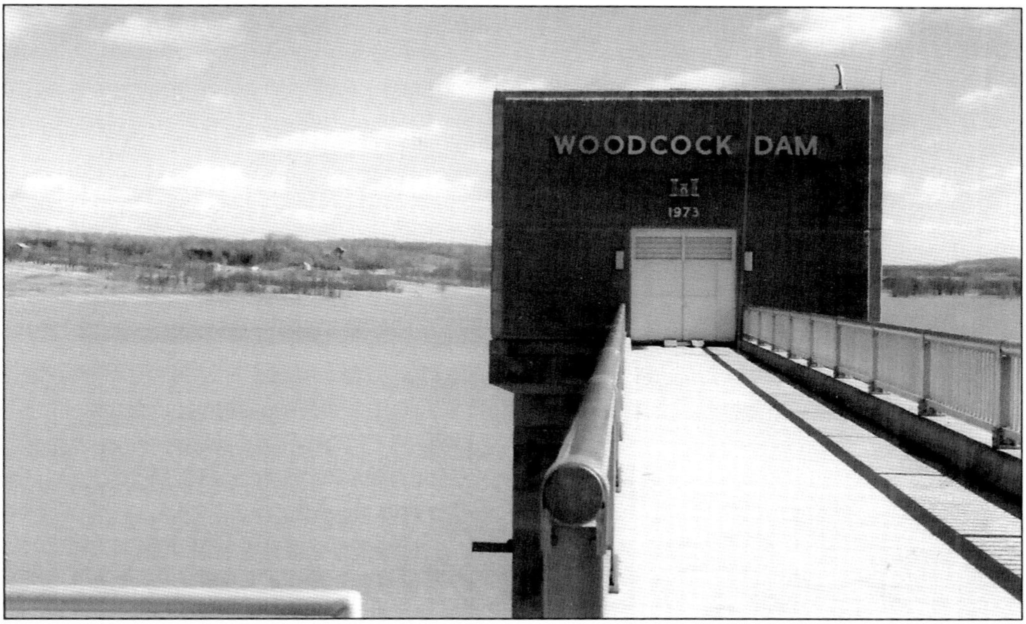

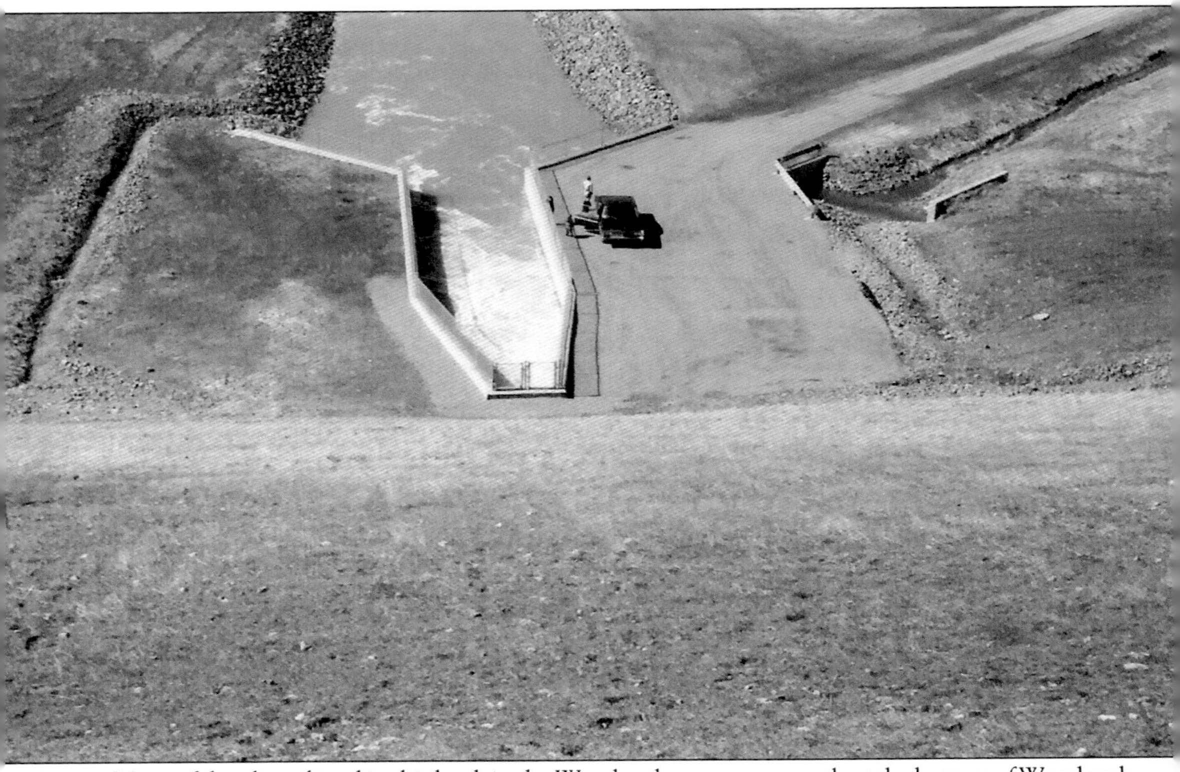

Many of the places listed in this book in the Woodcock area are currently at the bottom of Woodcock Lake. When the lake was established, houses, farms, and other buildings were submerged.

Four

The Rural Social Scene

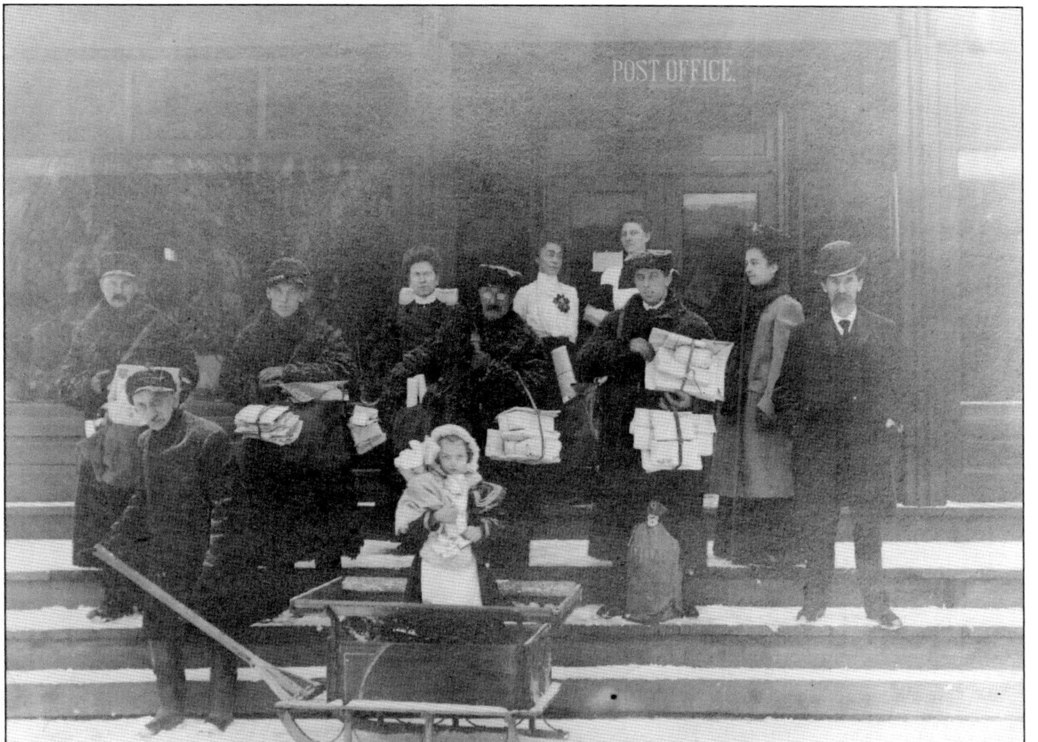

A gathering is seen here picking up packages from the Saegertown Post Office. Being winter, the number of packages could mean it is the Christmas season, but it cannot be confirmed.

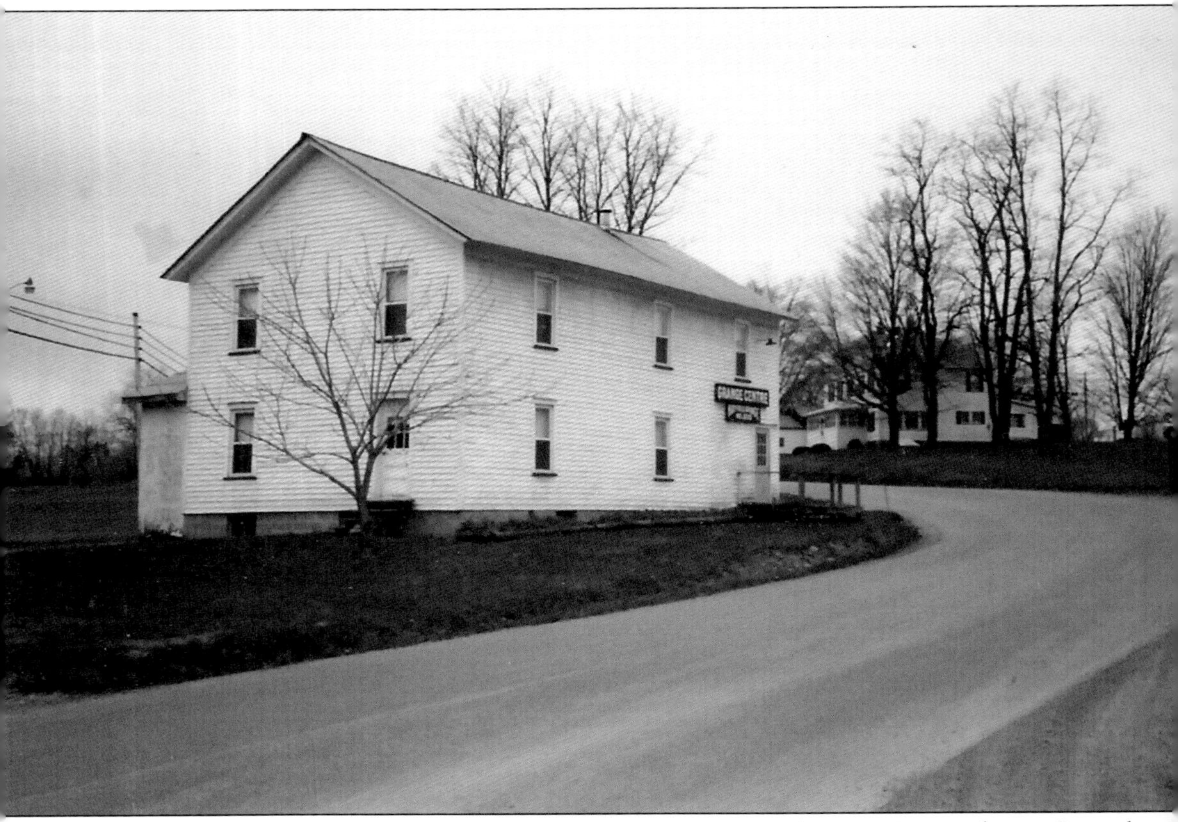

Hayfield Grange No. 800 was first organized on April 15, 1886, by state Grange deputy Samuel Dout. It rented its hall, originally a cheese factory, for four years before purchasing the structure for $200. Many improvements were made during this time, and the building has been in continual use for Grange business through the present day. Four Granges have consolidated with it over the years: Keystone Grange No. 901 from Little's Corners in October 1965, Meadville Grange in January 1987, Randolph Grange No. 190 in October 1993, and Woodcock Center Grange more recently. It currently holds the largest membership of any Grange in Crawford County. (Courtesy of Hayfield Grange No. 800.)

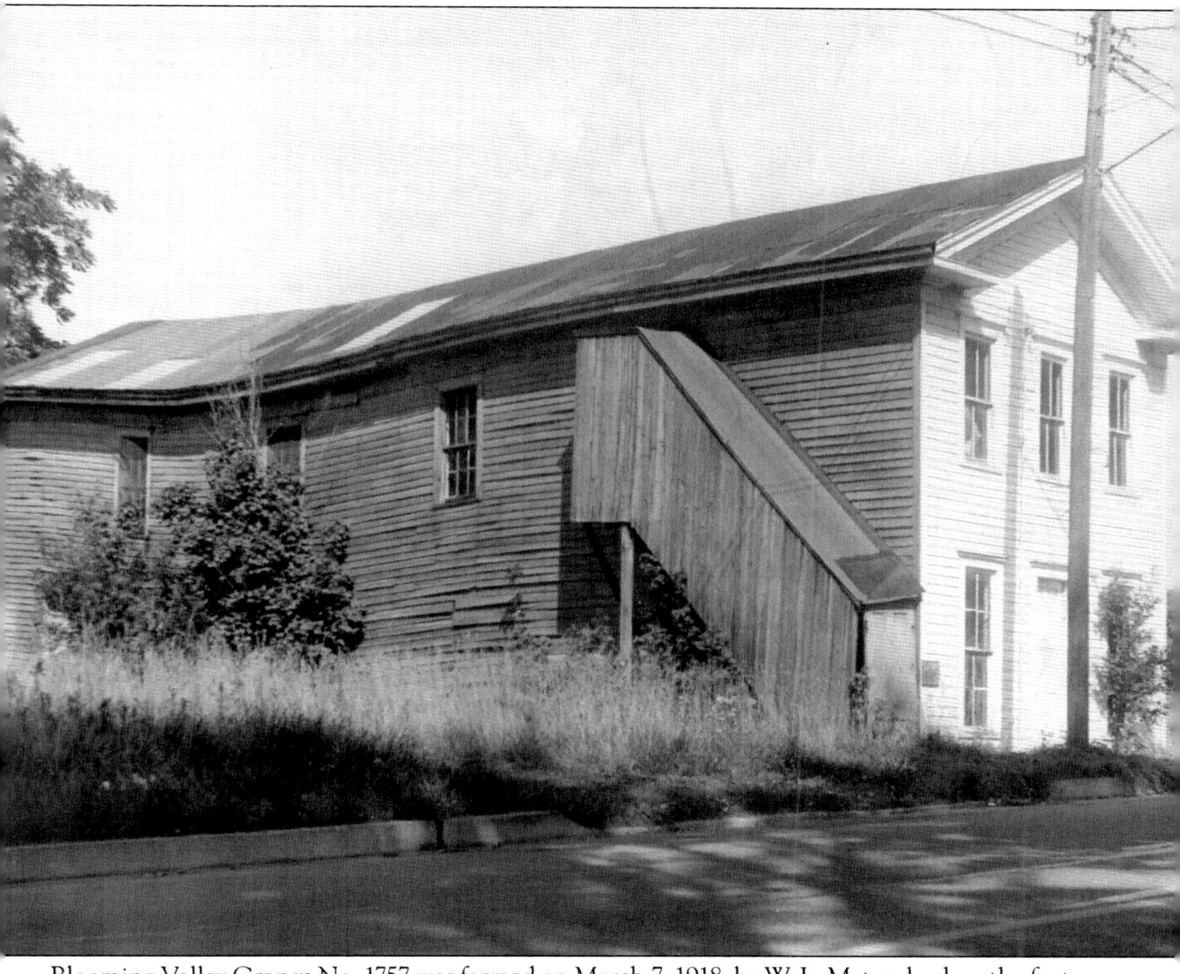

Blooming Valley Grange No. 1757 was formed on March 7, 1918, by W. L. Metzenbacher, the first master, in the old Hunter House Hotel with 71 charter members. It removed the eastern wing of the building due to safety issues and remodeled the remainder into a suitable meeting area and social hall. The Grange remained for over 40 years as the community hub until consolidating with Randolph Grange No. 190 on June 31, 1961.

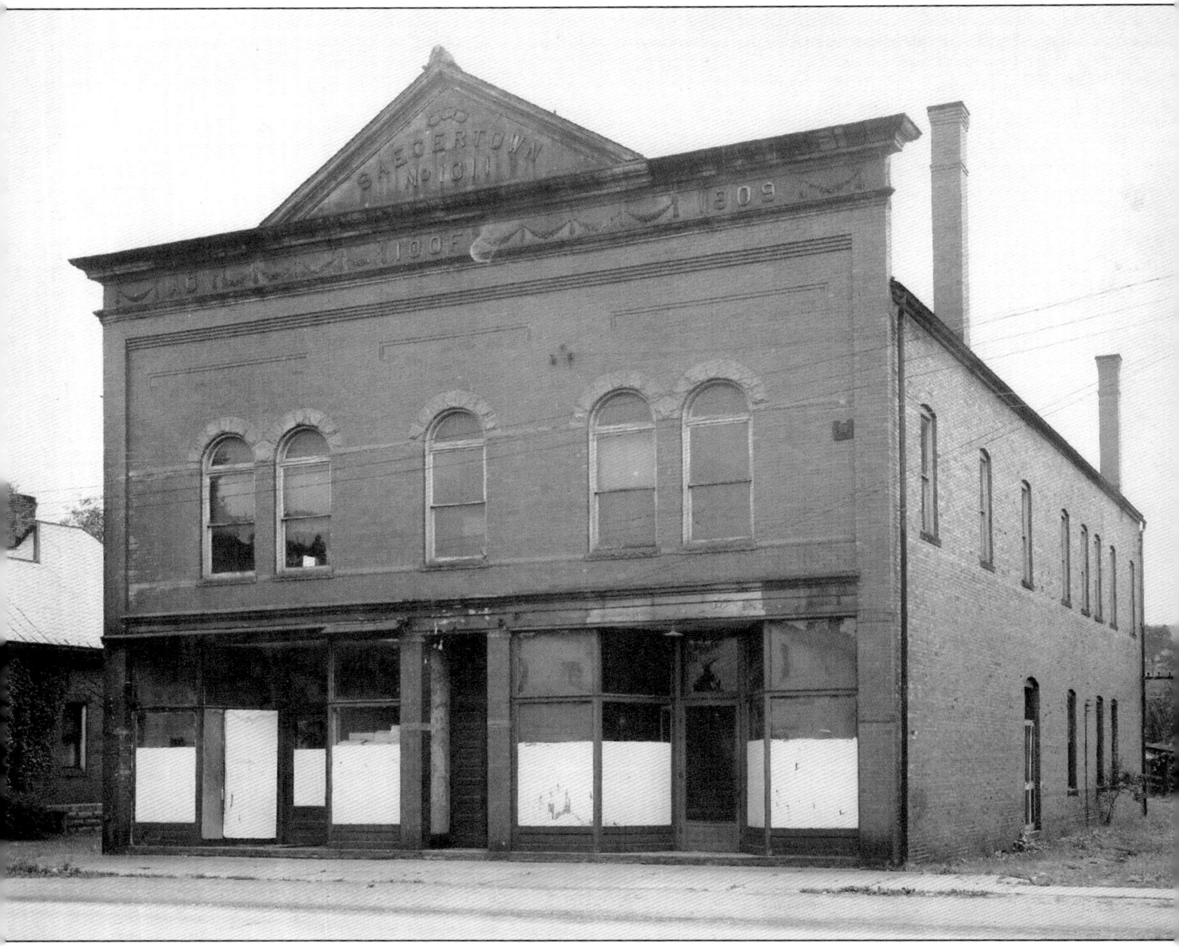

Built in 1909 as a replacement for the recently burned structure, the Independent Order of Odd Fellows building served as the organization's meeting area and social hall. Since that time, it has served as a telephone office, locker plant, bowling alley, pizza parlor, day care, and more uses in recent years. In 1944, at the time of this photograph, DWIN (Baldwin Laboratories' brand name) was using the second floor as part of its factory.

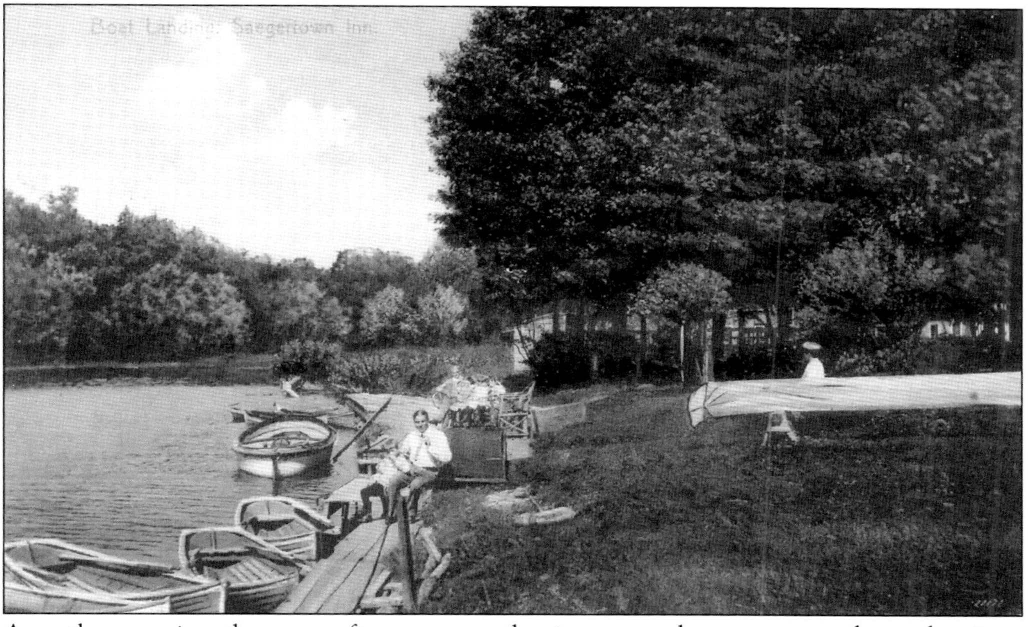

A gentleman enjoys the sunny afternoon near the river as another gets prepared to go boating.

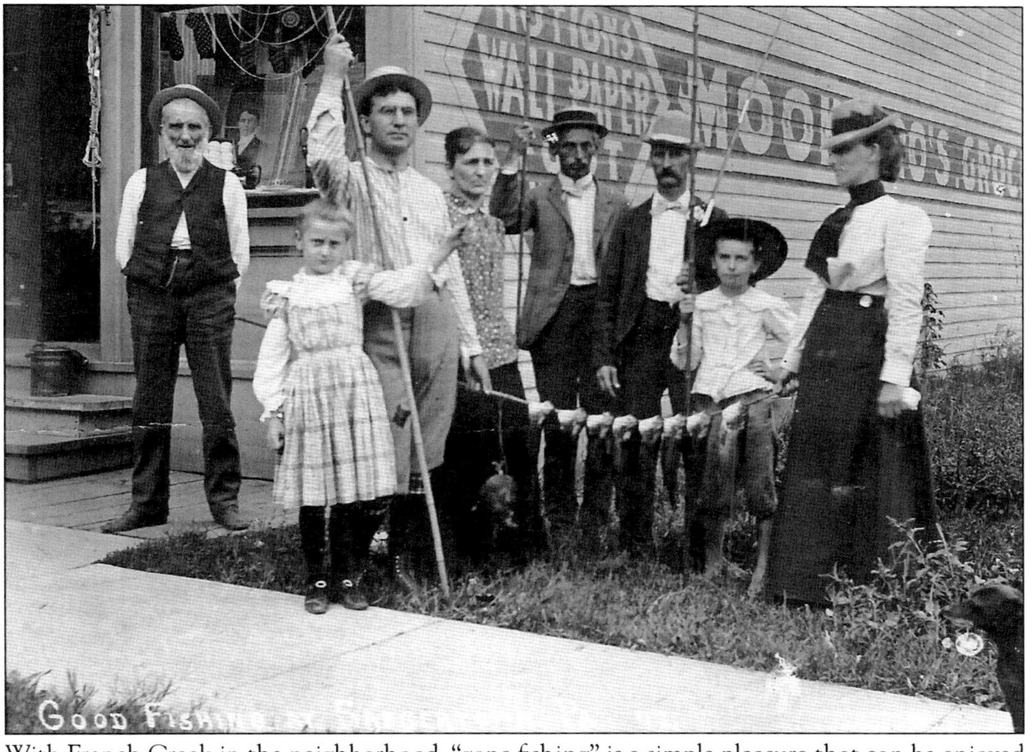

With French Creek in the neighborhood, "gone fishing" is a simple pleasure that can be enjoyed on a regular basis. Standing for this postcard, the group here shows its catch.

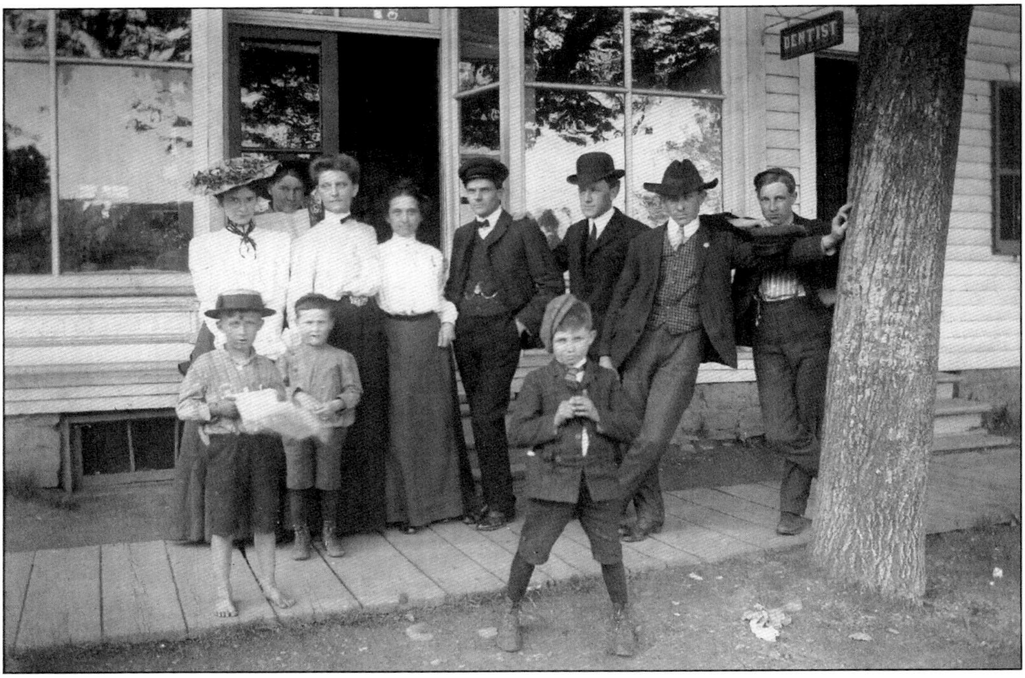

A group of residents is gathering in front of the local dentist office for a picture.

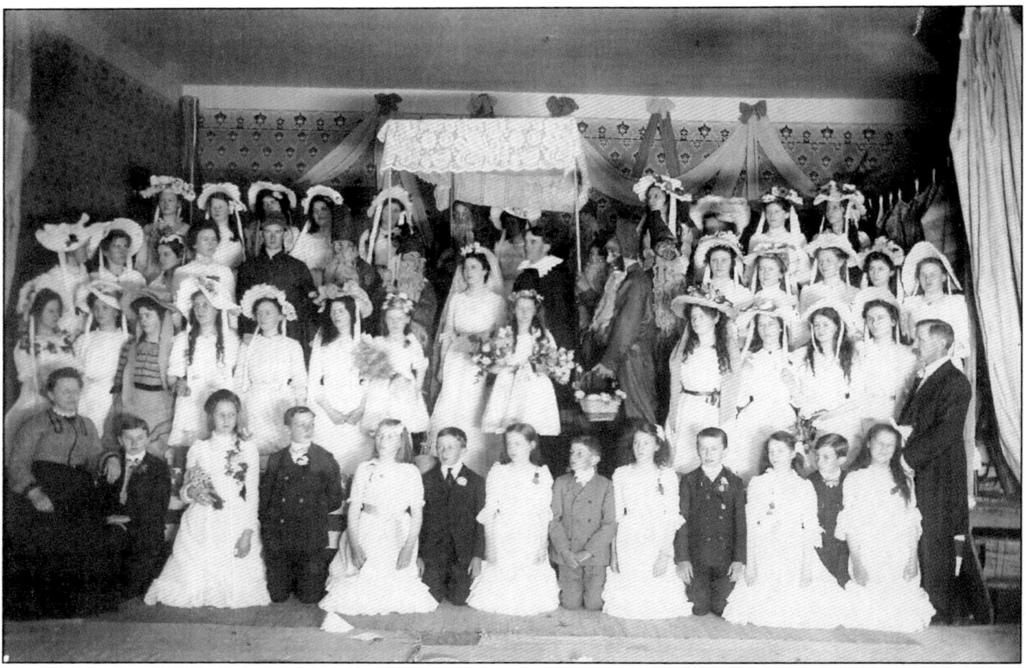

The Saegertown Inn, as with the other inns and hotels in the area, had one thing in great demand to citizens—free space. The ballroom at the inn was used frequently for community affairs, this one being a 1903 local production of *Snow White*.

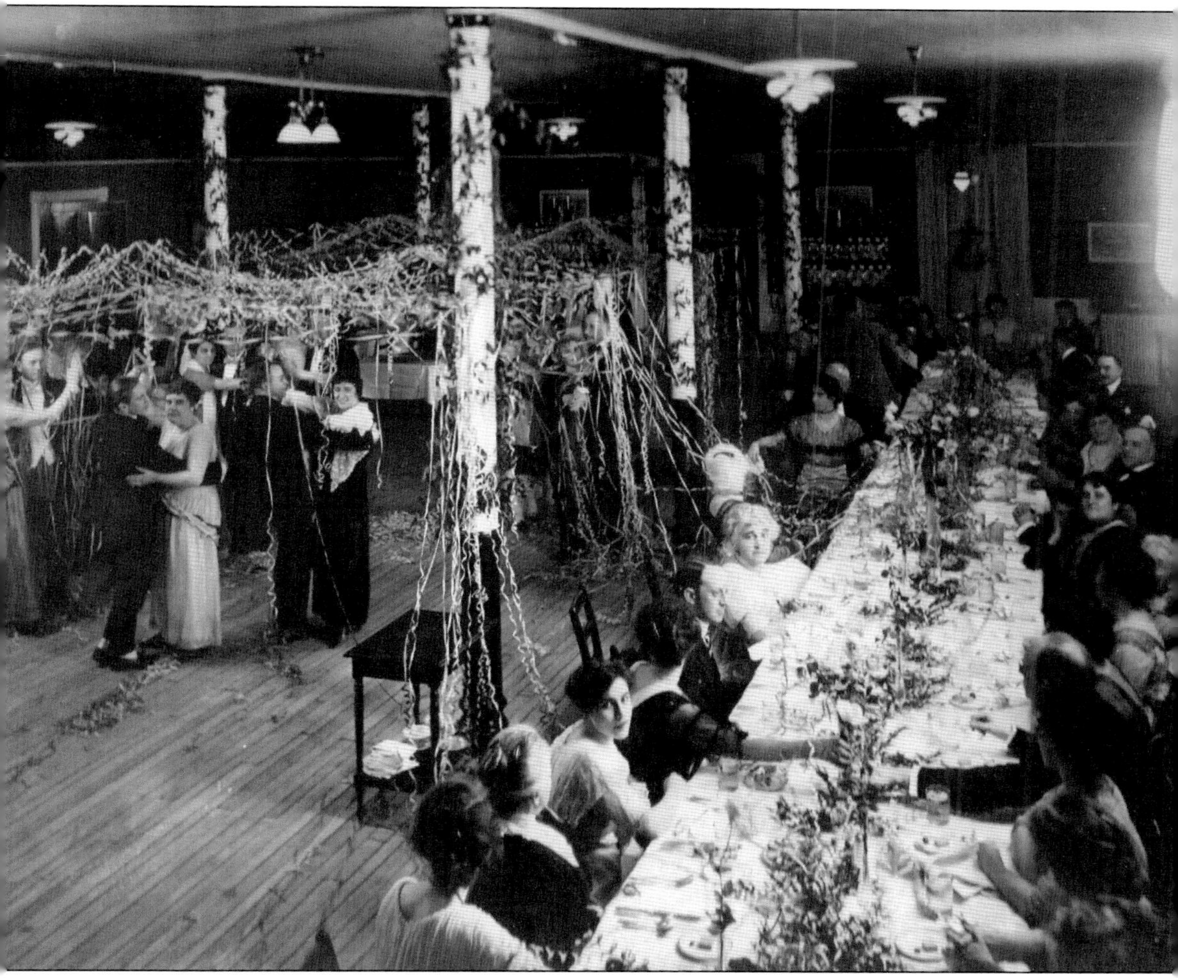

The Saegertown Inn hosted special dinners and events for holidays when it became well established. In its first year in business under the Fox family's proprietorship, it entertained four guests for Thanksgiving, two on Christmas, and three over New Year's. The Fox family expanded the inn and with this expanded its festivities, as can be seen at this New Year's party. During the 1915–1916 season, 151 guests attended Thanksgiving dinner, 67 celebrated Christmas here, and 96 guests were entertained over New Year's at the inn.

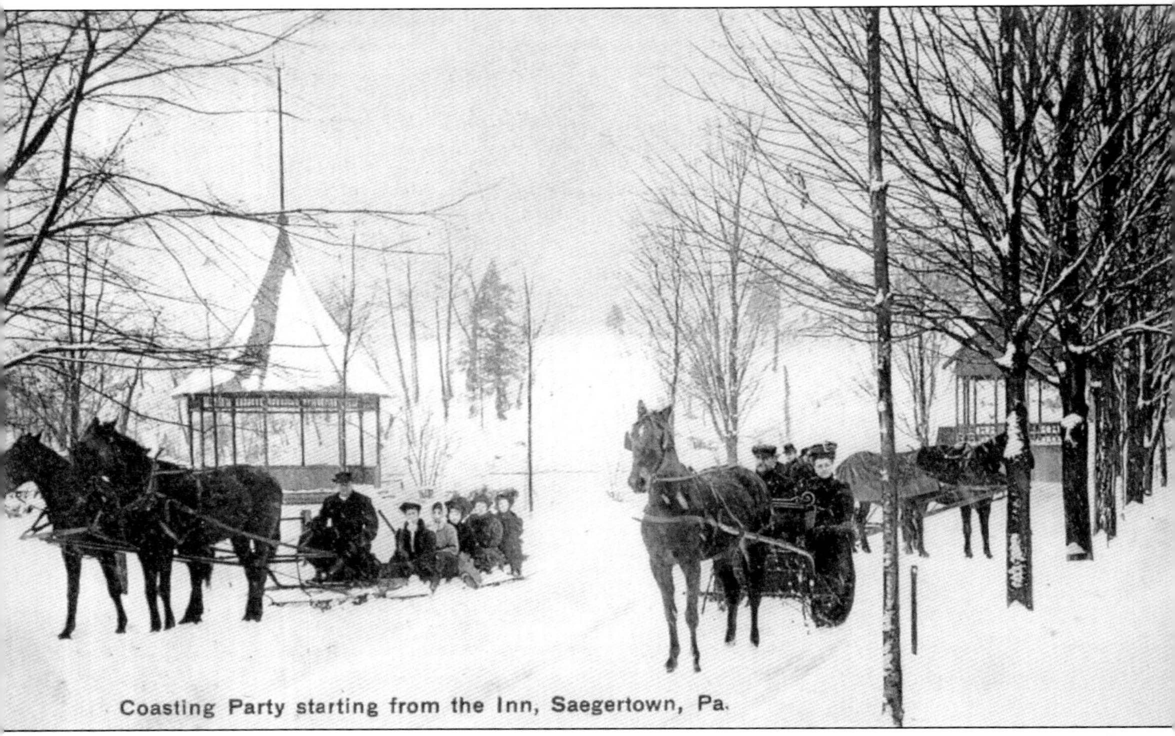

Long before the days of radio and television, winter brought with it a vast array of ways to be entertained in a small community such as Saegertown. The coasting (or sledding) party shown here could have been guests of the Saegertown Inn or just local residents having a bit of weekend fun. Regardless of who, this was truly a time when the simple pleasures were much better realized than in the current hectic world.

The Saegertown High School basketball team was formed with seven members in 1927. It played its games in the Grace Hotel.

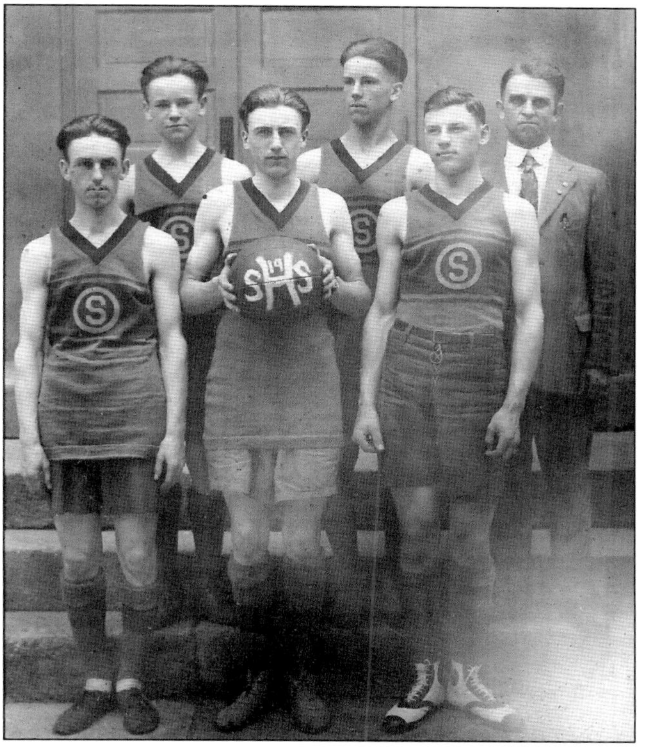

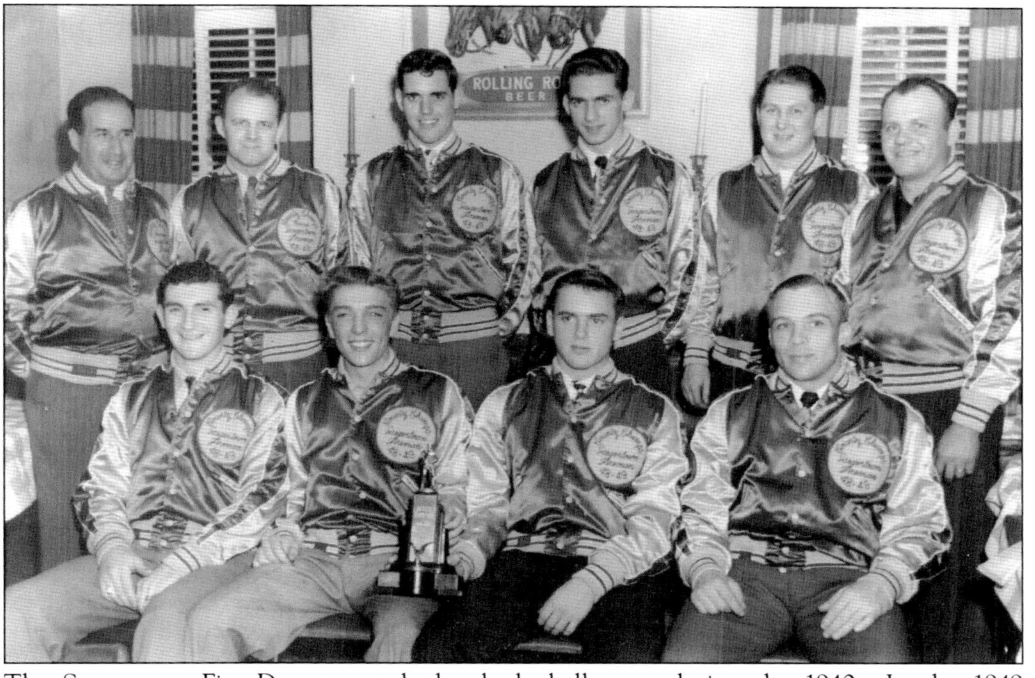

The Saegertown Fire Department had a basketball team during the 1940s. In the 1949 photograph shown here, the team sits for a picture with its trophy. Henry Ward Baldwin's (Baldwin Laboratories owner) son "Buzz" (Henry Jr.) is seen sitting second from the left.

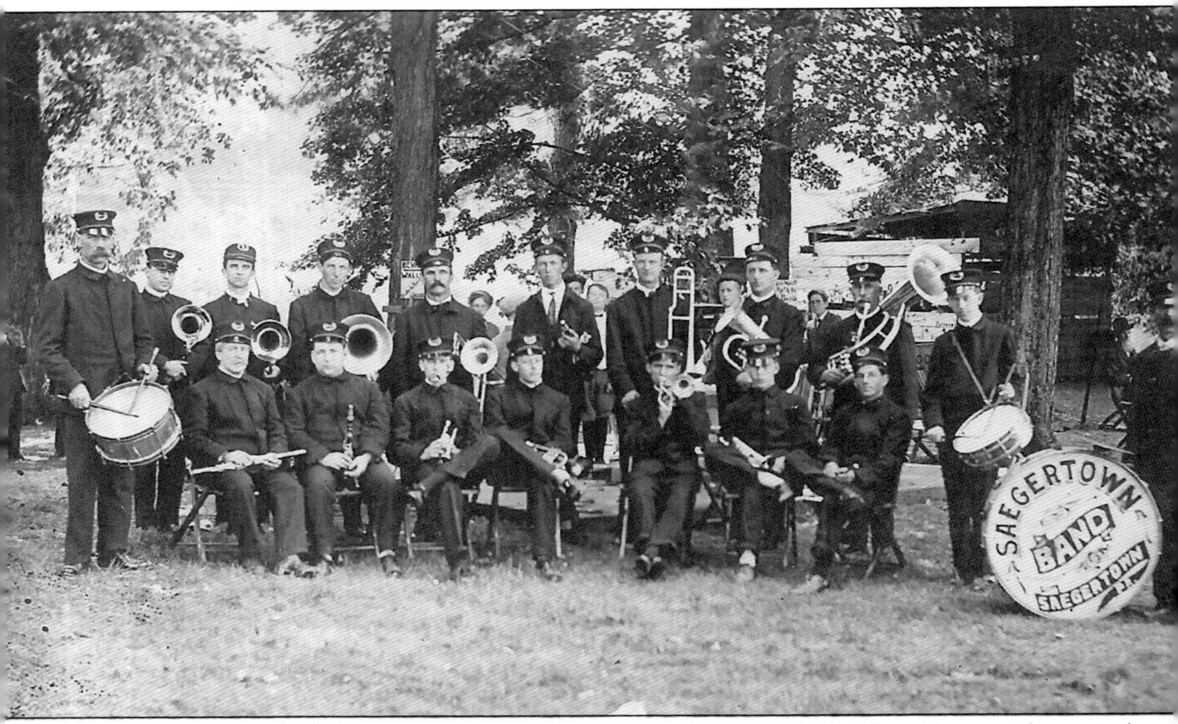

Before schools had their own sports teams and marching bands, local residents with musical ability formed town bands. Shown here in 1905, the Saegertown Band stands ready for a musical engagement of some sort. The Saegertown Band traveled by wagon twice during the 1890s, to play in the inaugurations of Grover Cleveland and William McKinley. It was renowned for its talent in this area and on a larger scale.

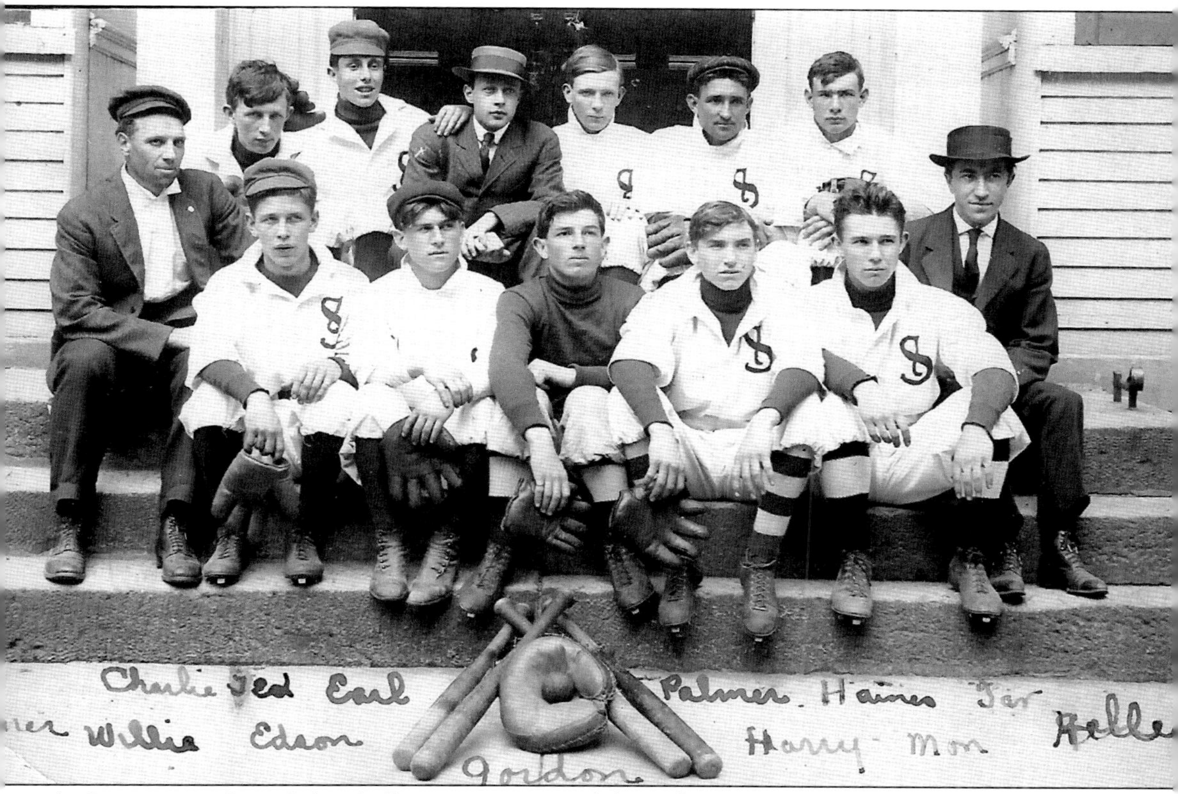

A Saegertown "town" baseball team is pictured here from either the late 19th or early 20th centuries. Incomplete names listed on the photograph are as follows, from left to right: (first row) "Miner," Willie, Edson, Gordon, Harry, "Mon," and Kelly; (second row) Charlie, Ted, Earl, Palmer, Haines, and "Jar."

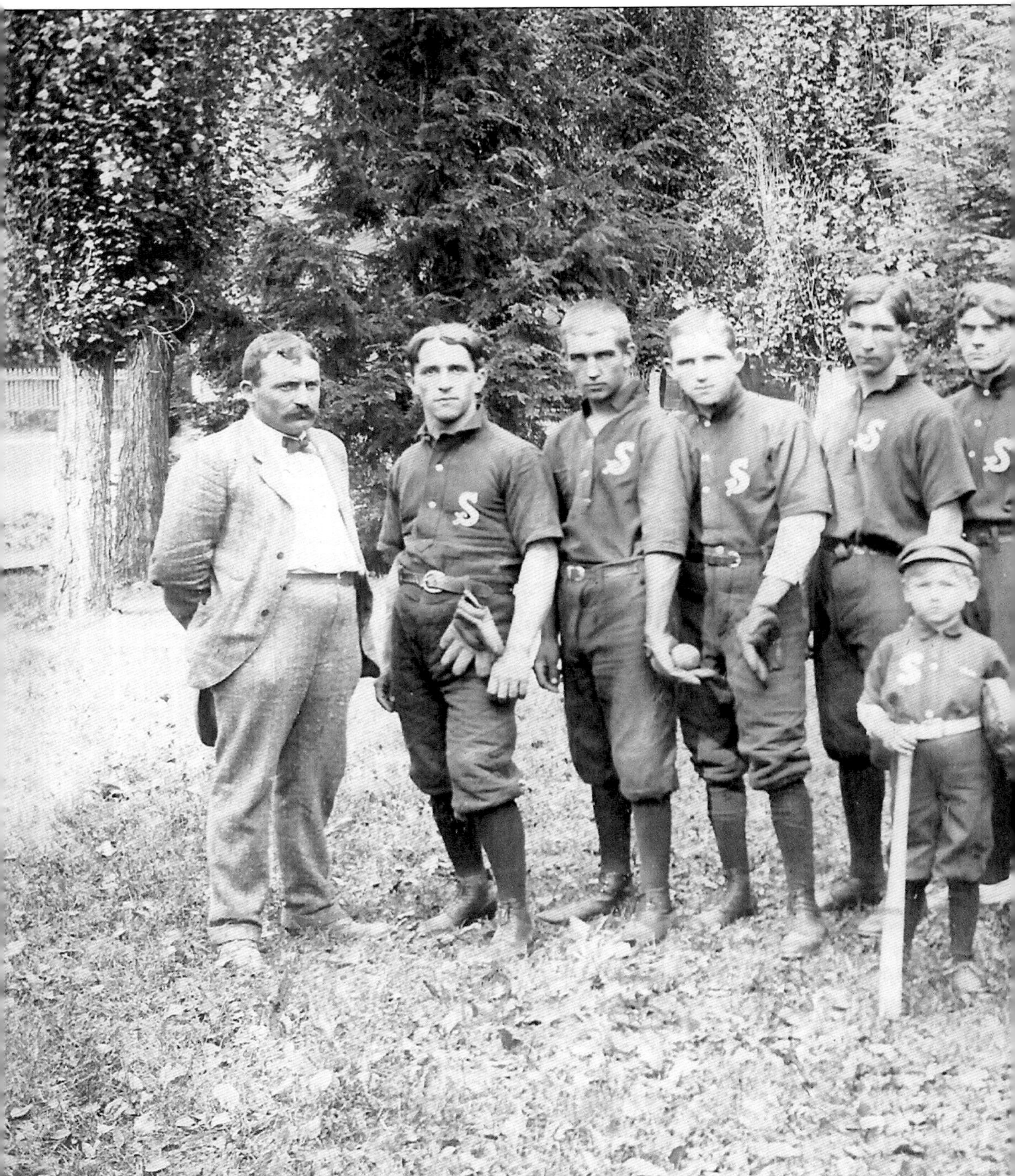

Baseball was a popular sport among small communities such as Saegertown throughout the 19th and 20th centuries. Groups such as churches, businesses, Granges, and other such organizations would often form their own community baseball teams and compete against others in the county. Meanwhile wives, children, and curious neighbors would congregate to these games,

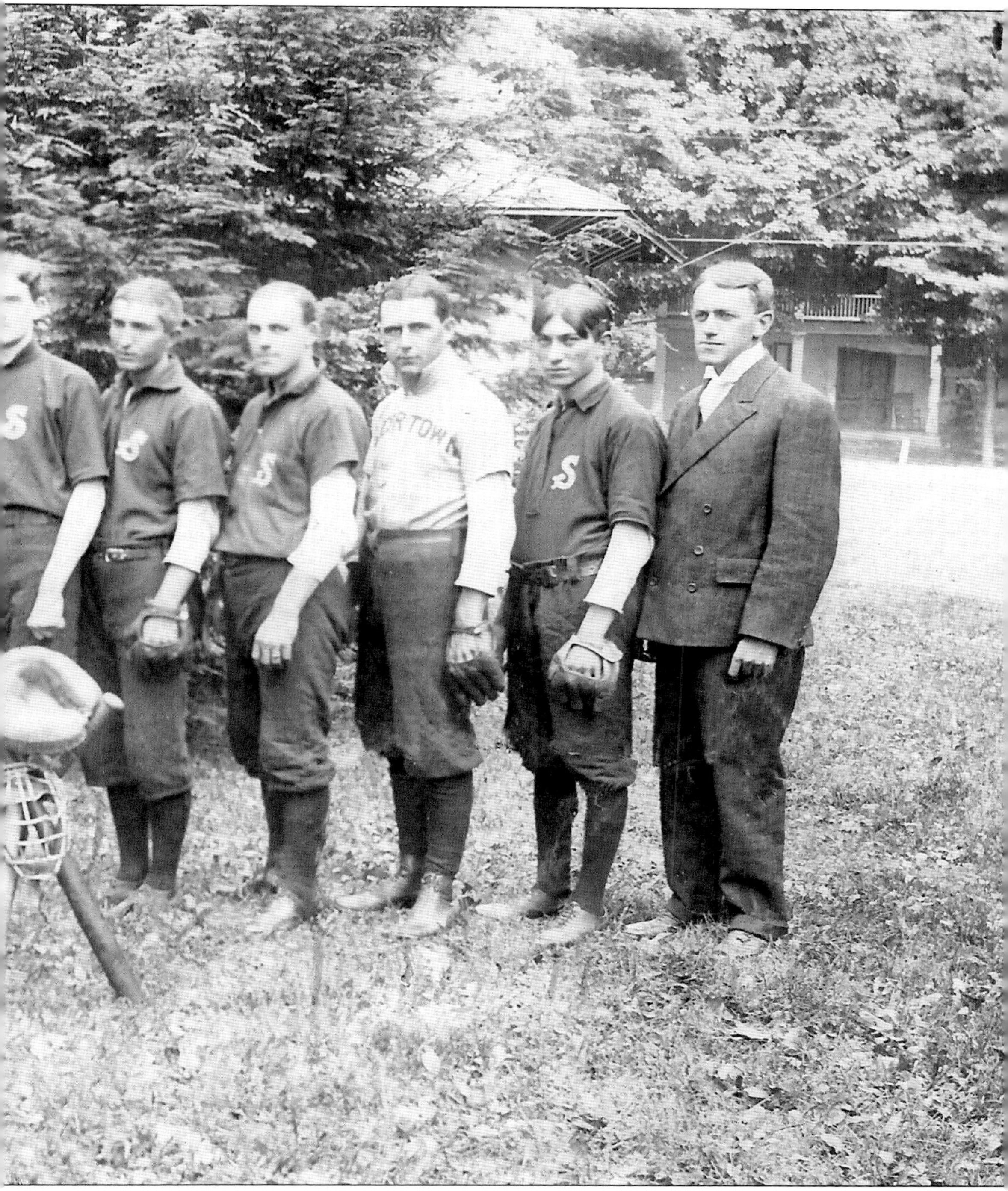

holding community get-togethers and picnics in this television- and radio-free era. Even though this started as a community event, Saegertown High School had its own team during the early and mid-1900s and won the Crawford County Class B championship several times during the 1940s and 1950s.

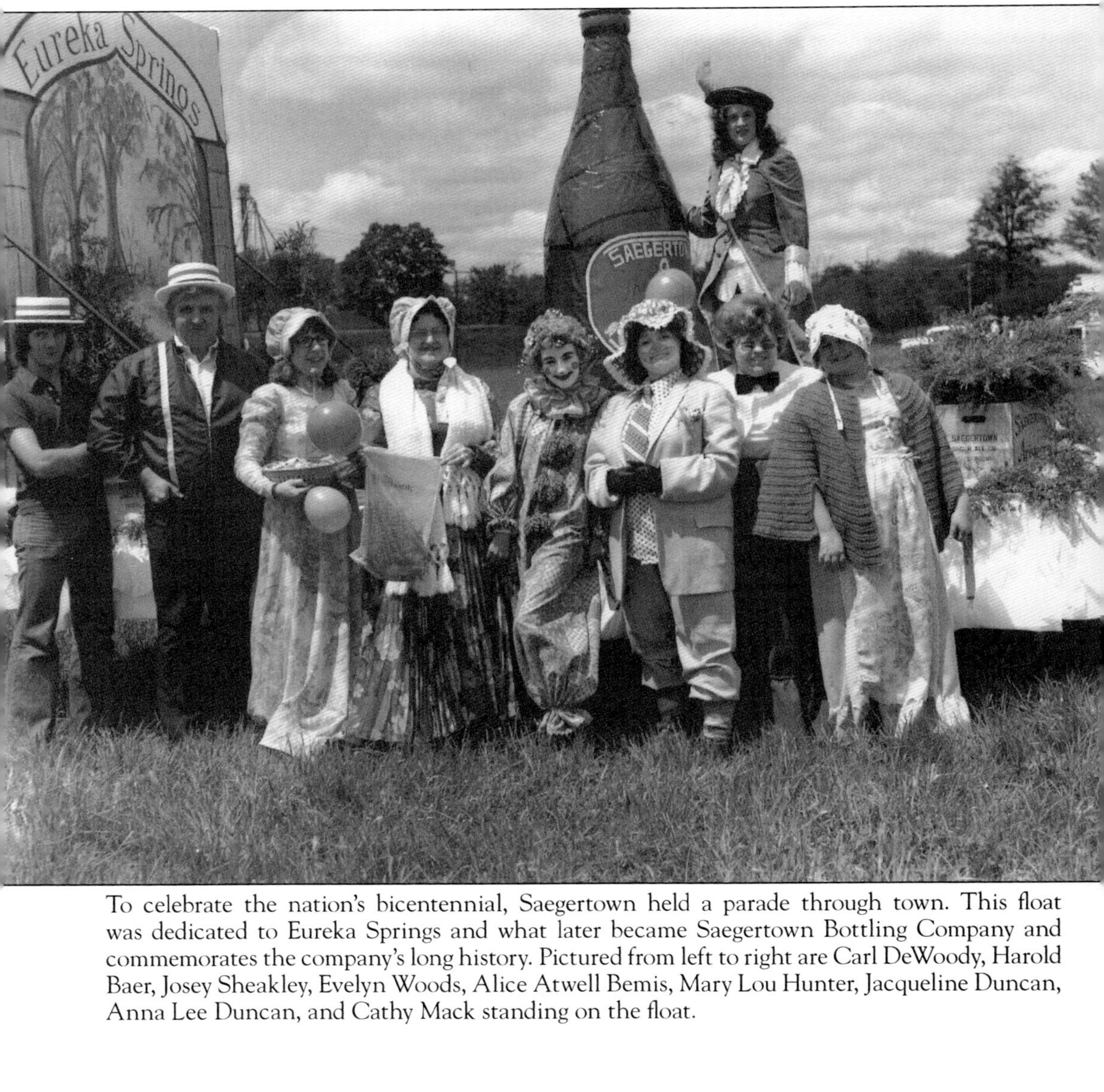

To celebrate the nation's bicentennial, Saegertown held a parade through town. This float was dedicated to Eureka Springs and what later became Saegertown Bottling Company and commemorates the company's long history. Pictured from left to right are Carl DeWoody, Harold Baer, Josey Sheakley, Evelyn Woods, Alice Atwell Bemis, Mary Lou Hunter, Jacqueline Duncan, Anna Lee Duncan, and Cathy Mack standing on the float.

Five

Small-Town Entrepreneurs

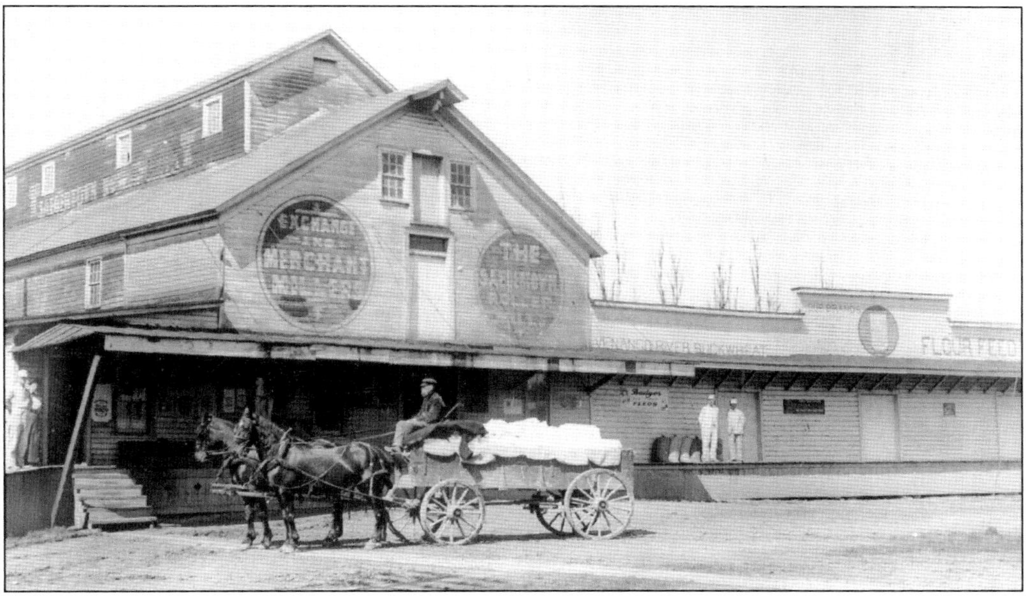

Long before it received its current name, Saegertown took the title of its first industry, Alden's Mills. Maj. Roger Alden built the first mill in 1801. The mill was powered by the waters of French Creek and was in operation as the Saegertown Roller Mills until 1913 when the east end of the dam washed out, ending operations.

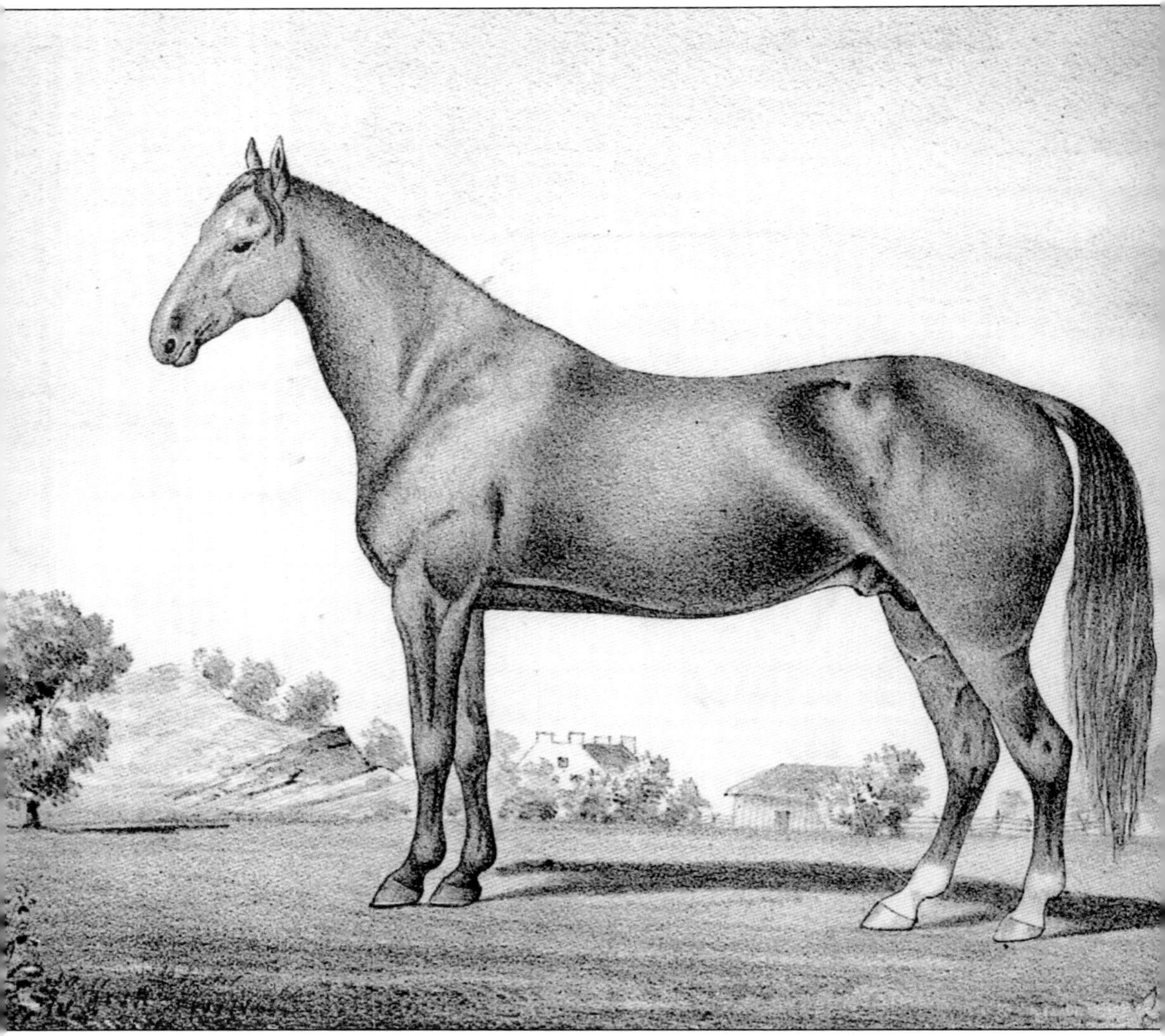

The horse pictured here belonged to Whipple and Densmore, millers in Saegertown. The Whipple brothers purchased the Saegertown Roller Mills originally owned by Maj. Roger Alden.

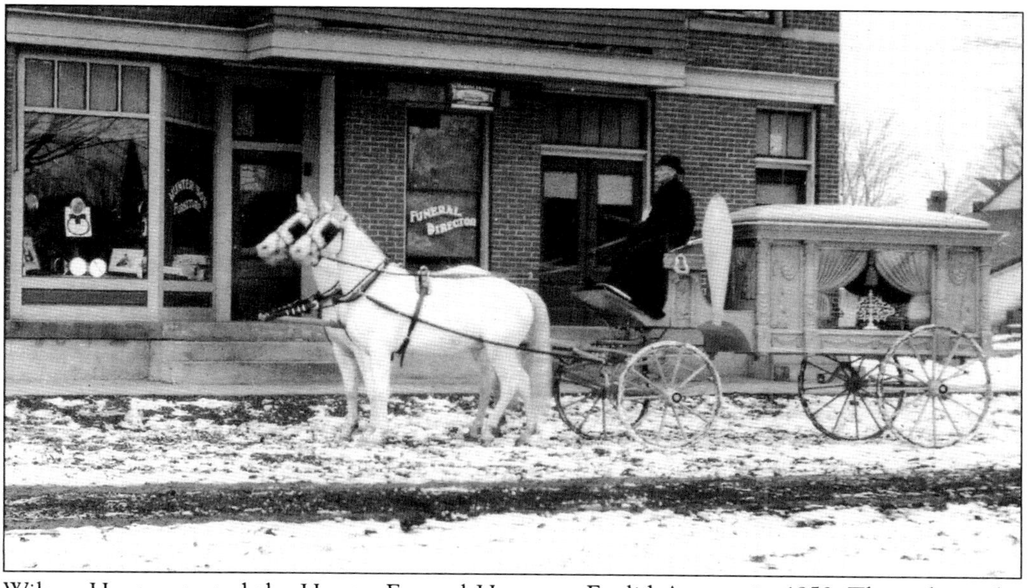

Wilson Hunter started the Hunter Funeral Home on Euclid Avenue in 1850. Throughout the 19th and early 20th centuries, Saegertown residents could also come here to purchase handmade furniture of all types. It was later moved to Broad Street, where the business is currently. The funeral home was operated by the Hunter family for over a century, as shown here, until the last undertaker, Kenneth Hunter, sold the business to Byham Miller Mizner Funeral Home of Meadville on March 1, 1985.

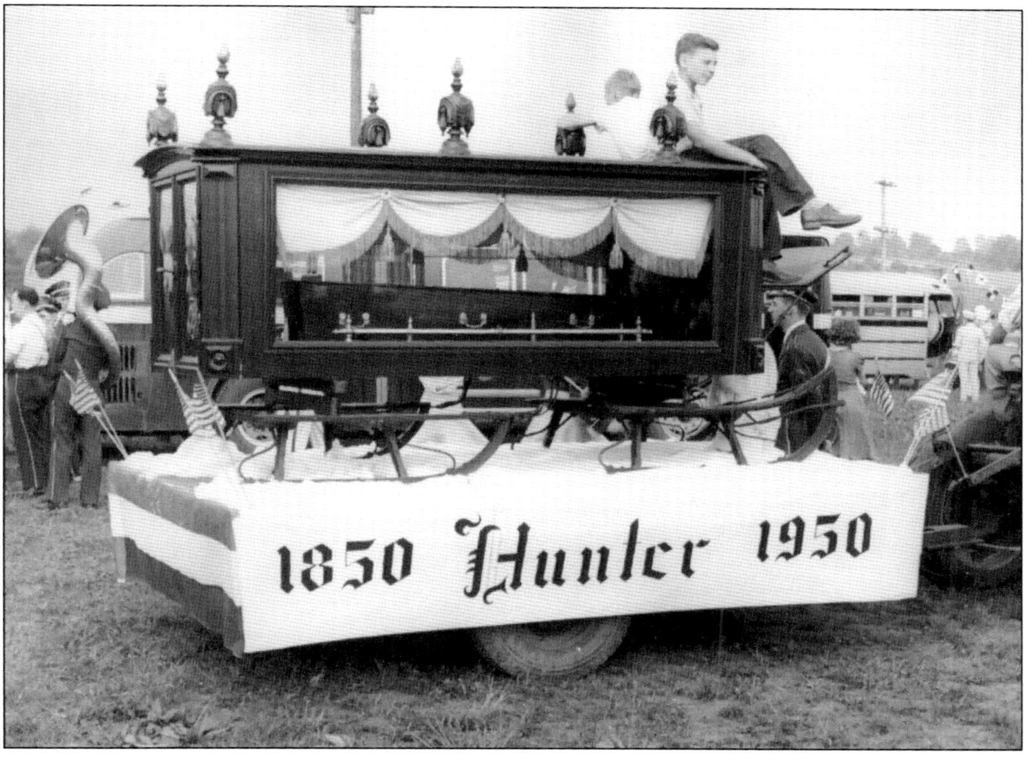

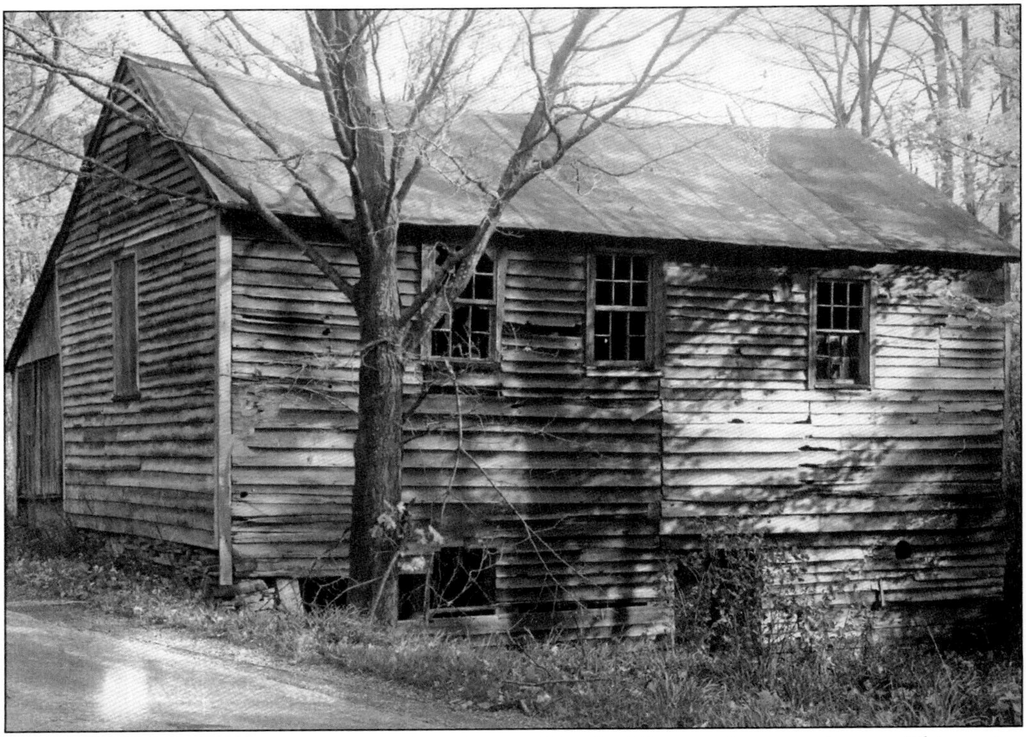

The Dickson family also owned a wool-carding mill in the Woodcock reservoir area. This entire area is now underwater with the formation of Woodcock Lake.

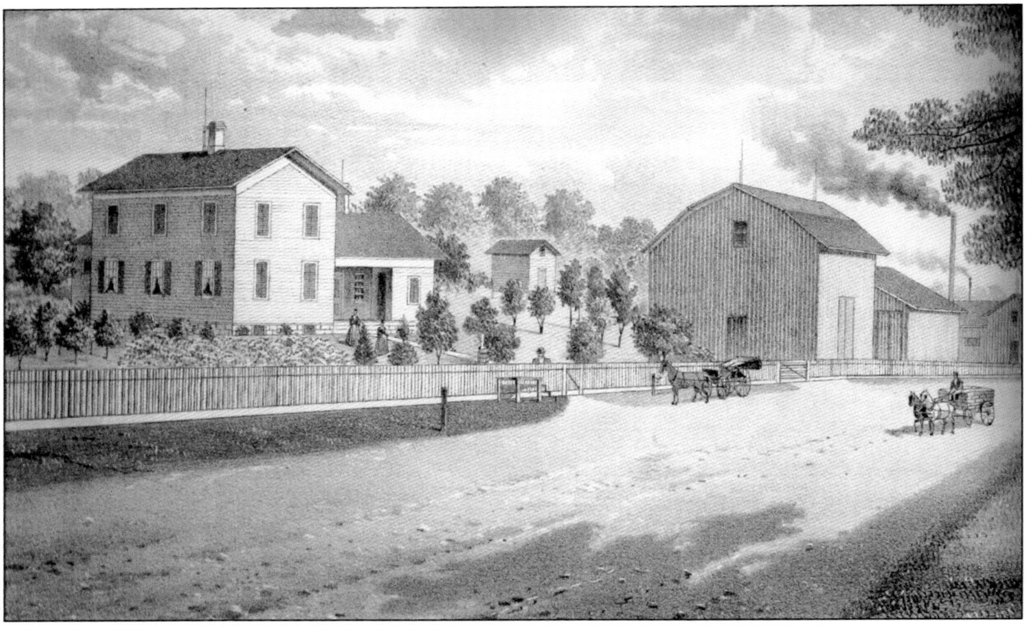

Porter J. Beebe owned and operated a handle-turning factory in Little's Corners for many years, owning 40 acres of land there.

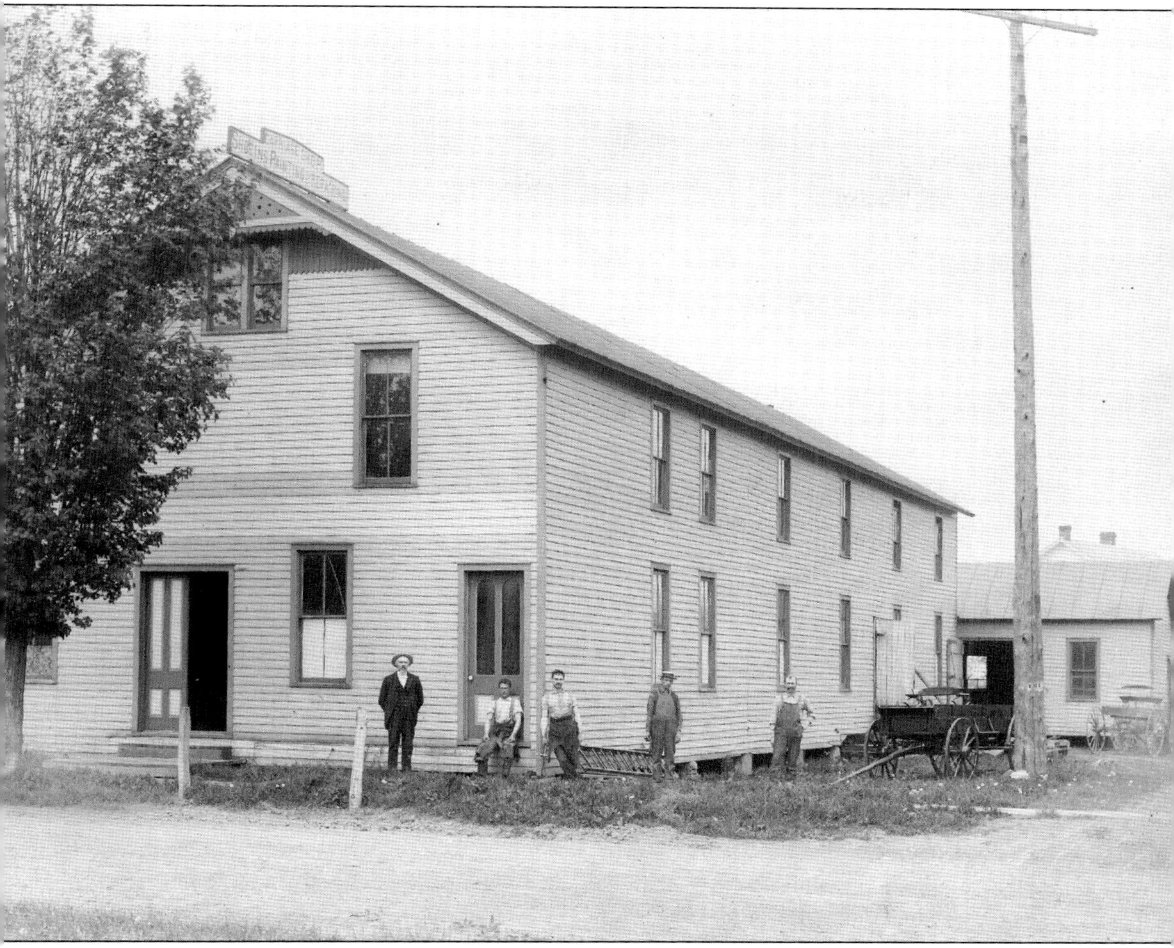

The Porter Carriage Works was in operation during the late 1800s. It was destroyed by fire in 1898. This was considered one of the worst fires in Saegertown's history, burning the carriage works, Rhodes' Store, and the Hornstein Furniture building. Hornstein was the only one of the three to rebuild.

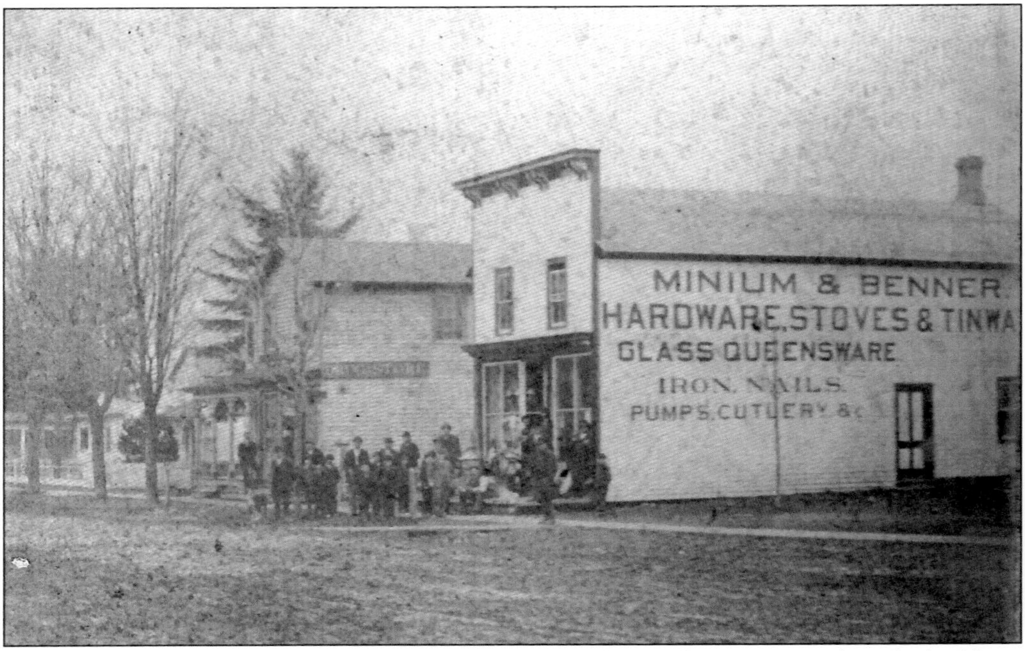

Minium and Benner is seen here from the side view, displaying the sign painted on the building.

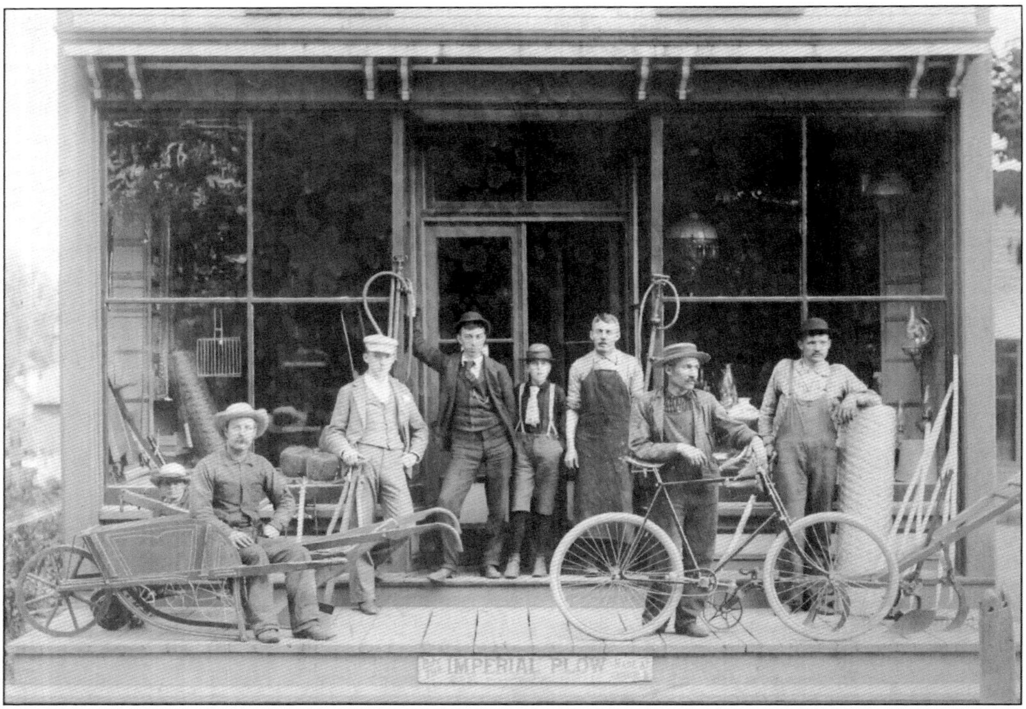

The following are shown from left to right in front of the Minium and Benner Hardware: unidentified, Dave Hunter (in wheelbarrow), unidentified, Jason and Loyd Minium, Wayne Benner (with apron), W. P. Benner (near bicycle), and John Cochran by the spool of wire.

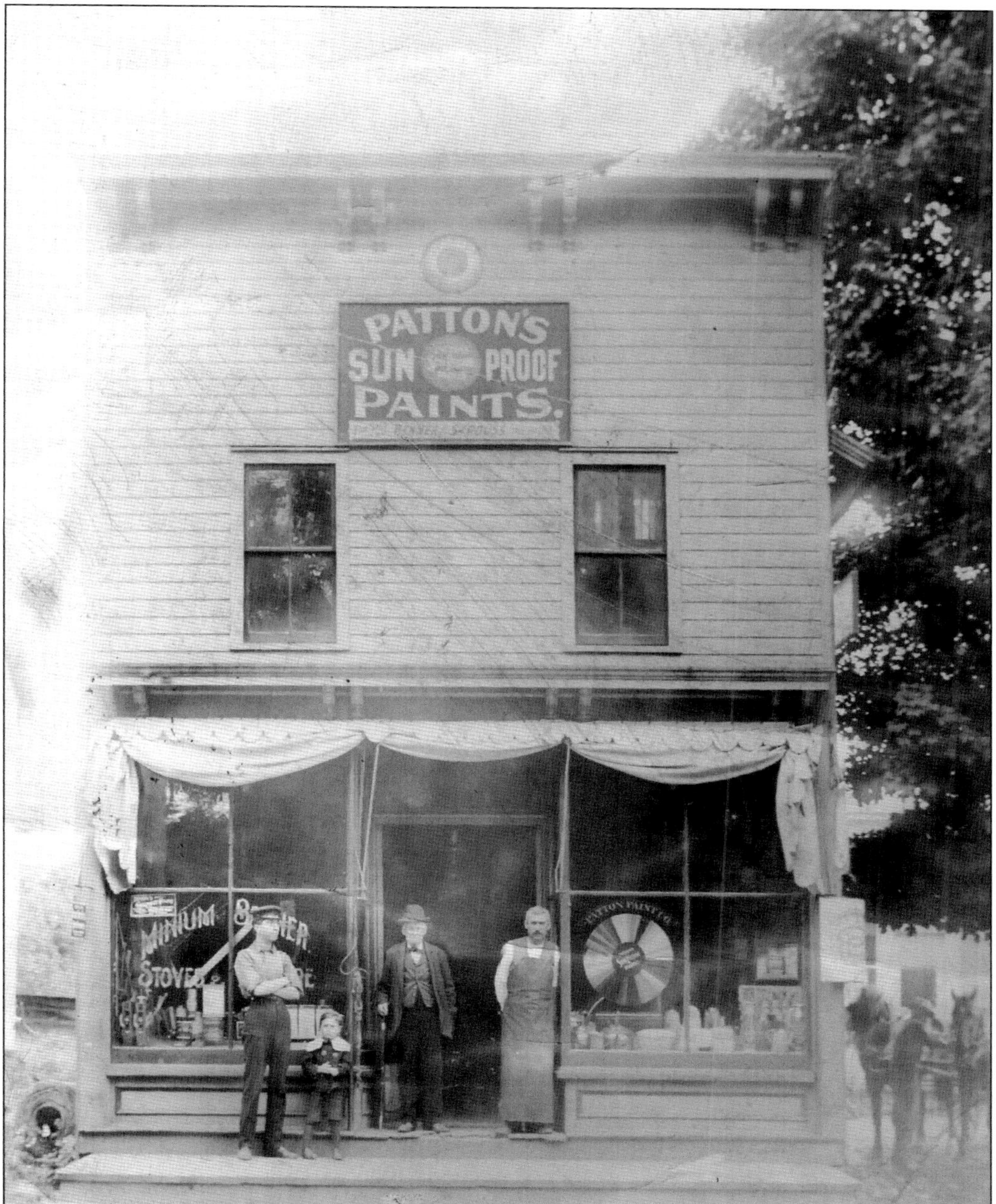

The first hardware store in Saegertown was opened in the late 1800s. At Minium and Benner, one could expect to find a full line of stoves from the Chicago and Erie Stove Company, Patton Paints, and all other hardware needs. W. P. Benner (wearing the apron) stands next to John Munich in the doorway to the building with the town square to the left side of the photograph.

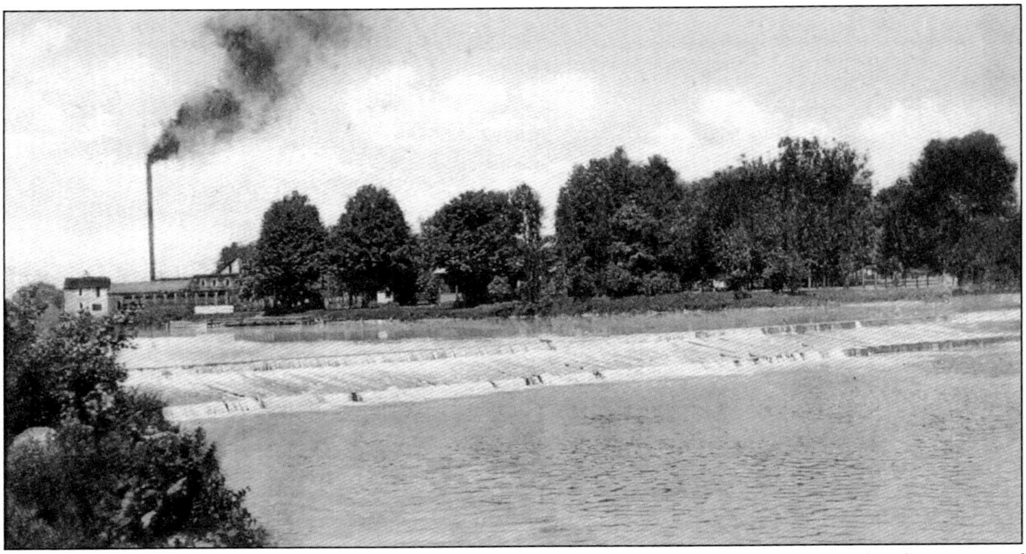

The Eureka Springs Hotel would have never been thought of had it not been for the discovery of "therapeutic" waters by Charles Benner in 1883. The laboratory at Allegheny College confirmed its mineral content, and an economic boom started in Saegertown that would not stop for decades. From the bottling works, mineral and carbonated waters as well as the famous Saegertown Ginger Ale were produced, and in 1900, the world's fair in Paris proclaimed Saegertown Ginger Ale was the best soft drink worldwide. The Aristocrat brand name was formed, and Saegertown Ginger Ale remained popular throughout much of the 20th century. Bottled water is still produced in Saegertown, making this industry well over 120 years old.

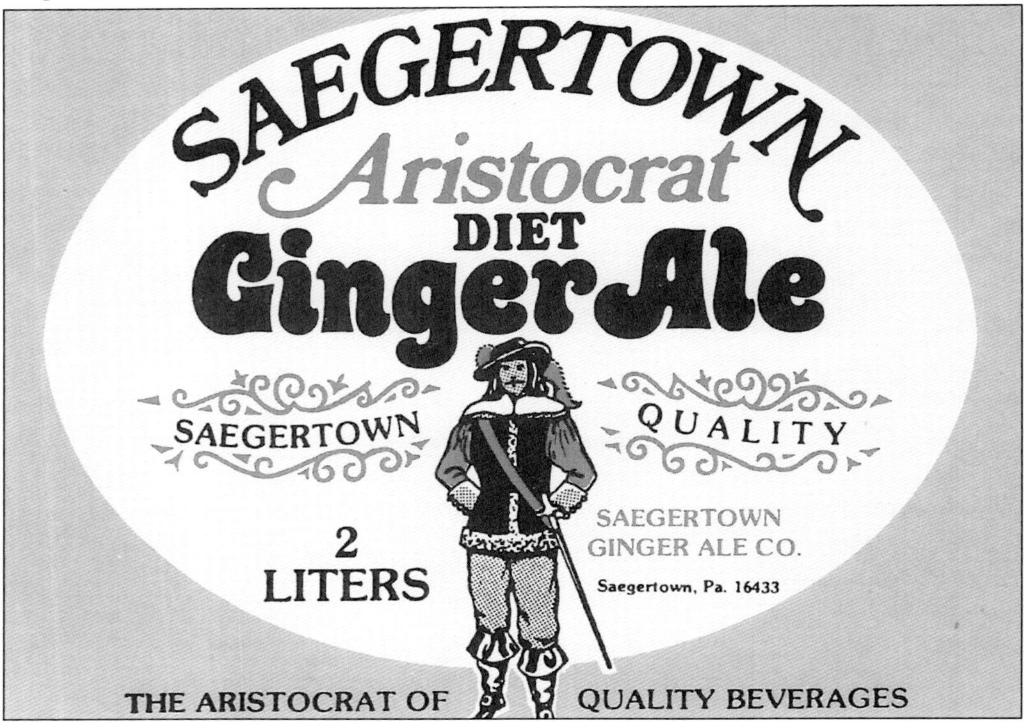

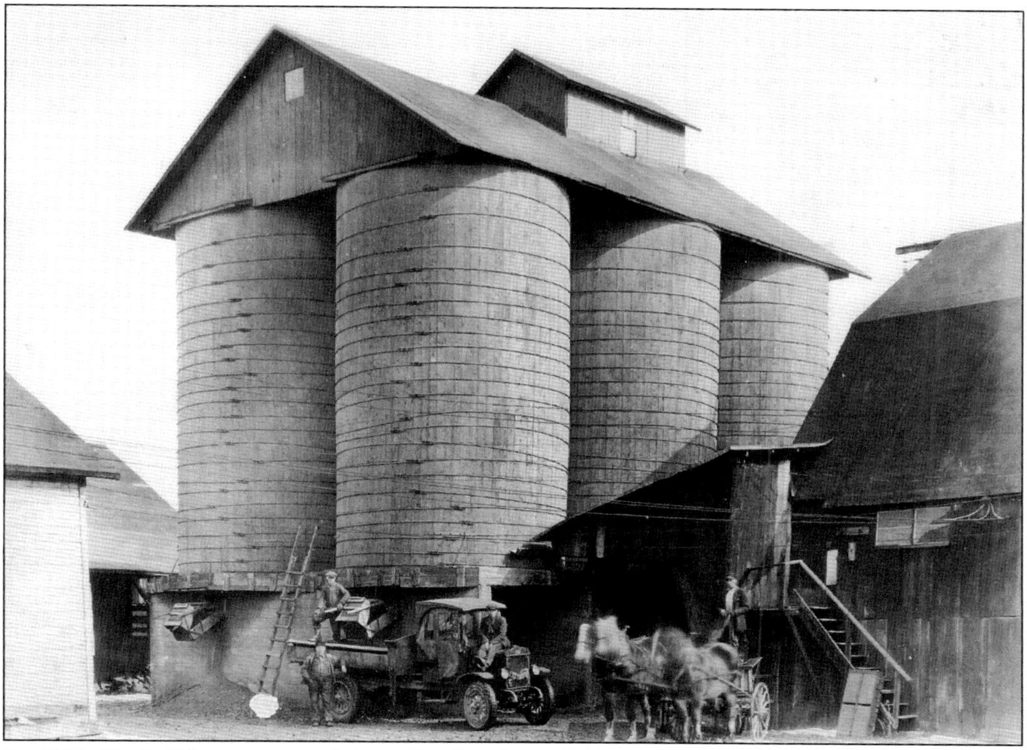

In 1919, D. A. Thomas moved from Pittsburgh to Saegertown. He purchased a hay and coal business from Frank Cottrell, who had operated it for 19 years. Upon retirement, his son Allan Thomas took over the business.

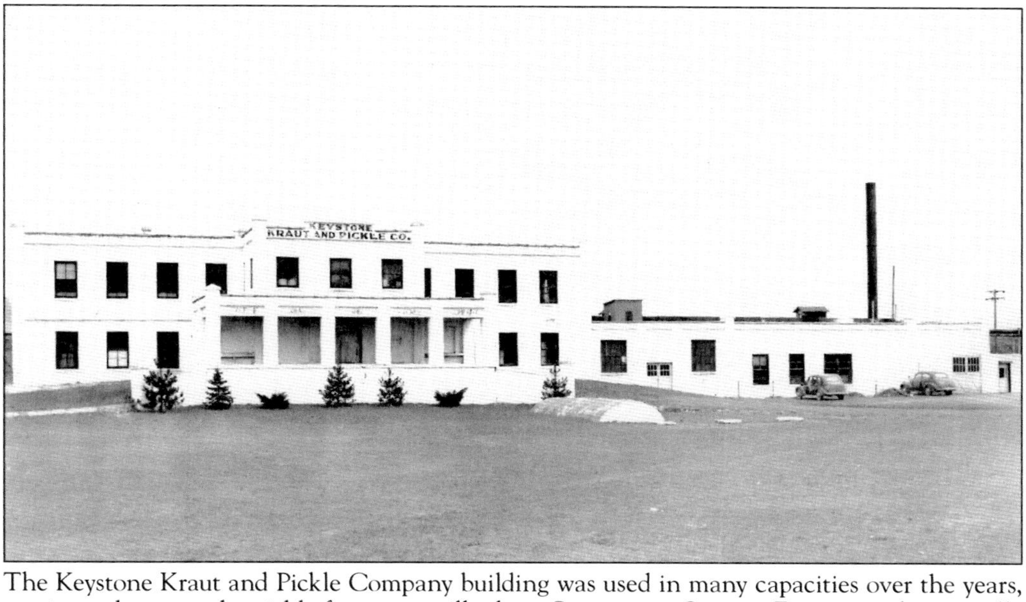

The Keystone Kraut and Pickle Company building was used in many capacities over the years, serving as home to the pickle factory, a milk plant, Saegertown Sausage Factory, and eventually Baldwin Laboratories. It has had many tenants since that time as well.

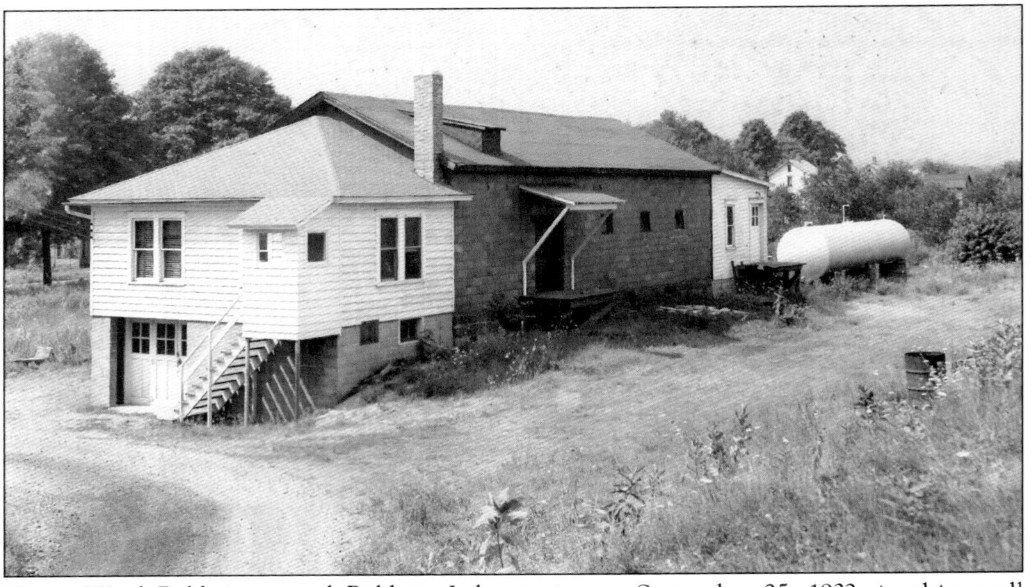

Henry Ward Baldwin started Baldwin Laboratories on September 25, 1932, in this small building. It soon expanded and moved to the same building that housed the Keystone Kraut and Pickle Company years earlier. Incorporating on June 14, 1933, DWIN Laboratories (Baldwin Laboratories' brand name) was a large employer in Saegertown and remained so for many years. (Courtesy of Lea Baldwin.)

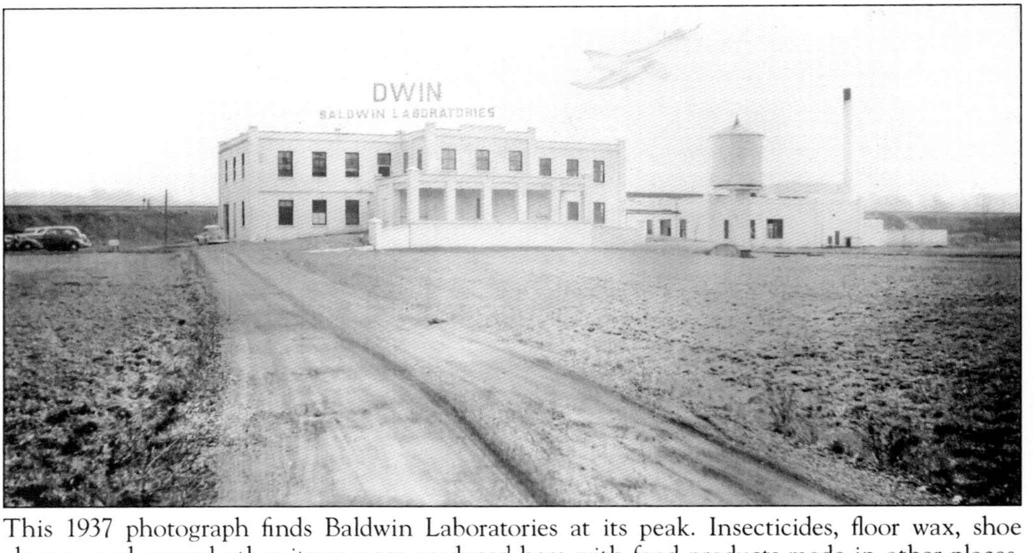

This 1937 photograph finds Baldwin Laboratories at its peak. Insecticides, floor wax, shoe cleaner, and several other items were produced here with food products made in other places. Baldwin Laboratories merged with the Aromatic Corporation of Chicago in the late 1930s. (Courtesy of Lea Baldwin.)

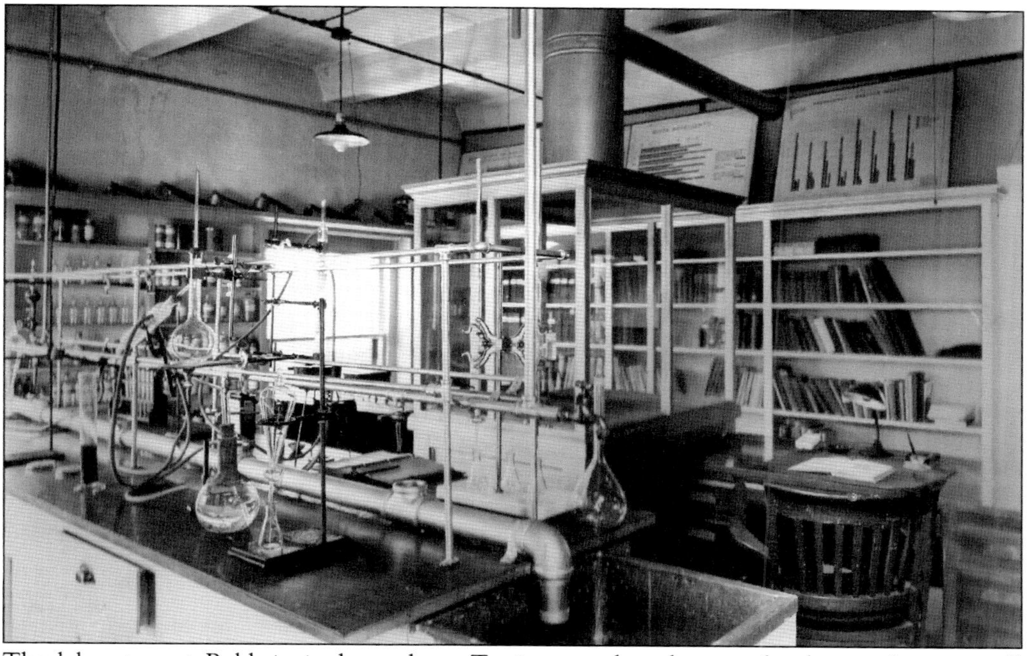

The laboratory at Baldwin is shown here. Testing was done here to develop products as well as test promising ones. Insects were bred and cared for at Baldwin Laboratories to be used in insecticide testing. (Courtesy of Lea Baldwin.)

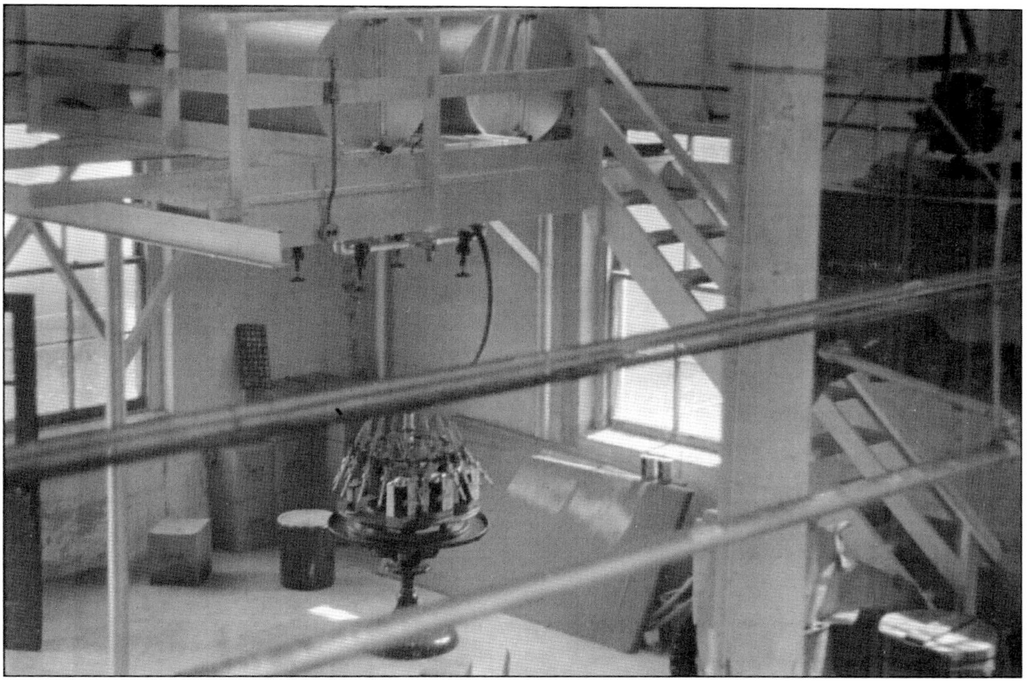

The interior of Baldwin Laboratories can be seen here. Boxes line the back wall to be shipped out to clients. Henry Ward Baldwin had quite an enterprise, marketing products to the inns in Saegertown as well as stores and companies worldwide. (Courtesy of Lea Baldwin.)

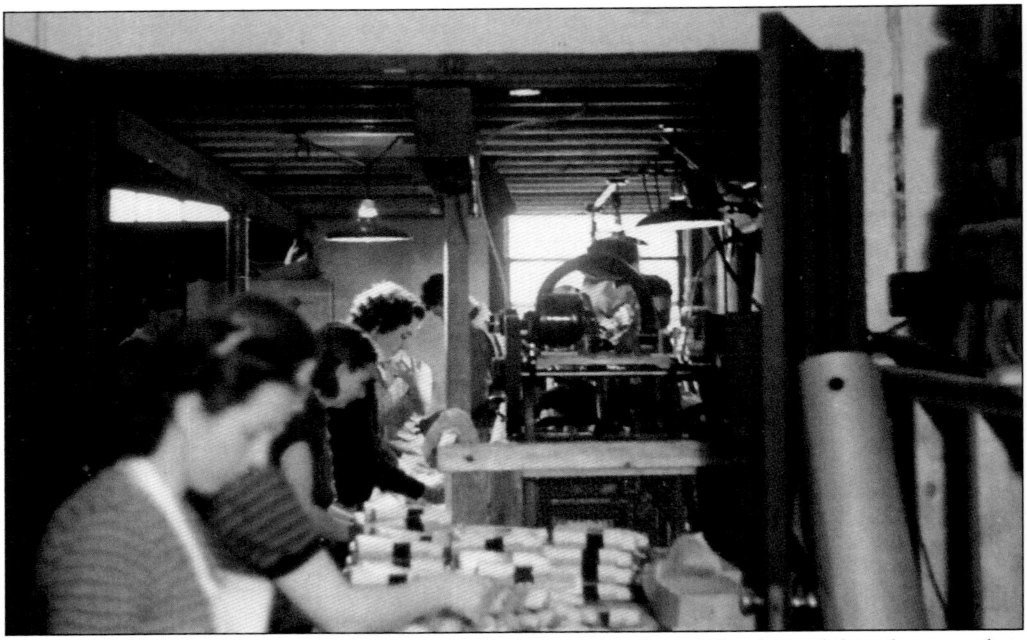

DWIN employees are seen here on an assembly line at the plant. The date of this photograph is not known. (Courtesy of Lea Baldwin.)

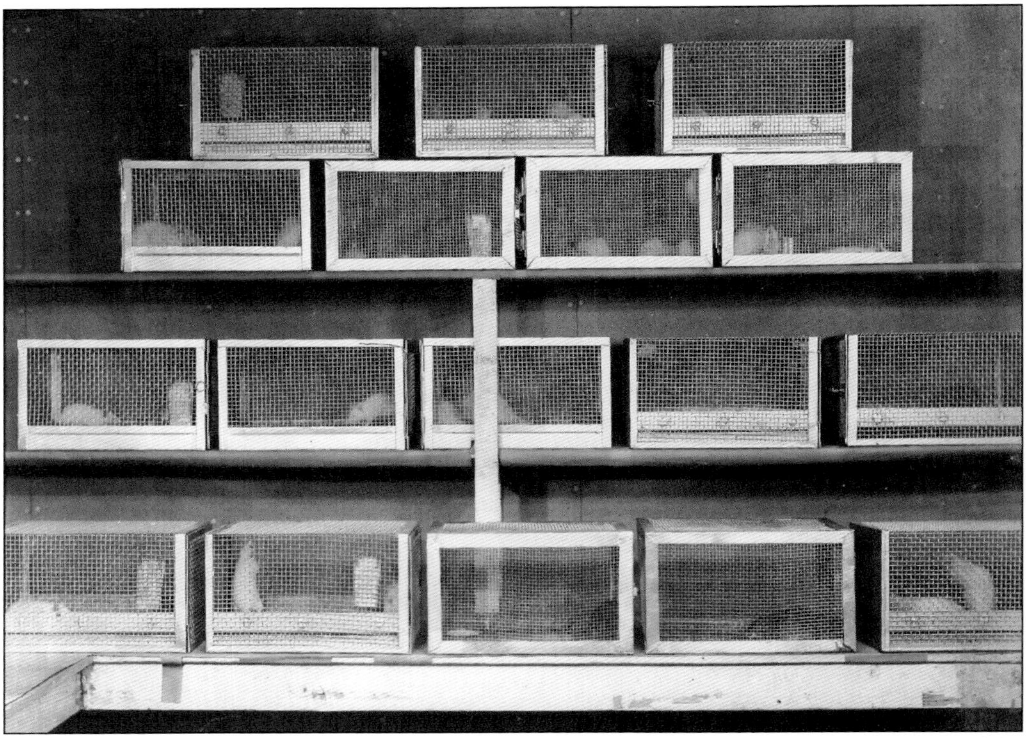

Large cages line the walls of this room at Baldwin Laboratories where white rats are used for product testing. (Courtesy of Lea Baldwin.)

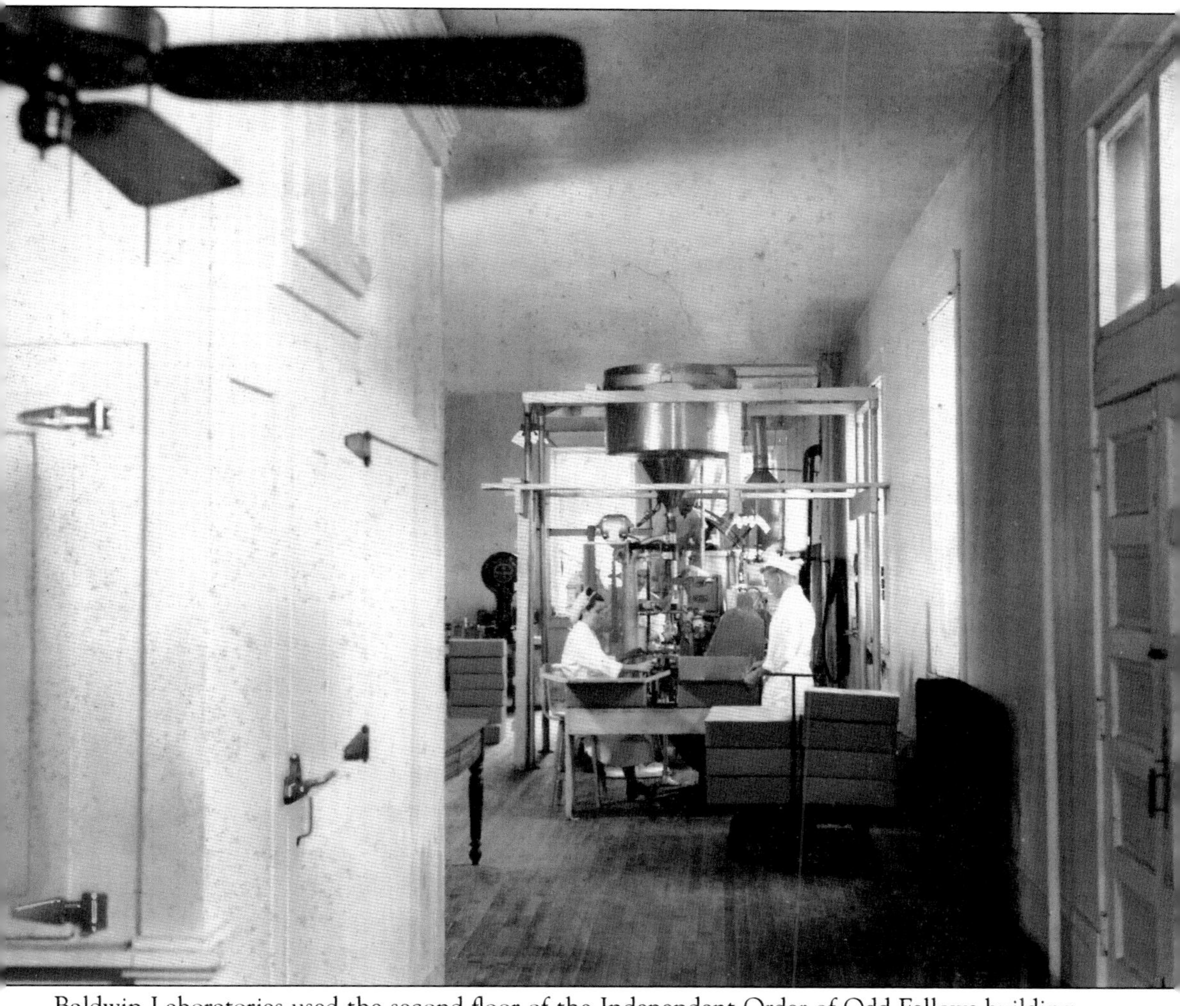

Baldwin Laboratories used the second floor of the Independent Order of Odd Fellows building for a time as an ideal place to produce mayonnaise. With fly powder and other chemicals being manufactured in the main factory, mayonnaise and sandwich spread could be made here without contamination. (Courtesy of Lea Baldwin.)

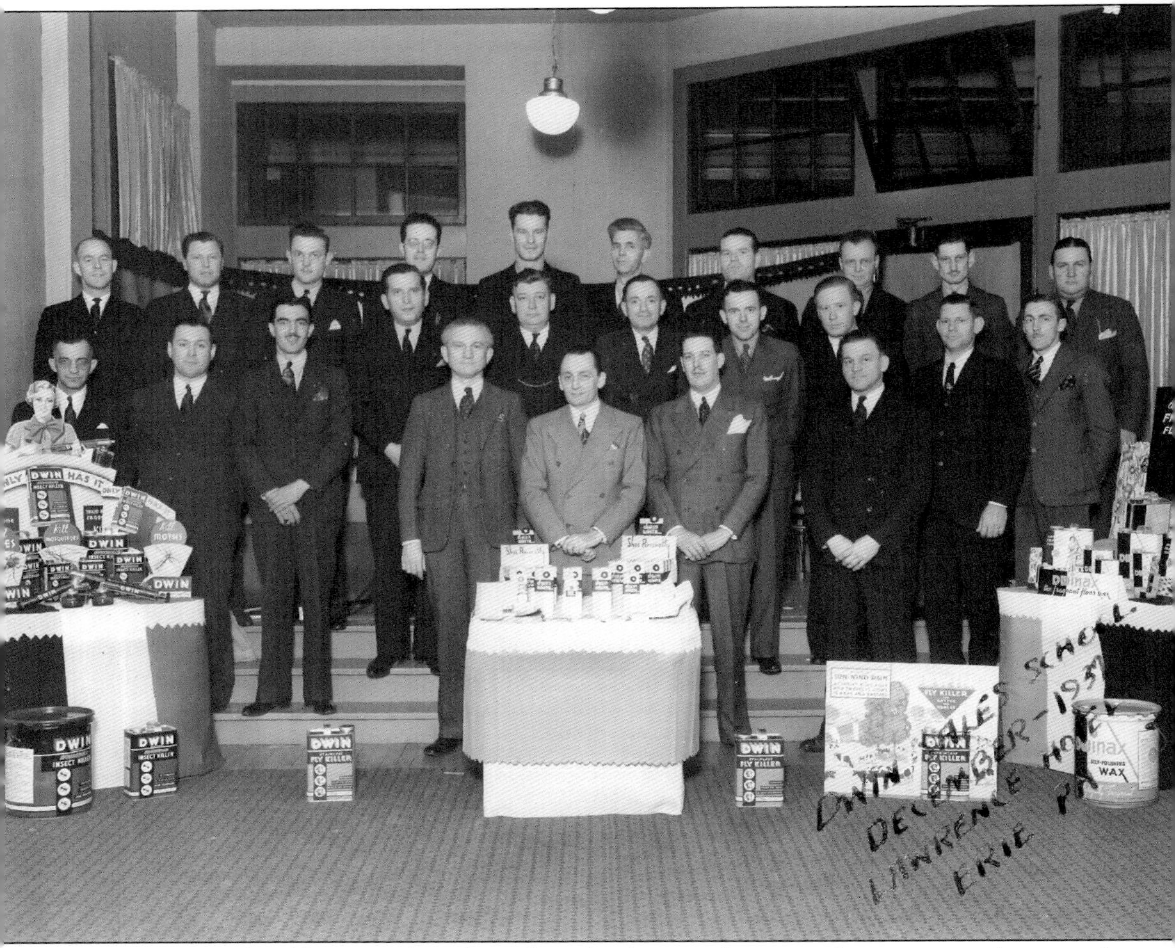

Henry Ward Baldwin conducted a sales school to teach new and existing employees to be effective salespeople to benefit the company. This seminar educated workers on new products, sales pitches, people skills, and all other necessities for the effective sale of products. The group shown here is at the DWIN sales school of December 1937 at Lawrence Hotel in Erie. Henry Ward Baldwin stands in the front center. (Courtesy of Lea Baldwin.)

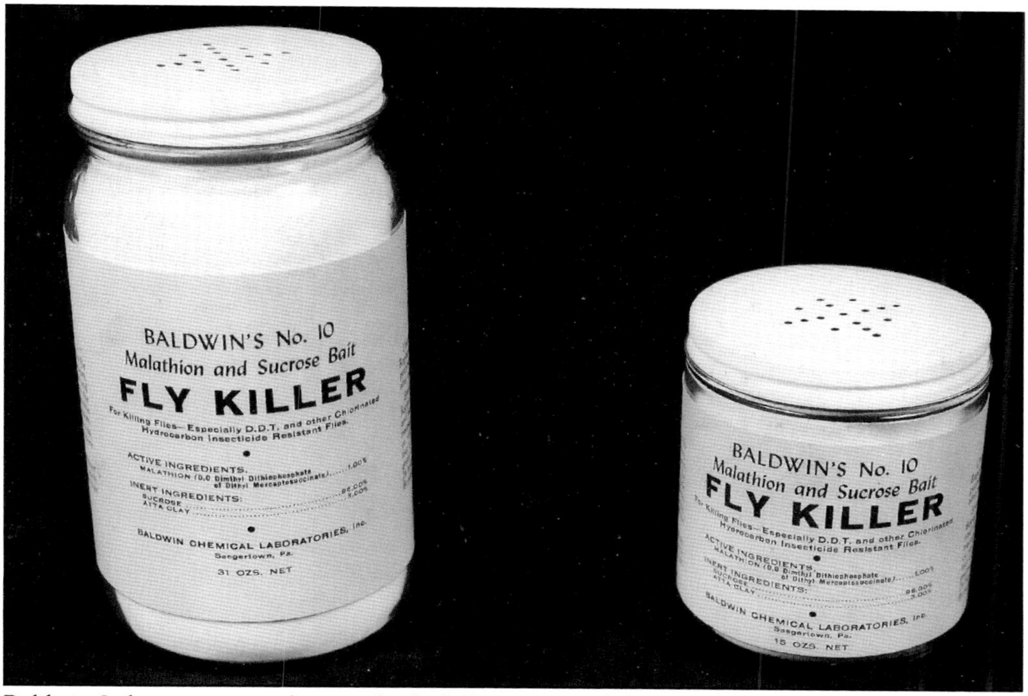

Baldwin Laboratories was known for fly killer in several forms. Shown here in a sprinkle can, this product was also manufactured in hand pump fumigators, the predecessor to aerosol cans. (Courtesy of Lea Baldwin.)

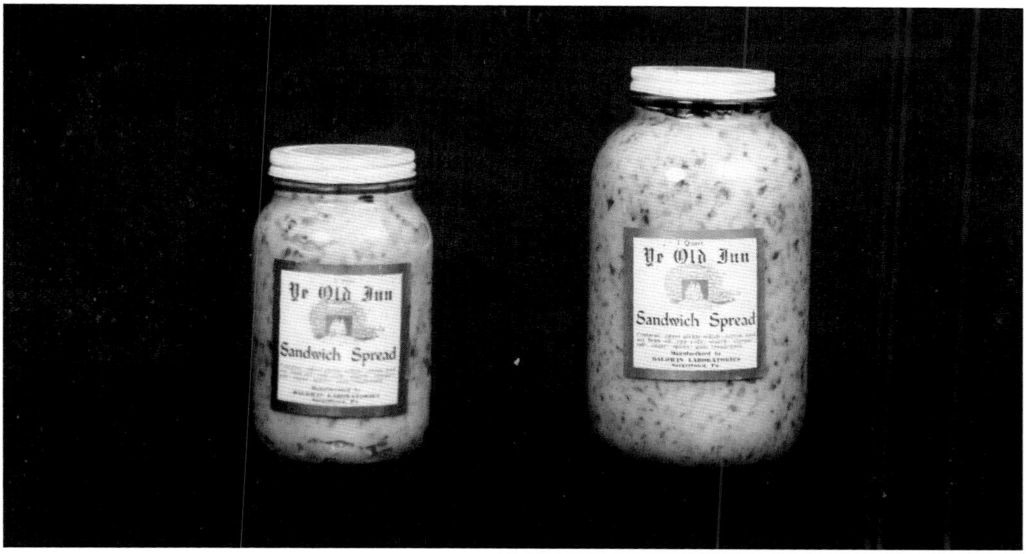

Baldwin Laboratories made sandwich spread for Ye Old Inn, the successor to the Saegertown Inn after Frank Fox passed away. (Courtesy of Lea Baldwin.)

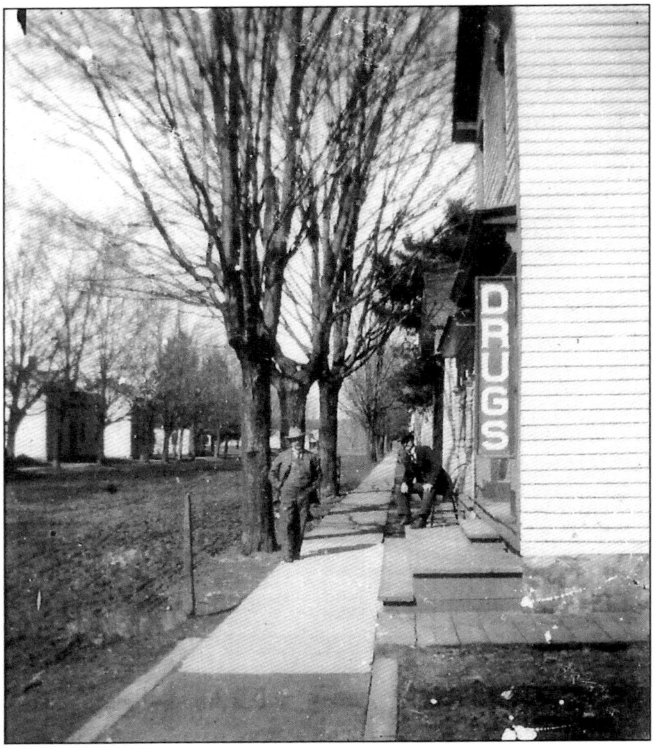

Cullen's Drug Store is shown here in 1901. It was located on the second floor of the hardware store.

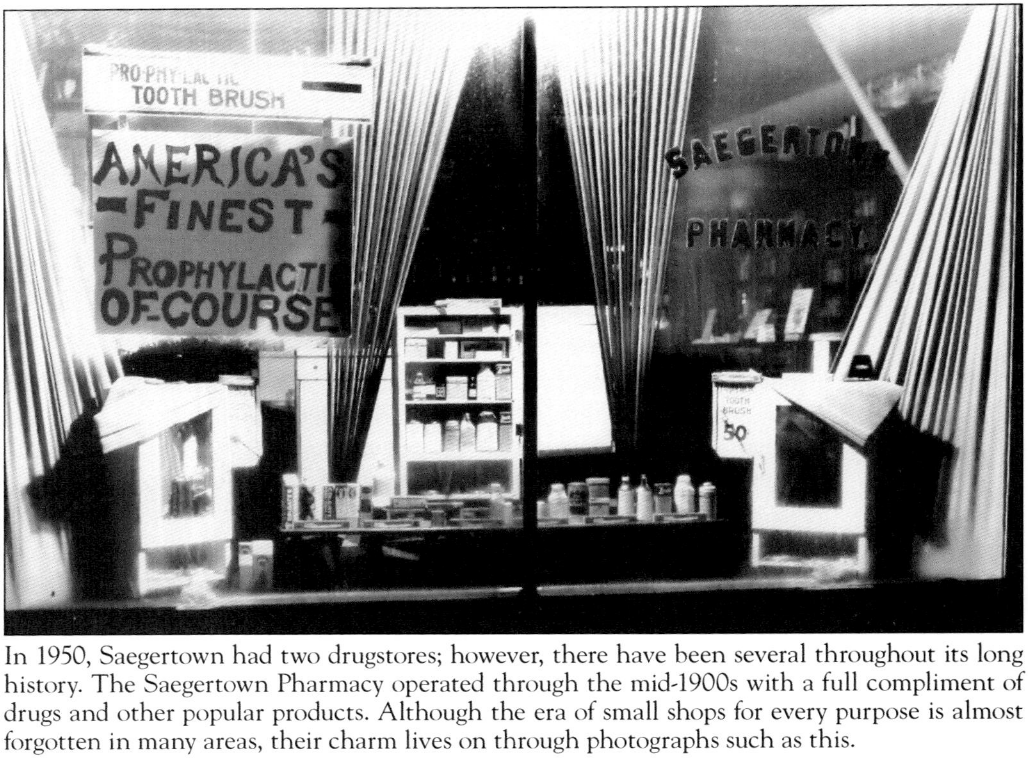

In 1950, Saegertown had two drugstores; however, there have been several throughout its long history. The Saegertown Pharmacy operated through the mid-1900s with a full compliment of drugs and other popular products. Although the era of small shops for every purpose is almost forgotten in many areas, their charm lives on through photographs such as this.

Before moving his office into his and his wife's home, Dr. Henry Emmons Smith used this office for his medical practice. He then practiced with their son Rodney until his death in 1920, when Rodney took over the entire practice.

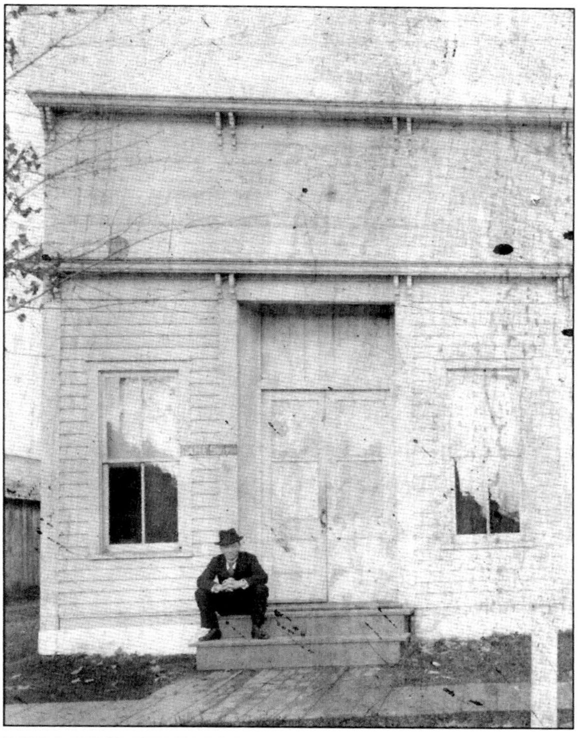

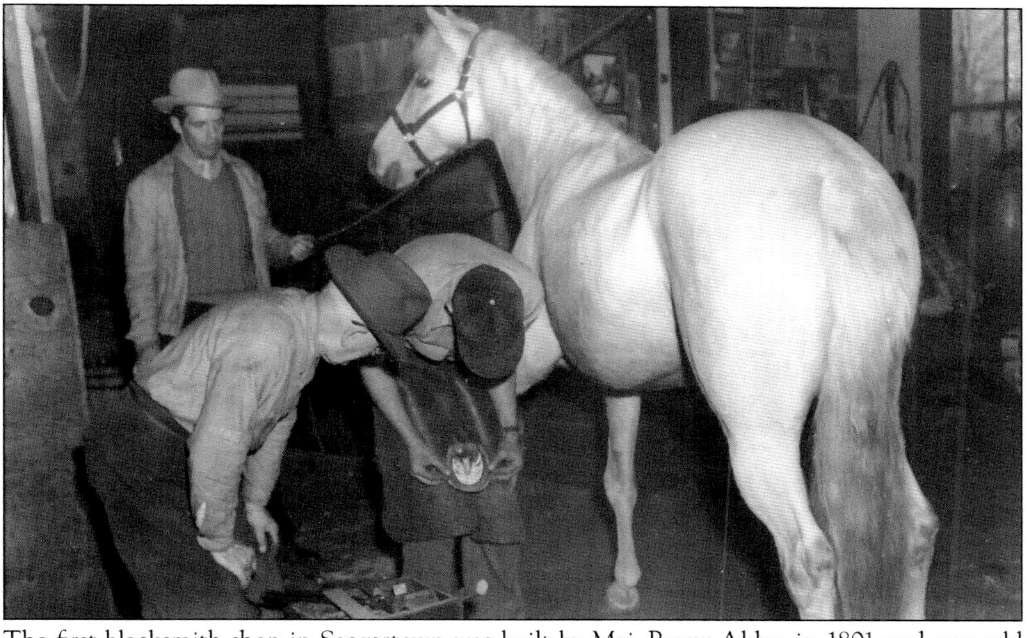

The first blacksmith shop in Saegertown was built by Maj. Roger Alden in 1801 and was sold two years later to George Peiffer Jr. In 1821, the shop was remodeled into the first schoolhouse in town. The blacksmith shop shown here was owned by George Waid and was located where the day care playground on Main Street is today. His shop burned at one point, after which he operated on a traveling basis.

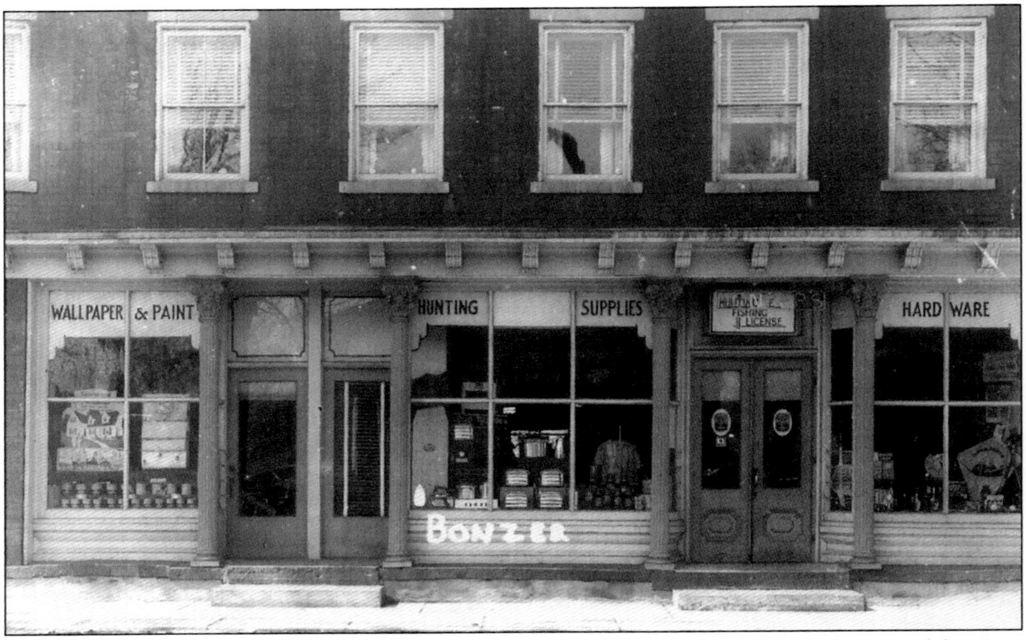

In 1829, Daniel Saeger opened a general store in a tavern building formerly owned by Pete Shaffer. The store stayed in the Saeger family through Oliver and Amos Saeger and then moved into the brick building it remained in for decades. Bernice Saeger sold the business in 1945, and it continued on as the Bonzer Store in the same location.

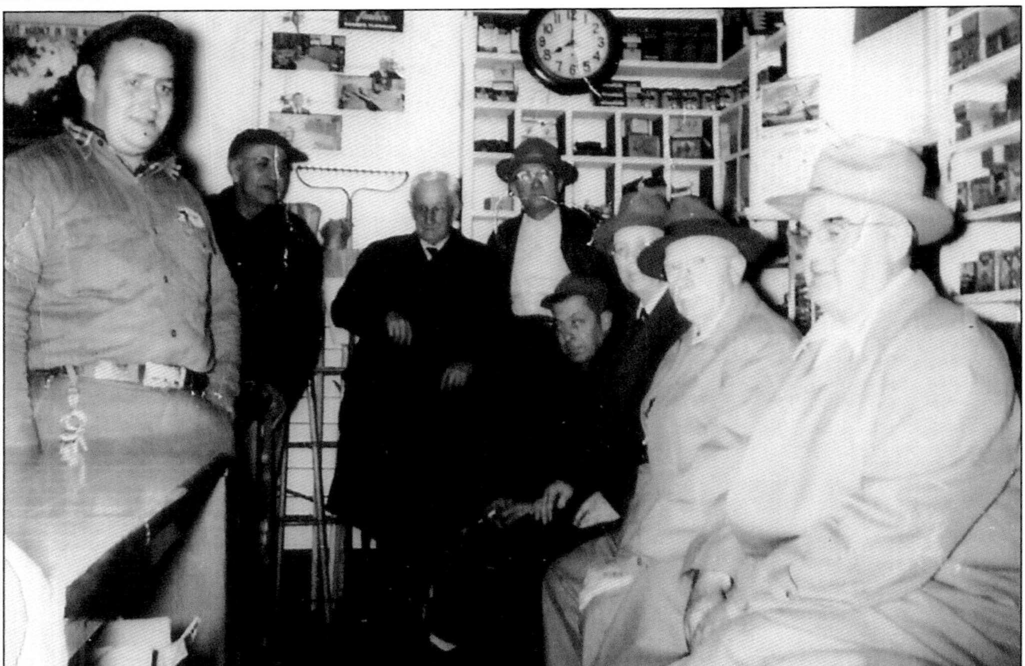

The Saeger store and its Bonzer successor was the gathering place where locals came to make purchases or just shoot the breeze. As one can see, "important business" is occurring here.

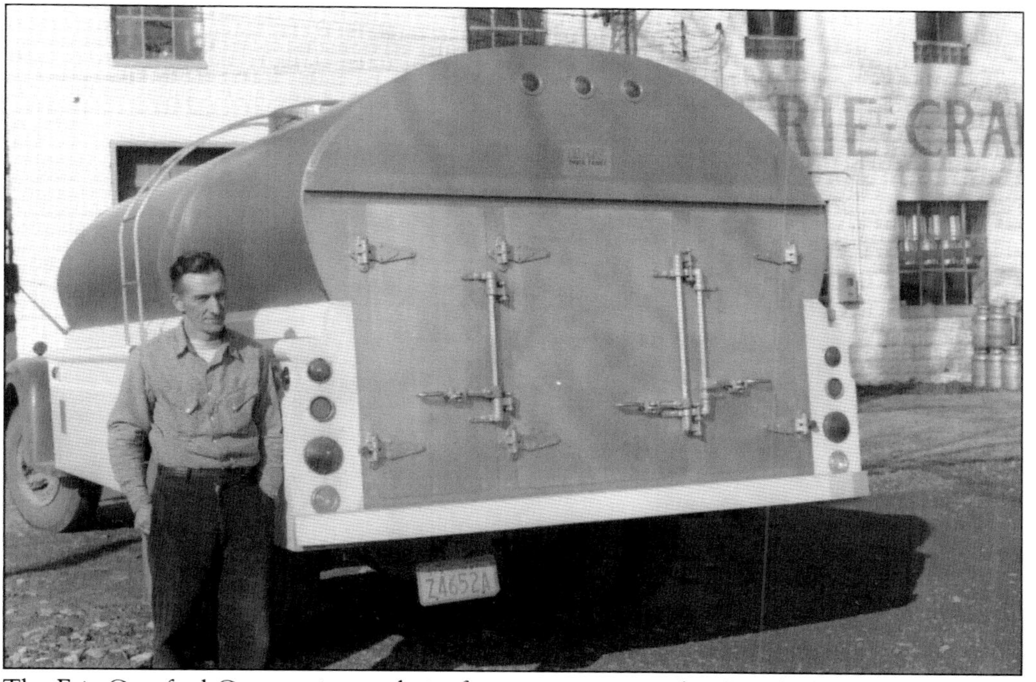

The Erie-Crawford Cooperative made its first appearance in the Crawford County telephone directory in 1942. It was farmer owned and operated and maintained a milk plant and feed store. Currently, of the two functions, the feed store is still in operation. Shown in this 1957 photograph (above), one of the haulers is taking milk to the plant. The other picture displays two more cooperative milk trucks.

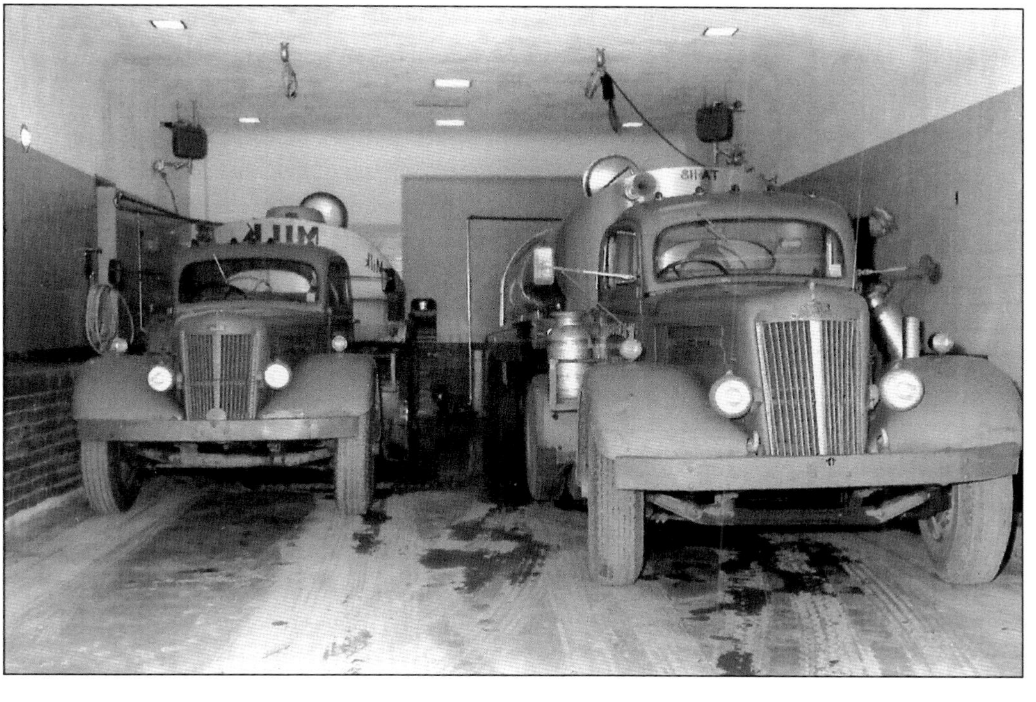

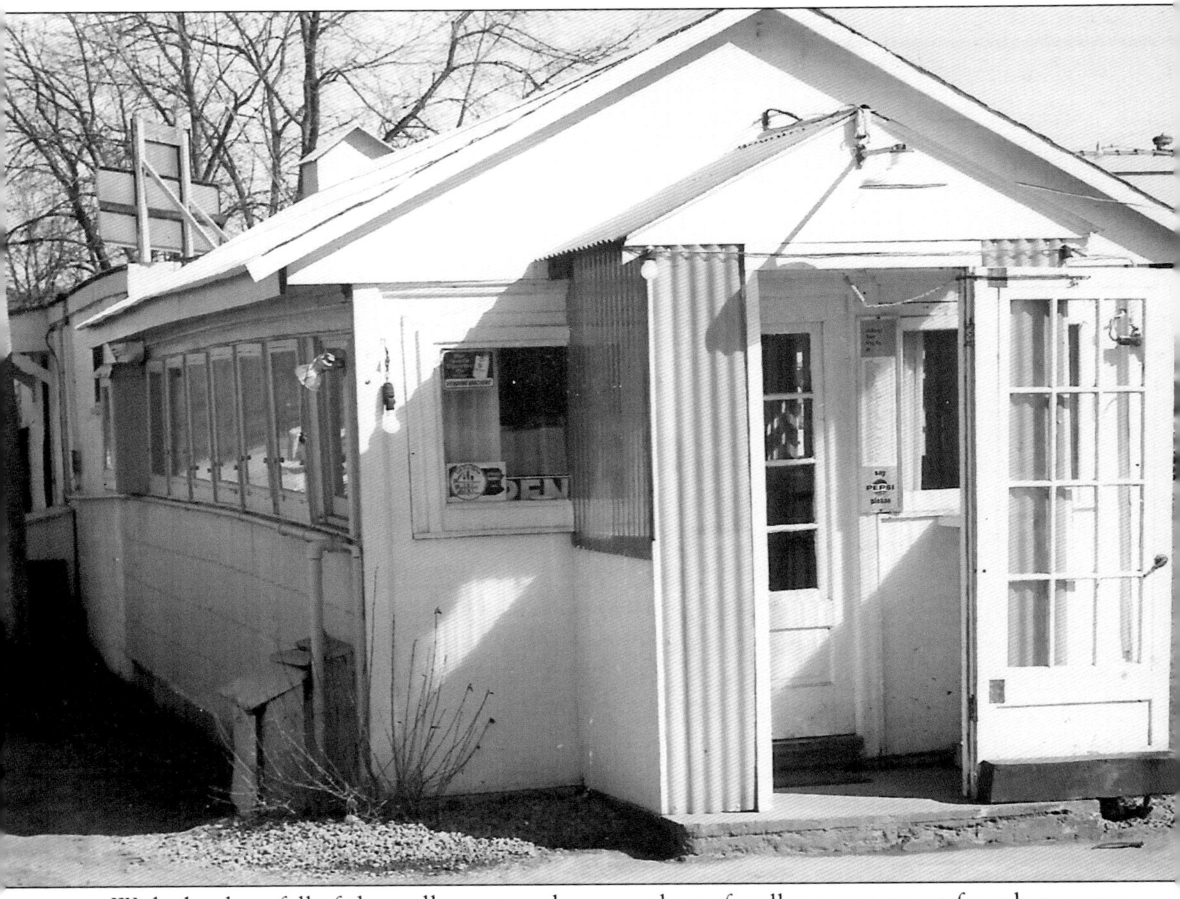

With the downfall of the trolley system, large numbers of trolley cars were up for sale or scrap. This modified trolley car, known as Bill's Diner, was a favorite eatery for Saegertown's residents. A quick lunch could be had here during a break from work or a sit-down informal meal with the family. (Courtesy of K. James Bertram.)

Six

RELIGION AND EDUCATION

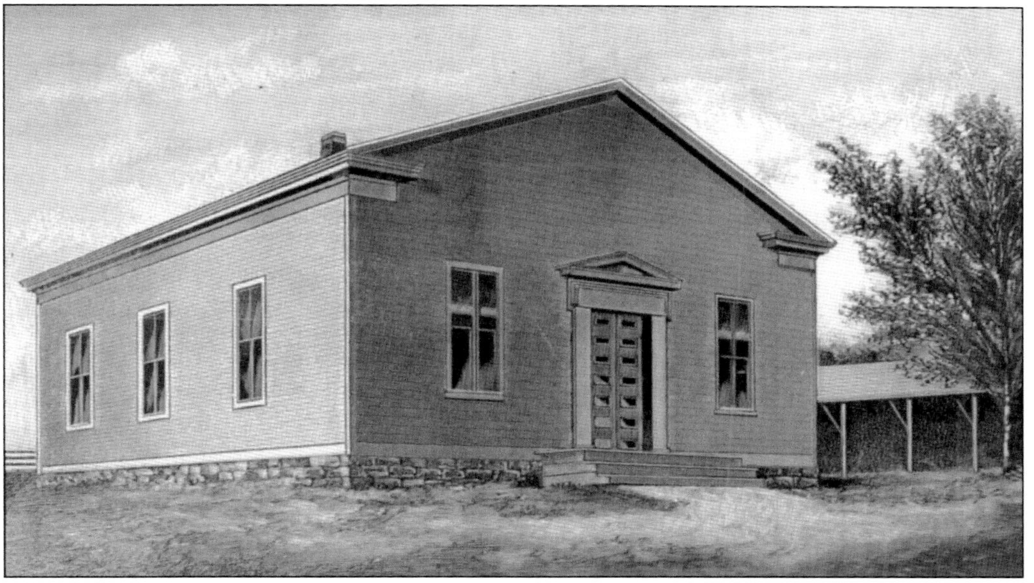

State Road Methodist was built in 1847. During the revivals of 1850–1851, hundreds of converts attended this church. Francis C. Waid recalled this in his memoirs, including many meetings and programs at the church between 1850 and roughly the beginning of the 20th century. State Road Methodist Church closed its doors in 1990 with fewer than 30 members left. (Courtesy of Francis C. Ward's Third Souvenir.)

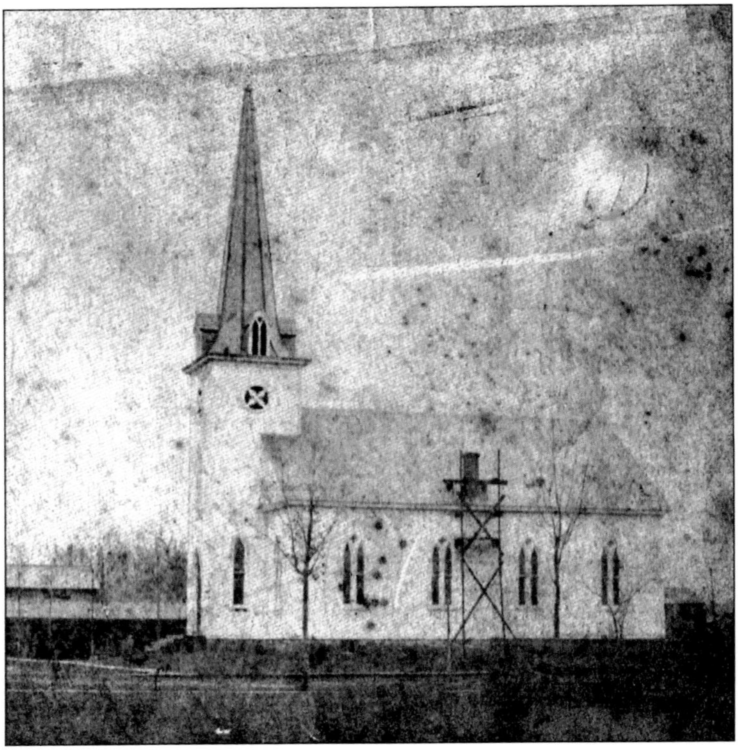

In 1839, a Methodist congregation built the first Methodist church in Saegertown. The original building was moved and sold to the Baptists in 1875, and a new church building was erected. The second building was struck by lightning and burned to the ground in June 1917.

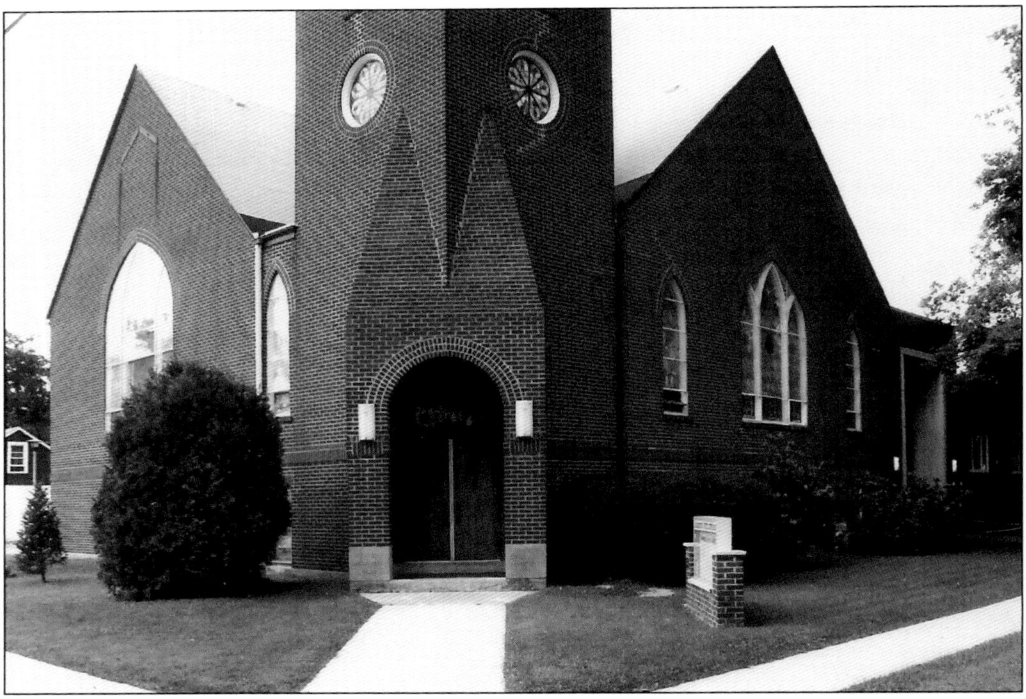

In 1918, the brick structure in use today was built by the Methodists at the cost of $20,000.

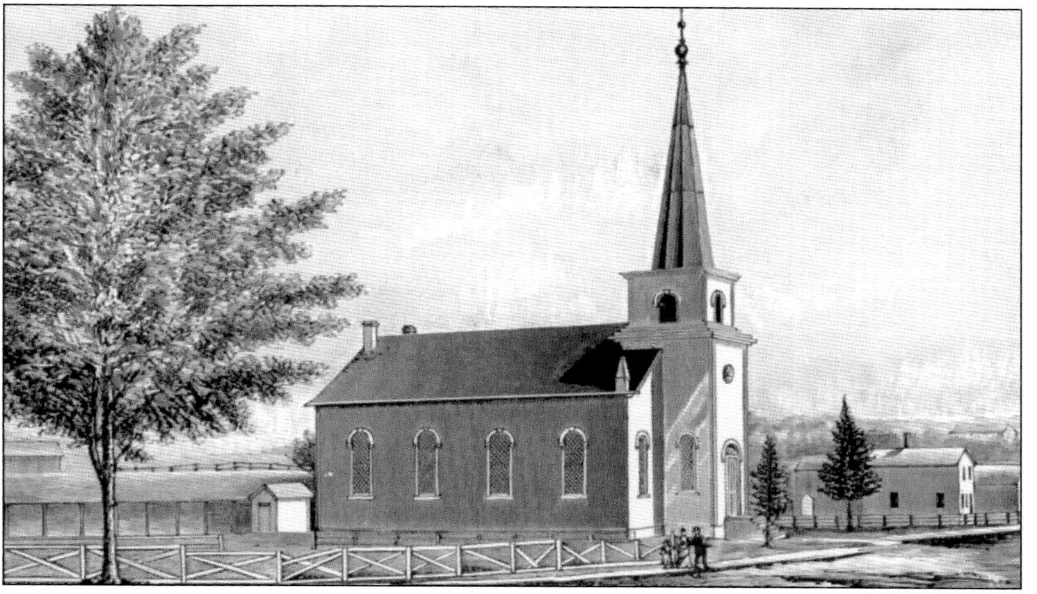

Blooming Valley Methodist Episcopal Church, located on what is now called Route 77, was built in 1874 at the cost of $4,500. A congregation met as early as 1835 nearly a mile north of the village in Cowan's school. (Courtesy of Francis C. Ward's Third Souvenir.)

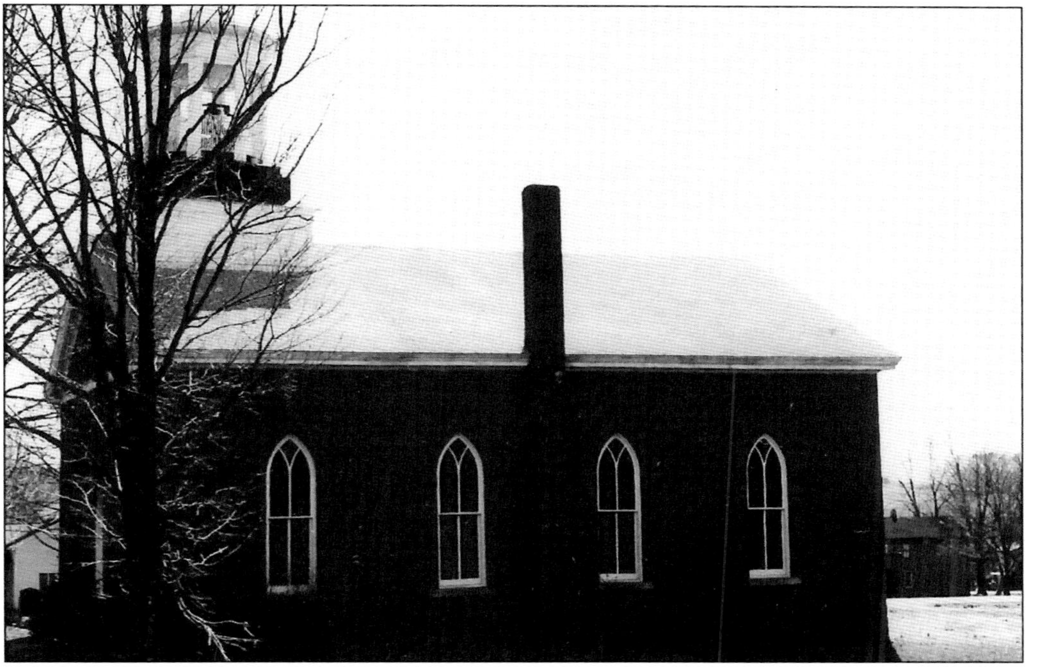

Beginning as Gravel Run Methodist Episcopal Church in 1844, Woodcock Methodist was referred to as the Rockville Methodist Episcopal Church. The first church built on this site was built between 1810 and 1817 and used until 1838 when the present building was built.

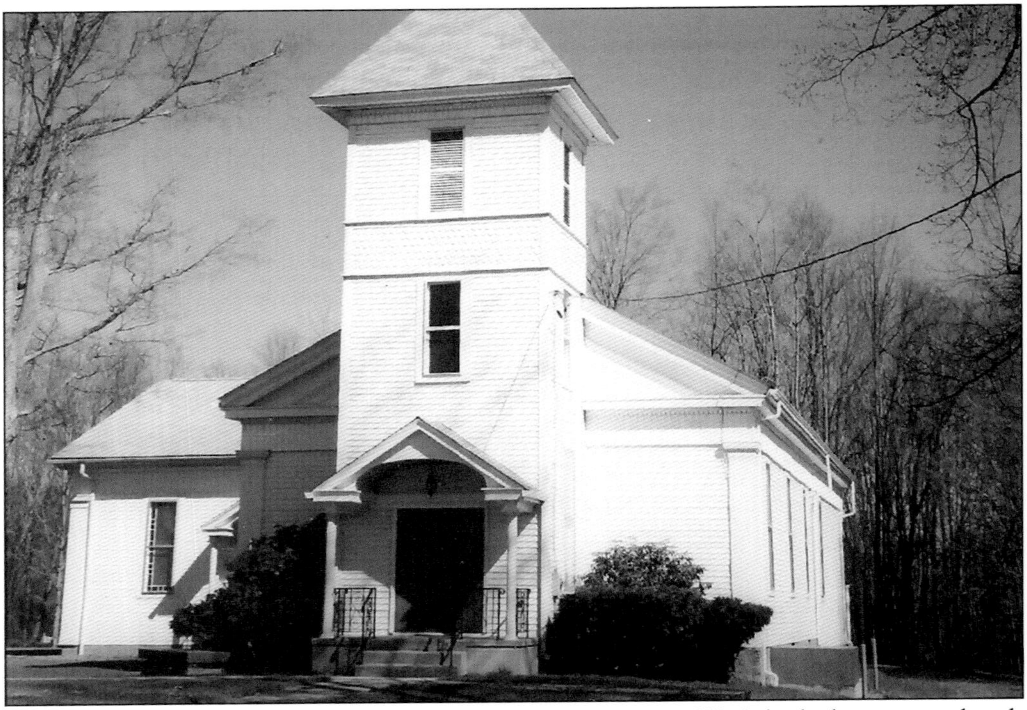

A Methodist congregation was organized in Little's Corners in 1852. It built the current church a year later in 1853. Although it has had at least one noticeable addition to the building since that time as well as much remodeling, the church's character remains intact.

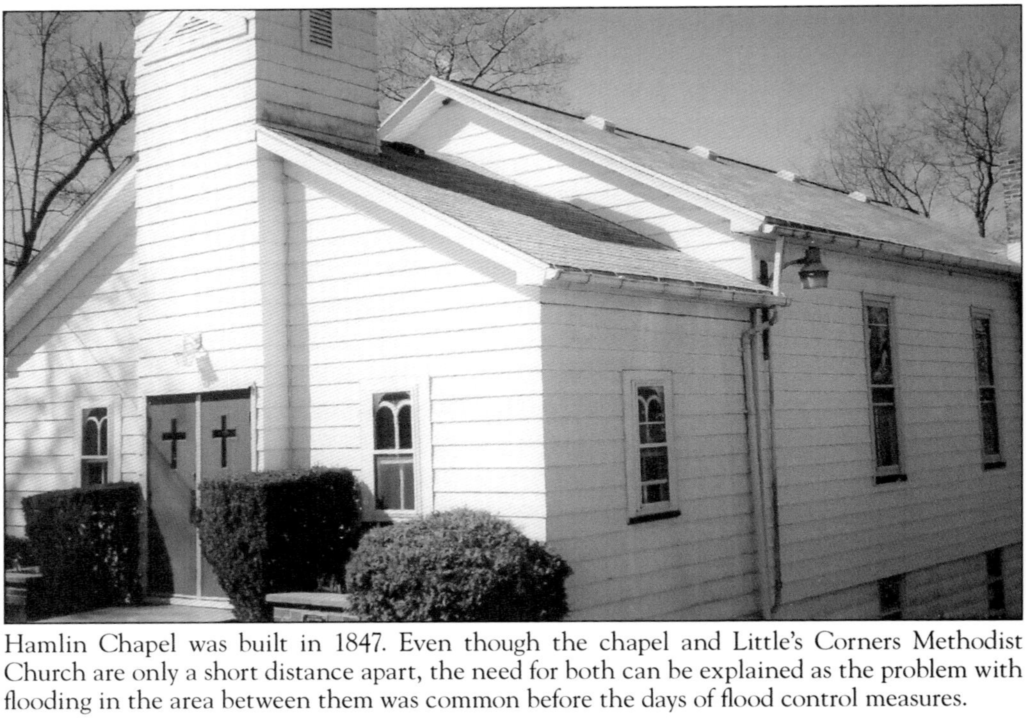

Hamlin Chapel was built in 1847. Even though the chapel and Little's Corners Methodist Church are only a short distance apart, the need for both can be explained as the problem with flooding in the area between them was common before the days of flood control measures.

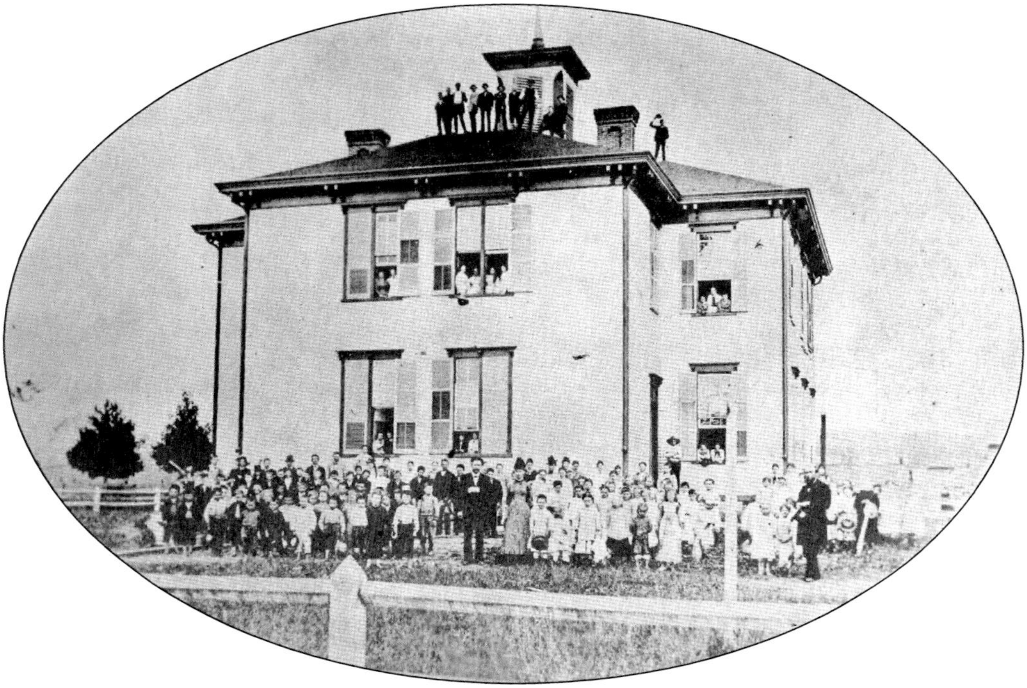

The Saegertown area has had a number of educational institutions in existence throughout its history. Over the last 200 years, one-room schoolhouses satisfied the population, followed by the Saegertown Academy, a high school with several additions, followed by several others until the 1970s structure used today was opened. This photograph displays many Saegertown residents in, on, and around the school building.

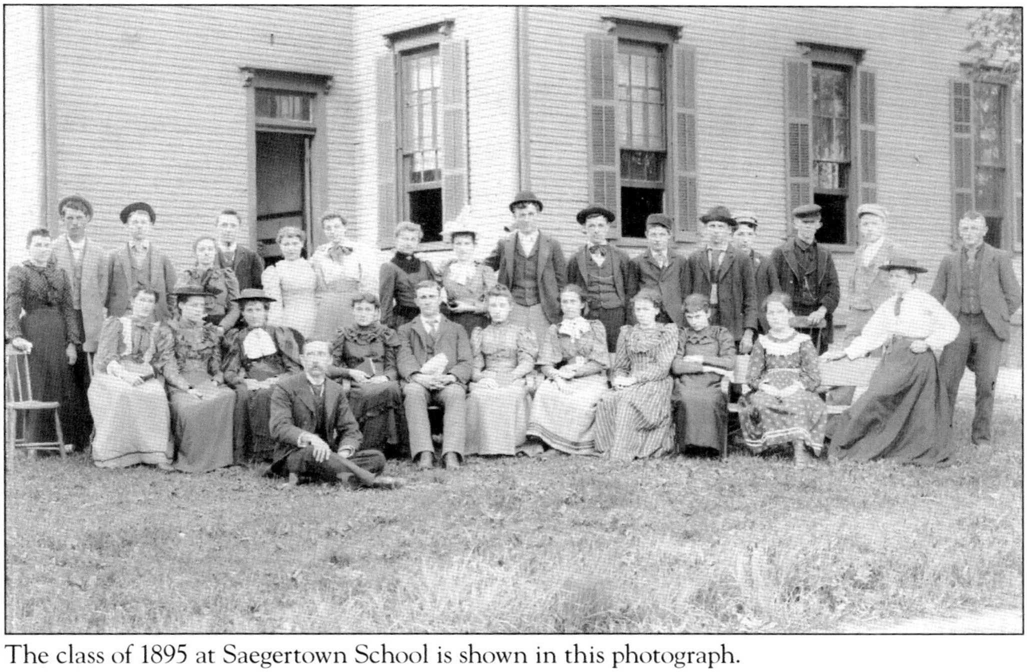

The class of 1895 at Saegertown School is shown in this photograph.

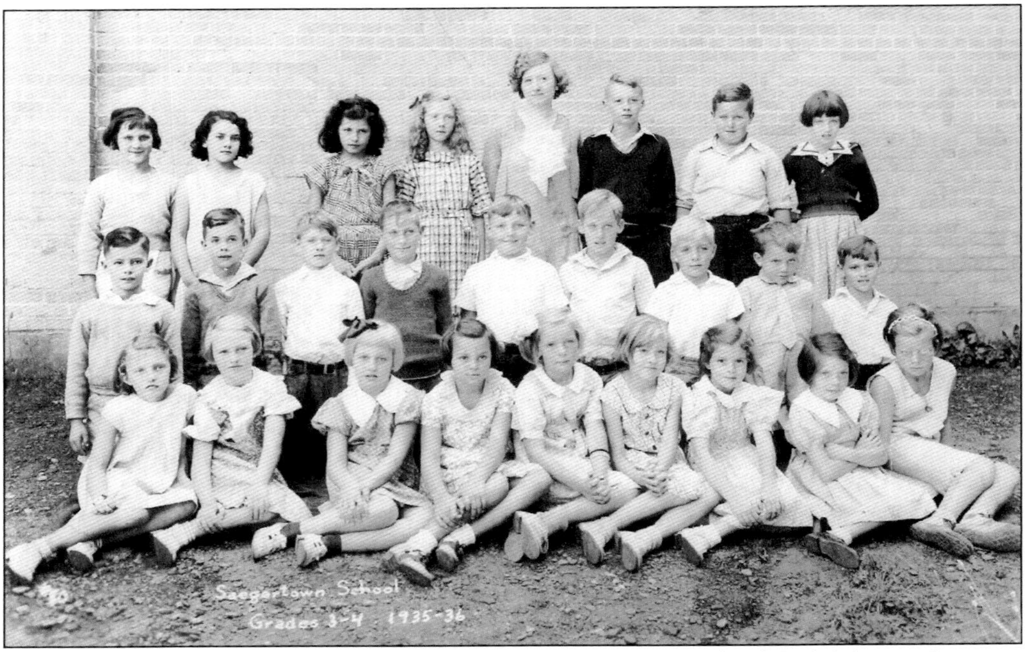

Built between 1870 and 1874, Saegertown School sits on the east side of Euclid Avenue between Washington Street and Broad Street. Classes were started in this building in 1875. Shown here are the third- and forth-grade classes during the 1935–1936 school year.

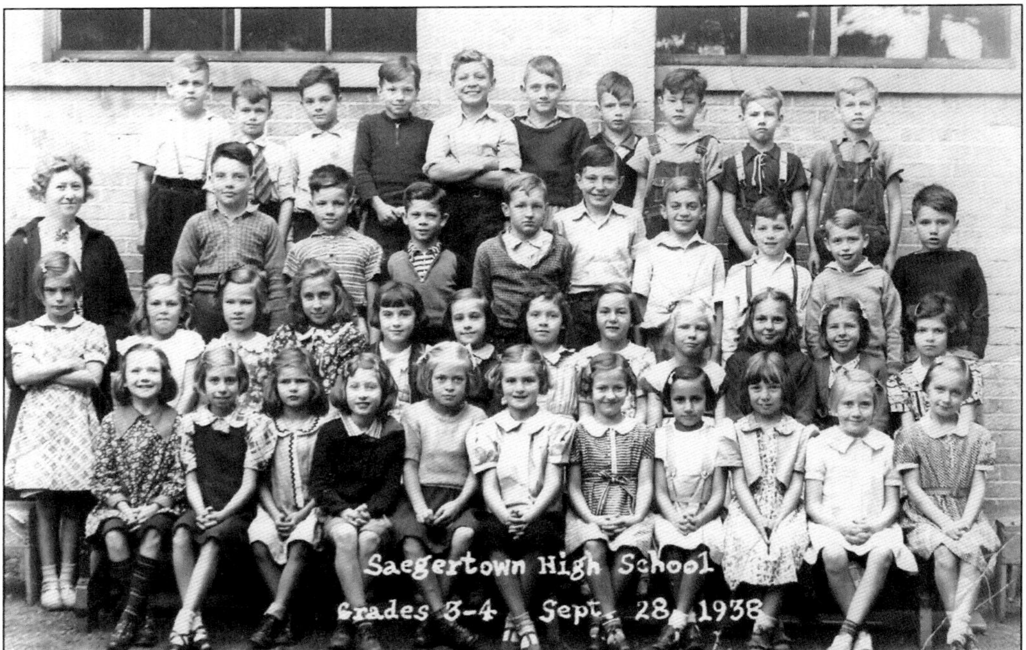

A gymnasium was added to the school in 1936, and six more classrooms were added in 1938 by the Public Works Administration. After 1952, it was used as an elementary school until it was closed in 1989. The third- and forth-grade classes are shown here in September 1938.

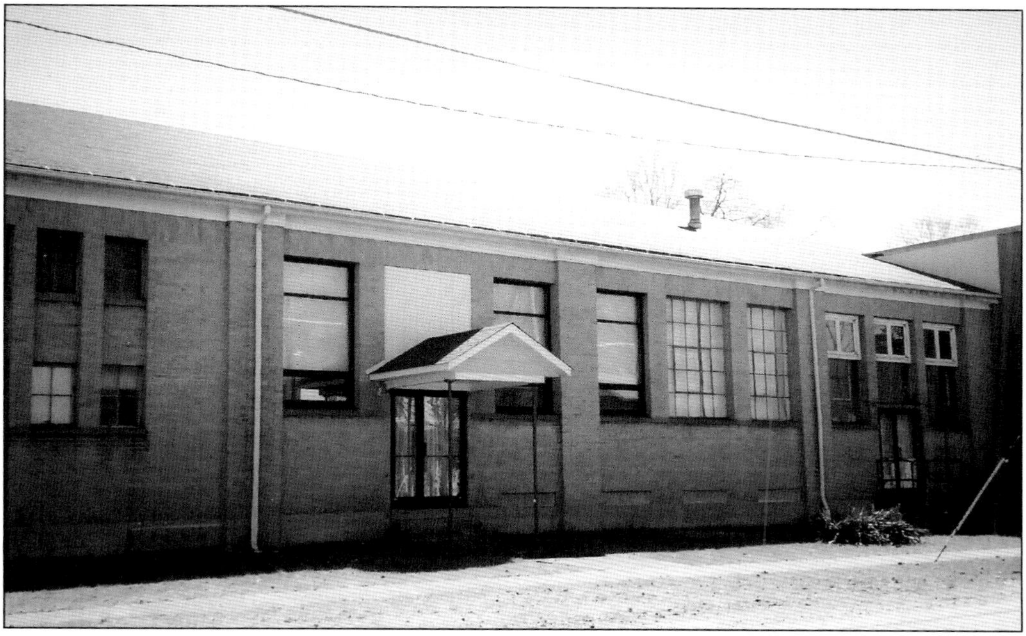

The school on Euclid Avenue is shown here in a modern photograph. It is now the home of a local ministry group.

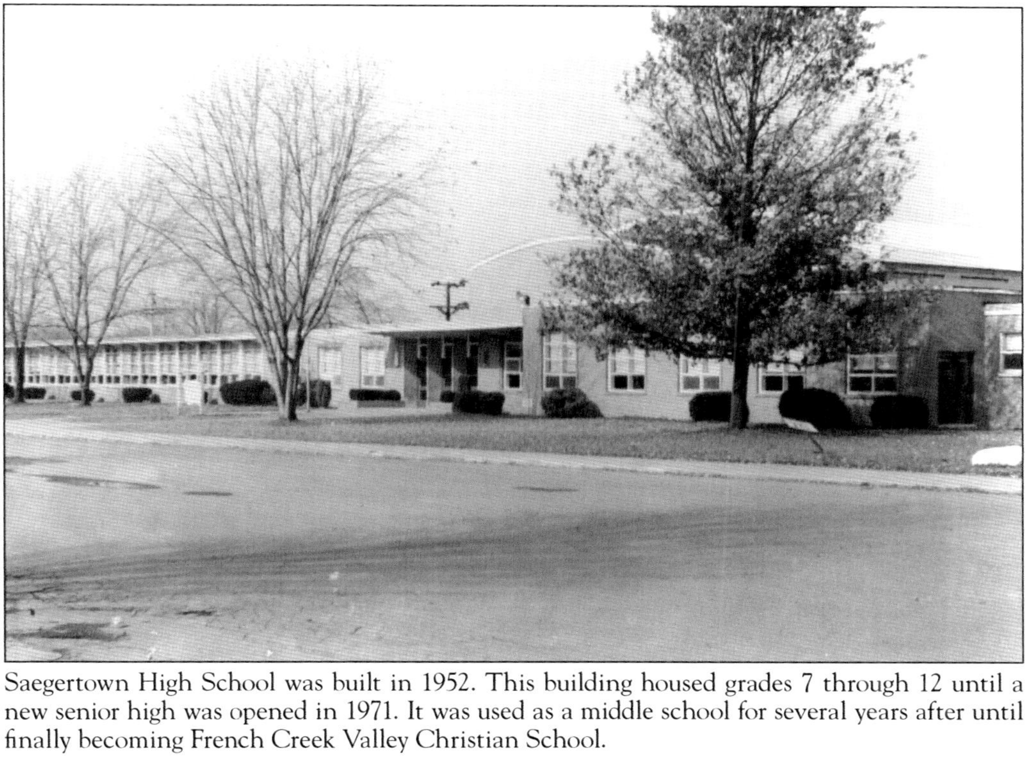

Saegertown High School was built in 1952. This building housed grades 7 through 12 until a new senior high was opened in 1971. It was used as a middle school for several years after until finally becoming French Creek Valley Christian School.

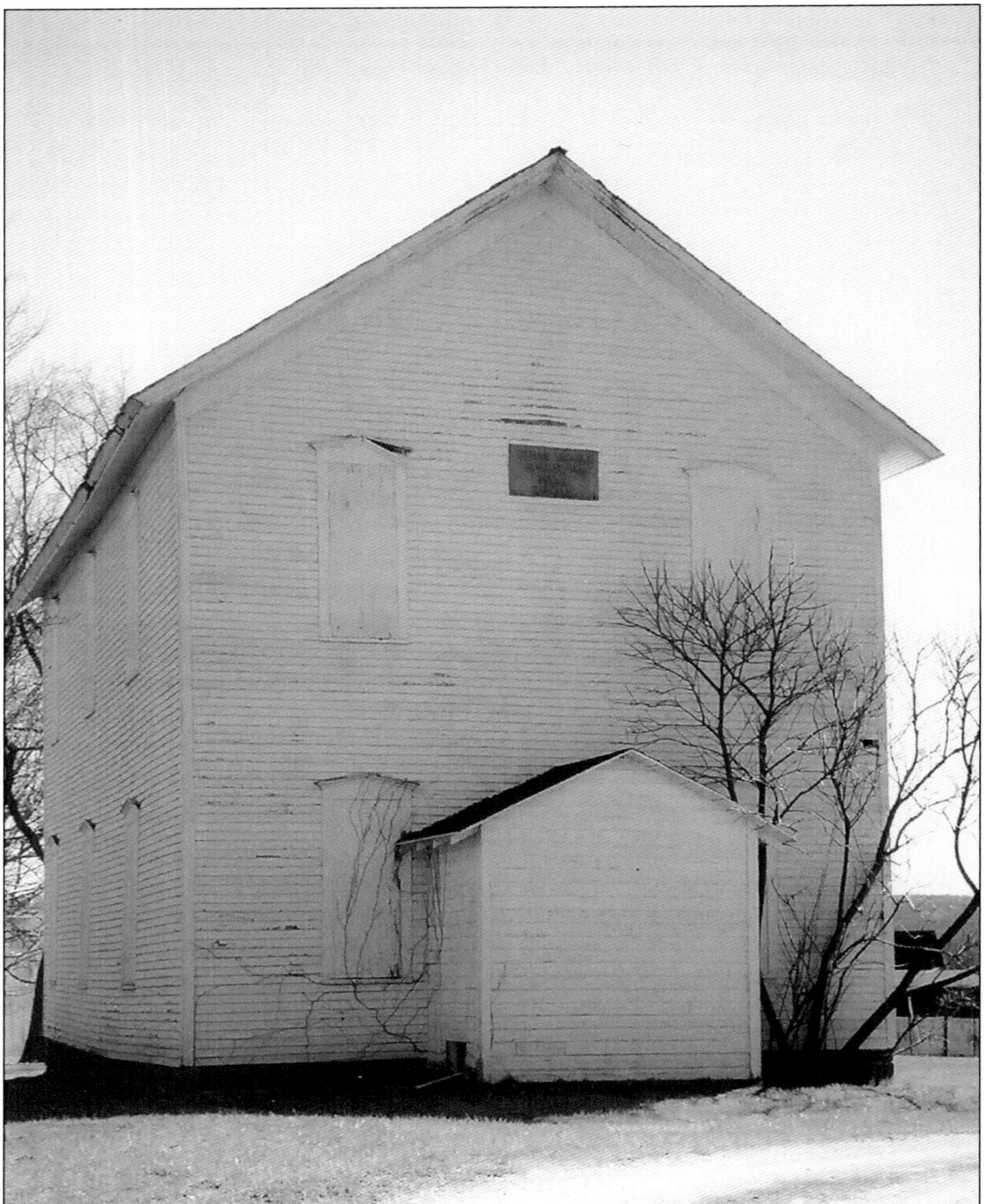

Hayfield Township was known for having the most one-room schoolhouses in Crawford County. Most of these schoolhouses covered grades 1 through 8 with a centralized school in the township for grades 9 through 12. Until it was consolidated with three others in 1947–1948, Little's Corners School was the only high school in the township. The building, shown in a more contemporary photograph here, is still in use as storage by Hayfield Township.

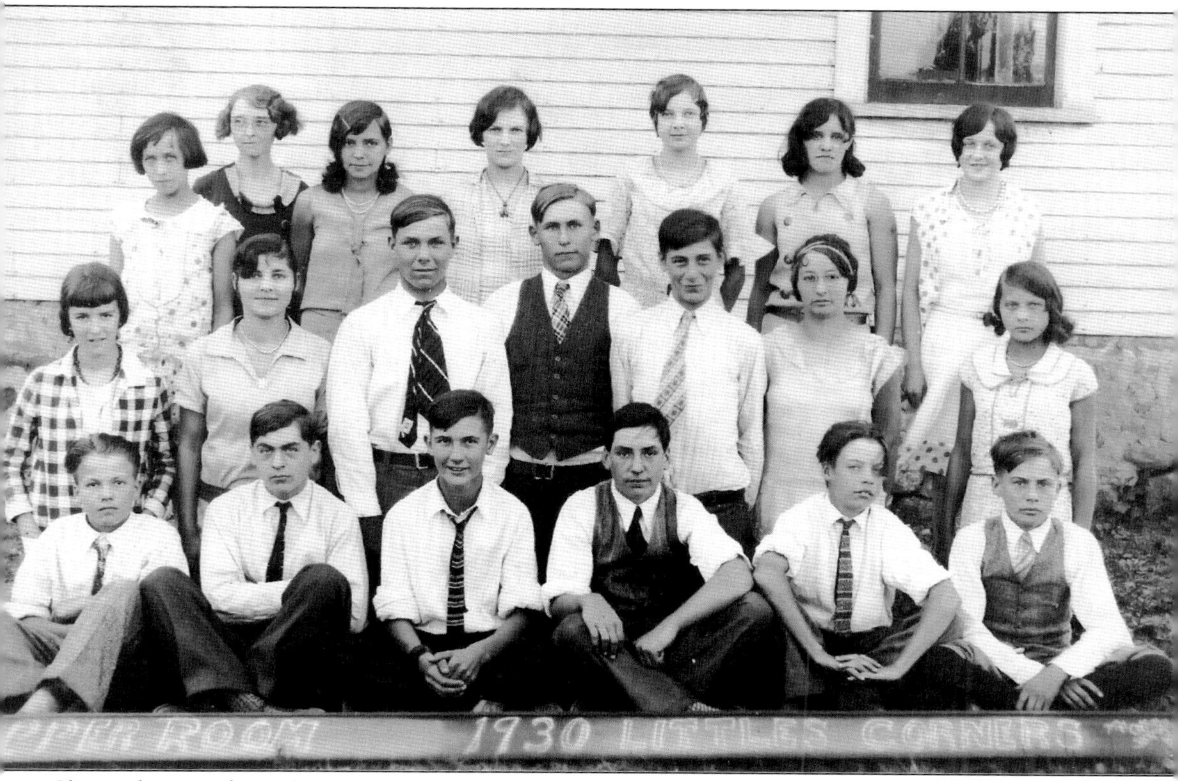

Shown here is the 1930 upper room class at Little's Corners School. Those shown here from left to right are (first row) Edwin Dillaman, Kingsly Doubt, Arthur Reichel, Lawrence Rung, Robert Newhard, and Irving McMillin; (second row) Nancy Ellen Nisley, Mary Raponel, Lester Hutchinson, Joe Daniells, Nevin Smith, Charlotte Weyman, and Geraldine Echan; (third row) Mary Mogush, teacher Jeanette McCullough, Ruth Young, Cecile Sturring, Virginia Graham, Pearl Prince, and Neva Smith.

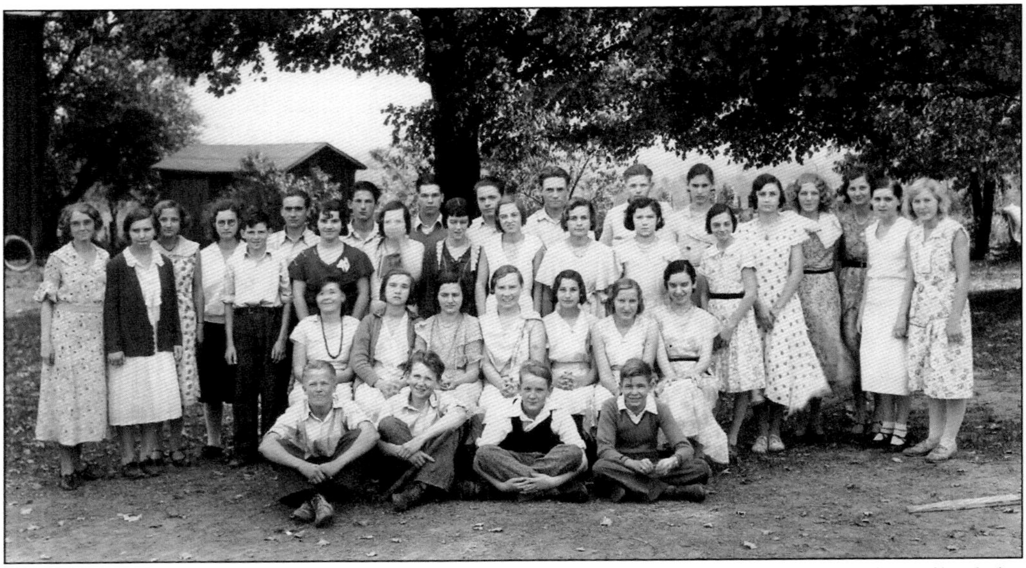

It is unknown when this Little's Corners School class photograph was taken, but all of the students can be identified. Jeanette McCullough, teacher at the school, is standing at the far left. Pictured from left to right are (first row) Clayton Dillaman, Joseph Mahoney, Neil Ingols, and Harry Hall; (second row) Audrey Camp, Margaret Paul, Mildred Dearborn, Ruth Ramsey, Mary Ann Constanovich, Anna Dearborn, and Inez Marie McGill; (third row) Julia Paul, Edna Dillaman, Mary Luchansky, Phillip Mahoney, Paul Locke, Mary Bair, John Yocina, Mary Mahoney, Stanley Dillaman, Nancy E. Nisley, Arthur Doubt, Addie McMillin, Arthur Ramsey, Anna Kapanik, Leo Deets, Sara Stanford, Louise Koehler, Mary Gordon, Gayle DeRoss, Cecile Mook, Esther Dillaman, Virginia Scott, and Elizabeth Luchansky.

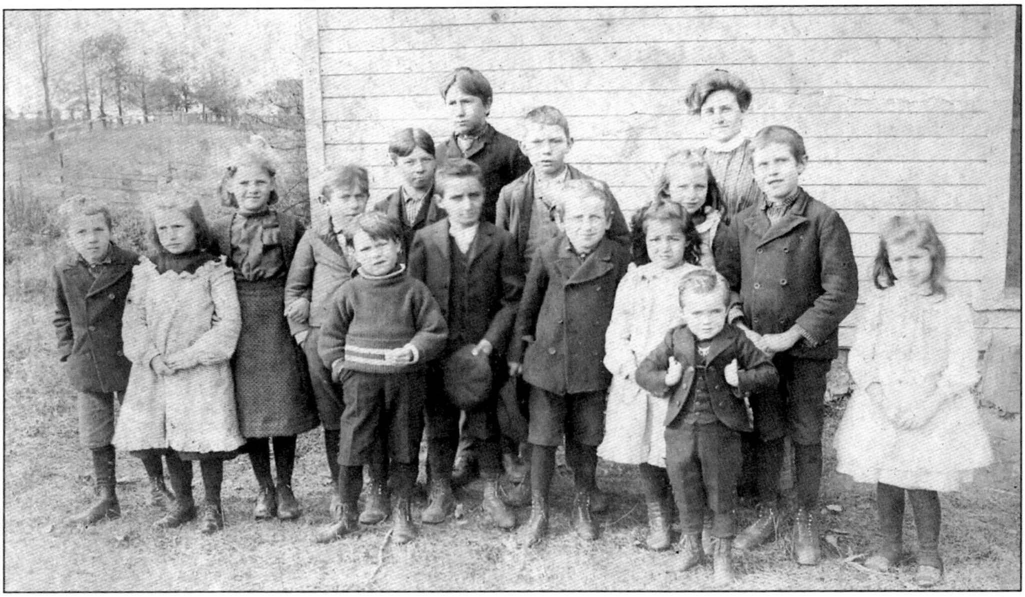

Peiffertown, like many other one-room schoolhouses, served its local community until joining the Saegertown School System after the advent of automobile transportation. The class photograph shown here was taken between approximately 1905 and 1910.

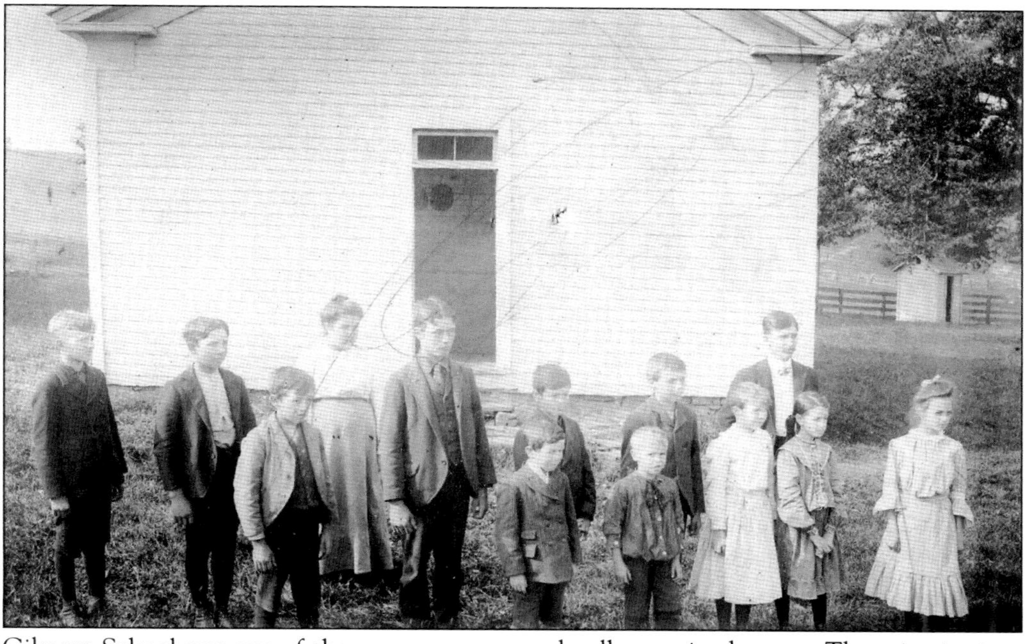

Gilmore School was one of the many one-room schoolhouses in the area. These institutions served local corners and communities and were paid for and maintained by local residents and parents of students. They usually served grades 1 through 8, and high schools were separate buildings traveled to if an education beyond the eighth grade was desired.

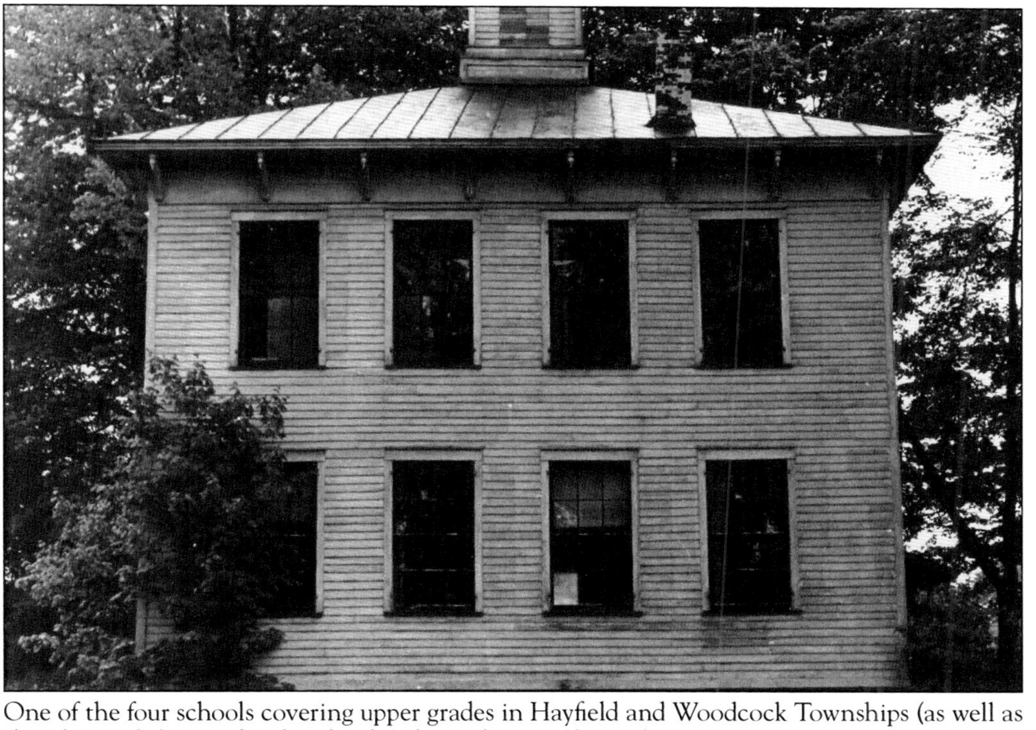

One of the four schools covering upper grades in Hayfield and Woodcock Townships (as well as their boroughs), Woodcock School is shown here in the mid-1900s.

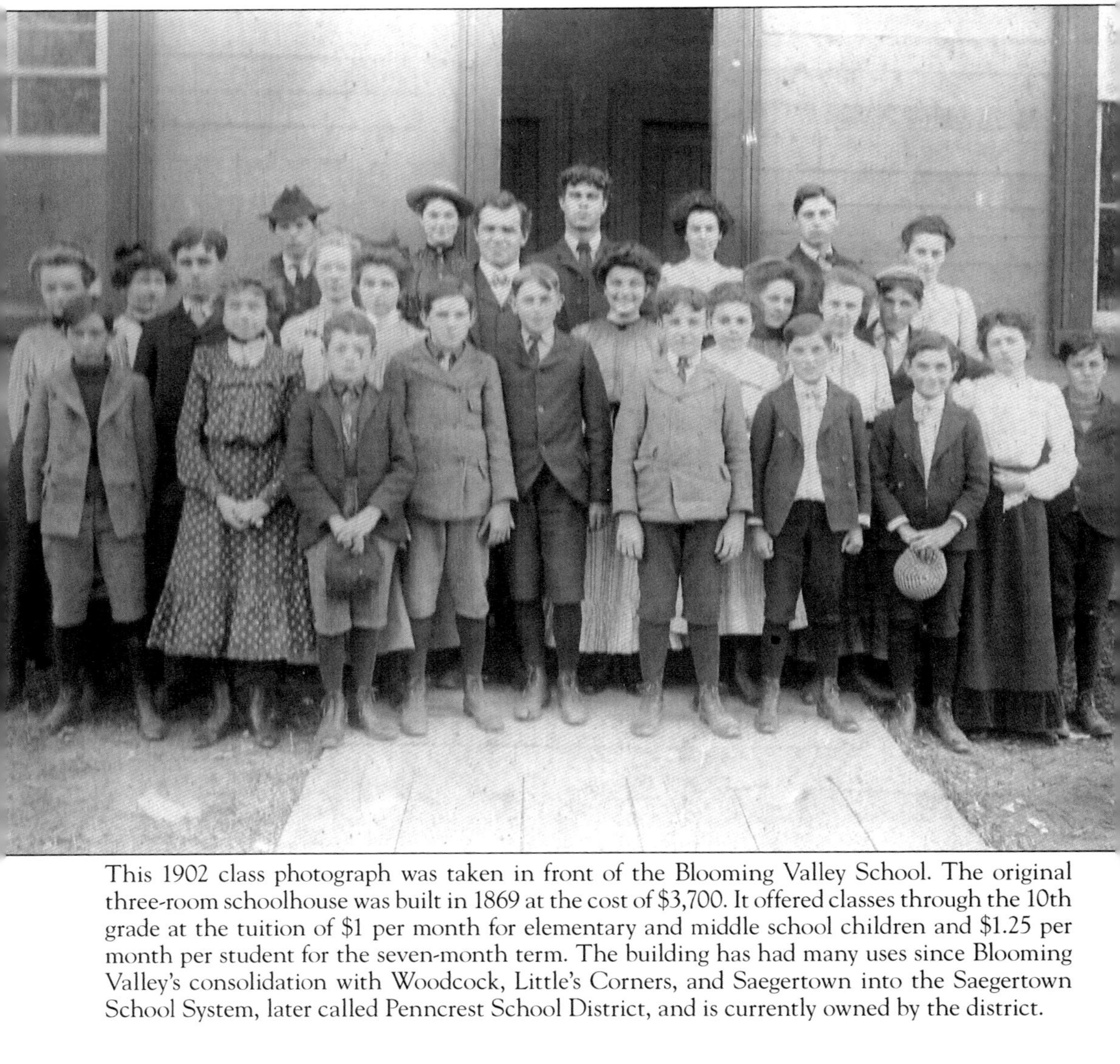

This 1902 class photograph was taken in front of the Blooming Valley School. The original three-room schoolhouse was built in 1869 at the cost of $3,700. It offered classes through the 10th grade at the tuition of $1 per month for elementary and middle school children and $1.25 per month per student for the seven-month term. The building has had many uses since Blooming Valley's consolidation with Woodcock, Little's Corners, and Saegertown into the Saegertown School System, later called Penncrest School District, and is currently owned by the district.

Seven

A Place to Get Away from It All

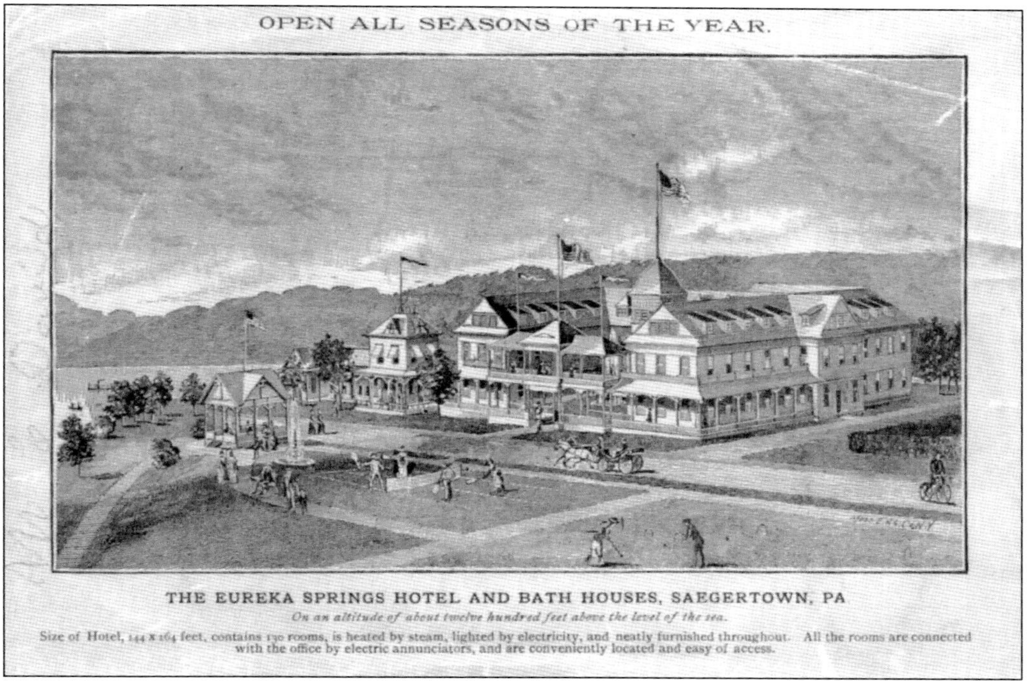

This advertisement for the Eureka Springs Hotel announces the 144-by-164-foot structure has 130 rooms. It is steam heated, electrically lit, and has electric annunciators connecting each room to the office to get attention or service.

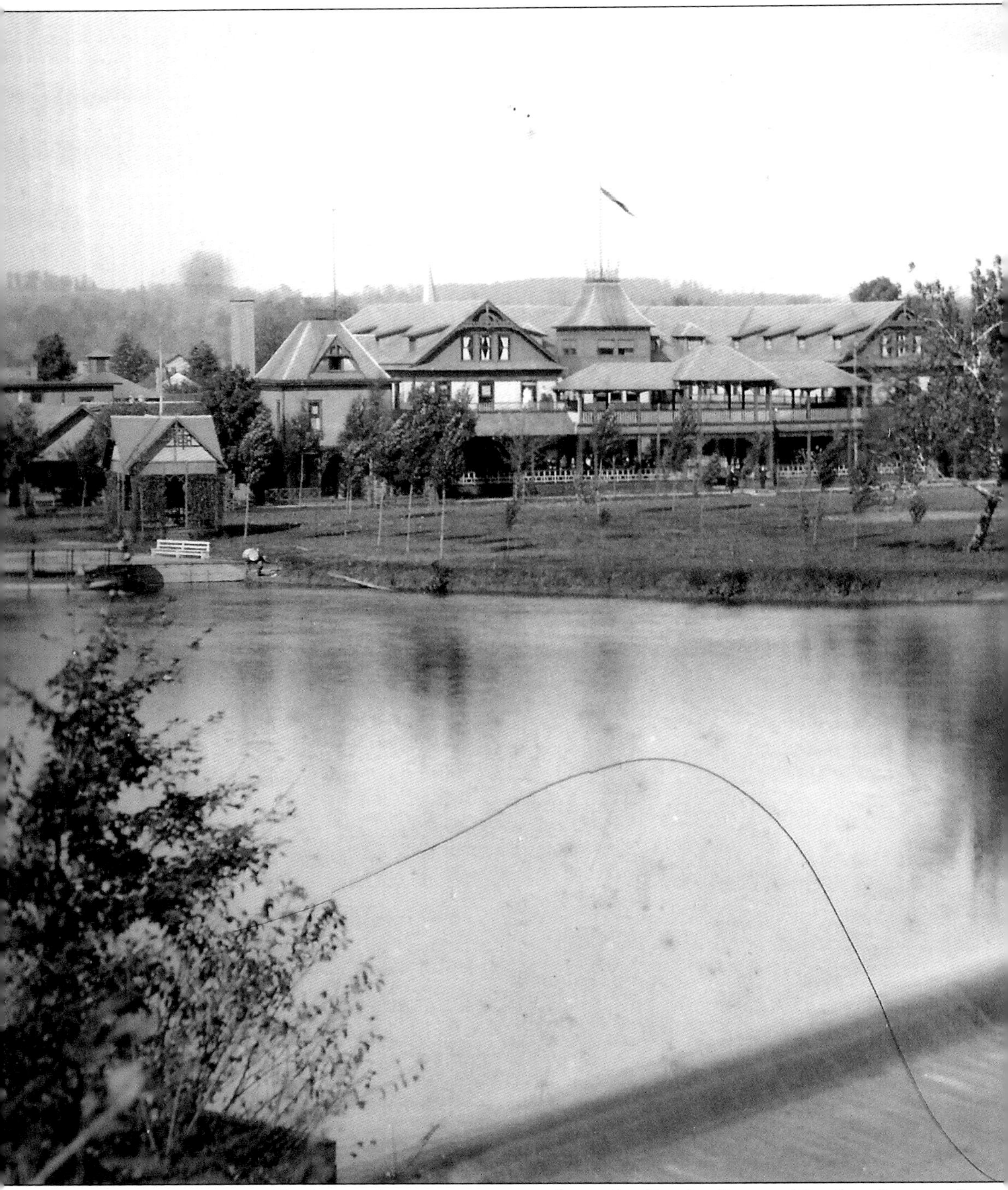

In 1885, someone felt the need to write a poem about the Eureka Springs Hotel and mineral water. It was included in pamphlets and speaks as advertisement in itself, proclaiming, "Eureka! Yes 'tis true we found it—Life's elixir let us sound it, to the world that all may try it, and be relieved from suffering by it. It will cure dyspepsia, salt rheum, sick headache, and constipation,

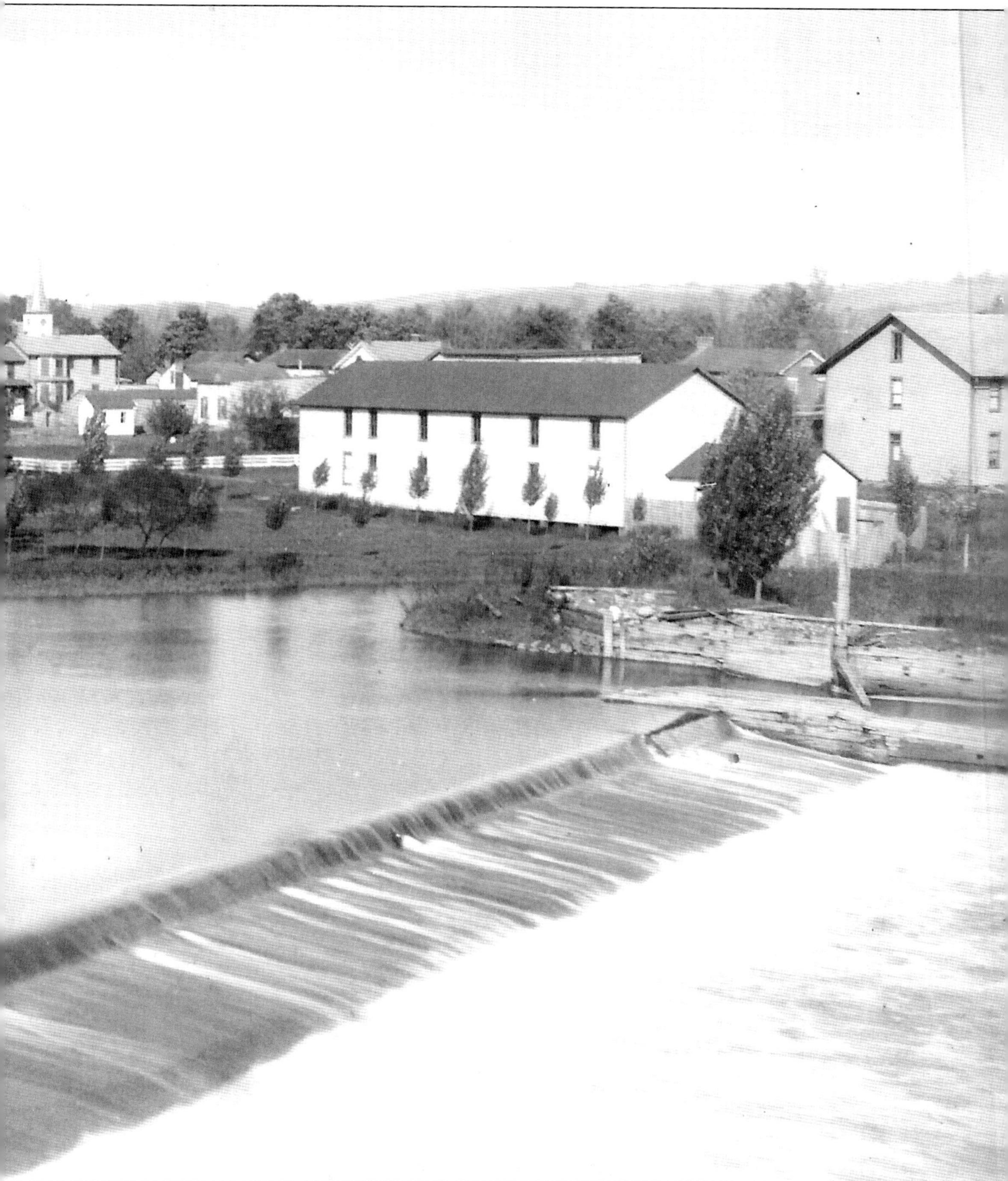

neuralgia, rheumatism, gout and ills accomp'ing these throughout. All these disease we have name, all skin diseases just the same, yield to this water, we're assured by scores of people who've been cured."

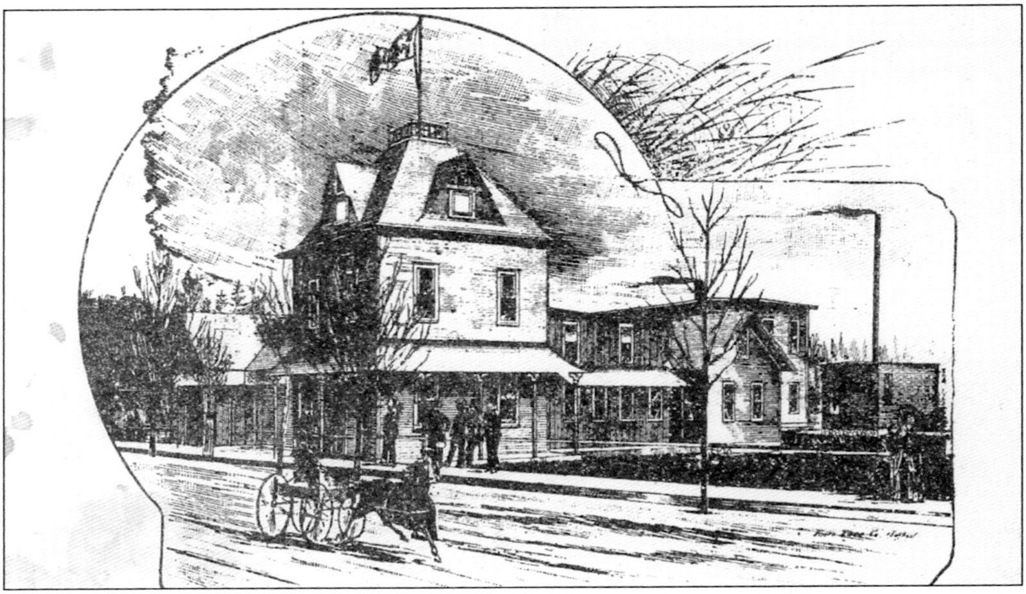

Alexander and Charles Benner built the Eureka Springs Hotel in 1888 to accompany the Eureka Springs Bottling Works. Ten years later, Horace Fox bought the property from the Benners for $20,000.

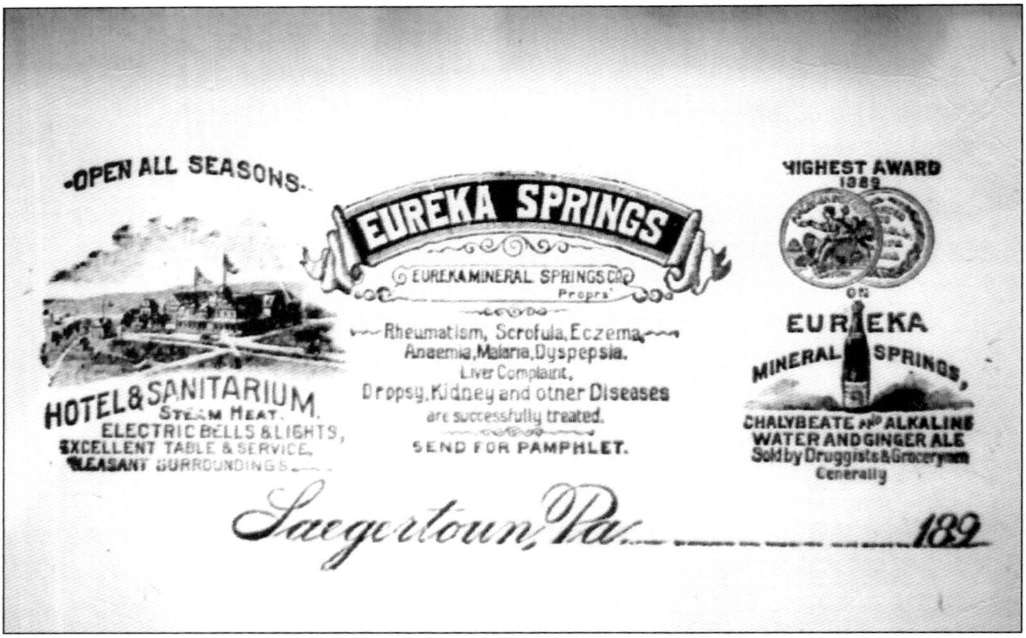

This advertisement from the 1890s displays the entire list of ailments Eureka Springs' mineral waters were supposed to cure as well as the highlights of the Eureka Springs Hotel.

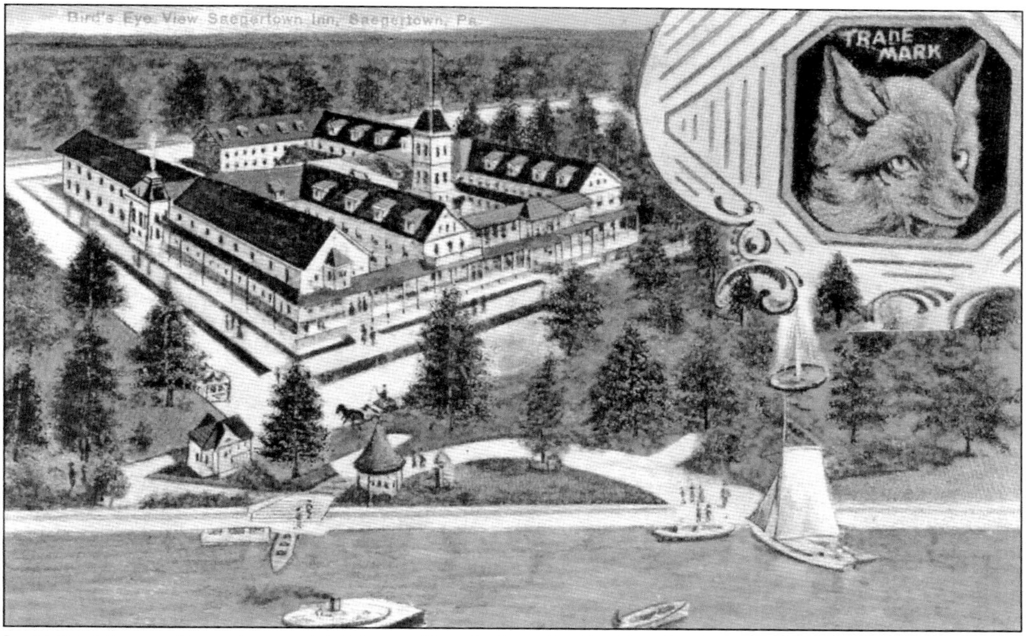

In 1898, Horace Fox, along with his son Frank, bought the Eureka Springs Hotel from the Benner Brothers and renamed it the Saegertown Inn. The inn offered 90 bedrooms, and local tradition claims notables such as John D. Rockefeller spent time at the inn when visiting Meadville.

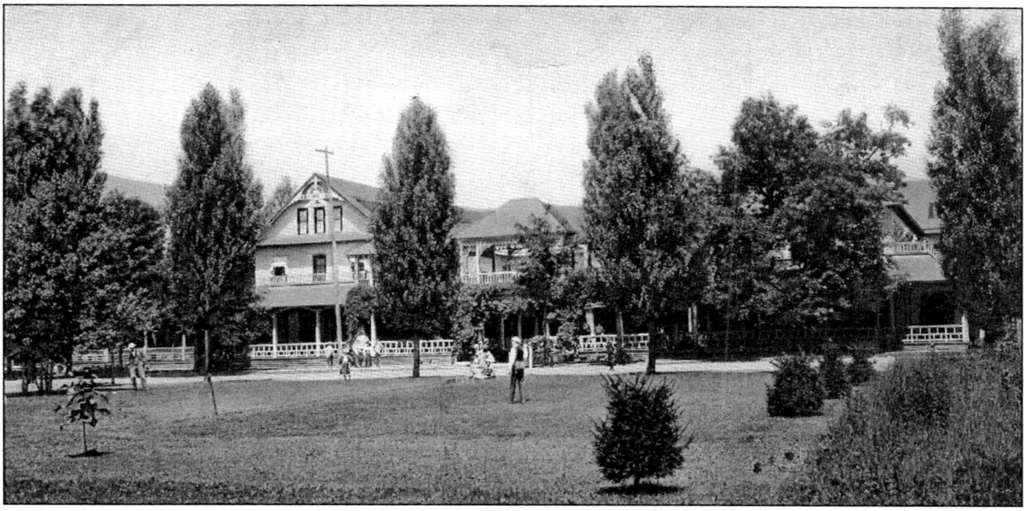

Upon his father's death in 1907 and his mother's in 1909, Frank Fox ran the thriving Saegertown Inn until his own death in 1919. The mineral springs were renamed after Horace's death to be called Frank M. Fox and Company. Upon Frank's death, his wife maintained the business for a time, remarrying and running it with her new husband.

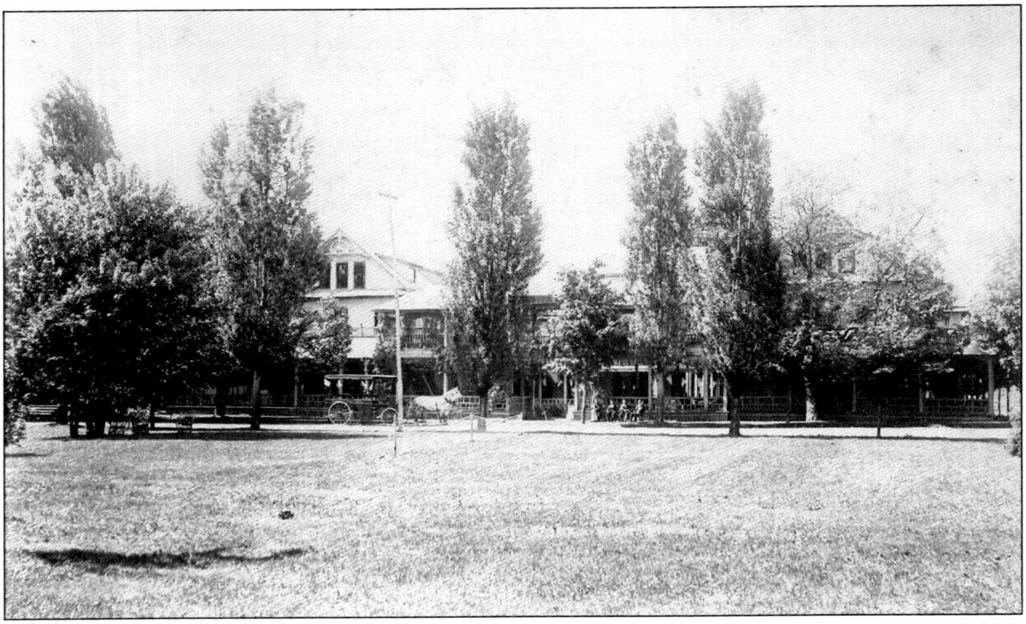

The inn is shown here with a carriage parked in front, possibly bringing or taking guests to their desired locations.

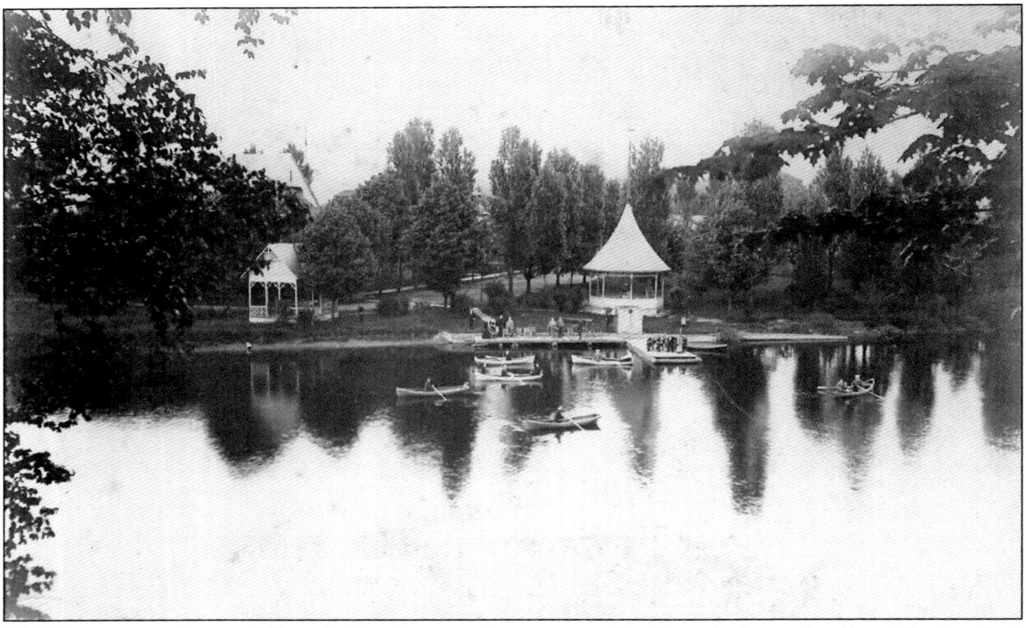

The Saegertown Inn and French Creek were what one could call made for each other. The inn had an area where boats could be used by guests on the creek for relaxation and enjoying the scenery.

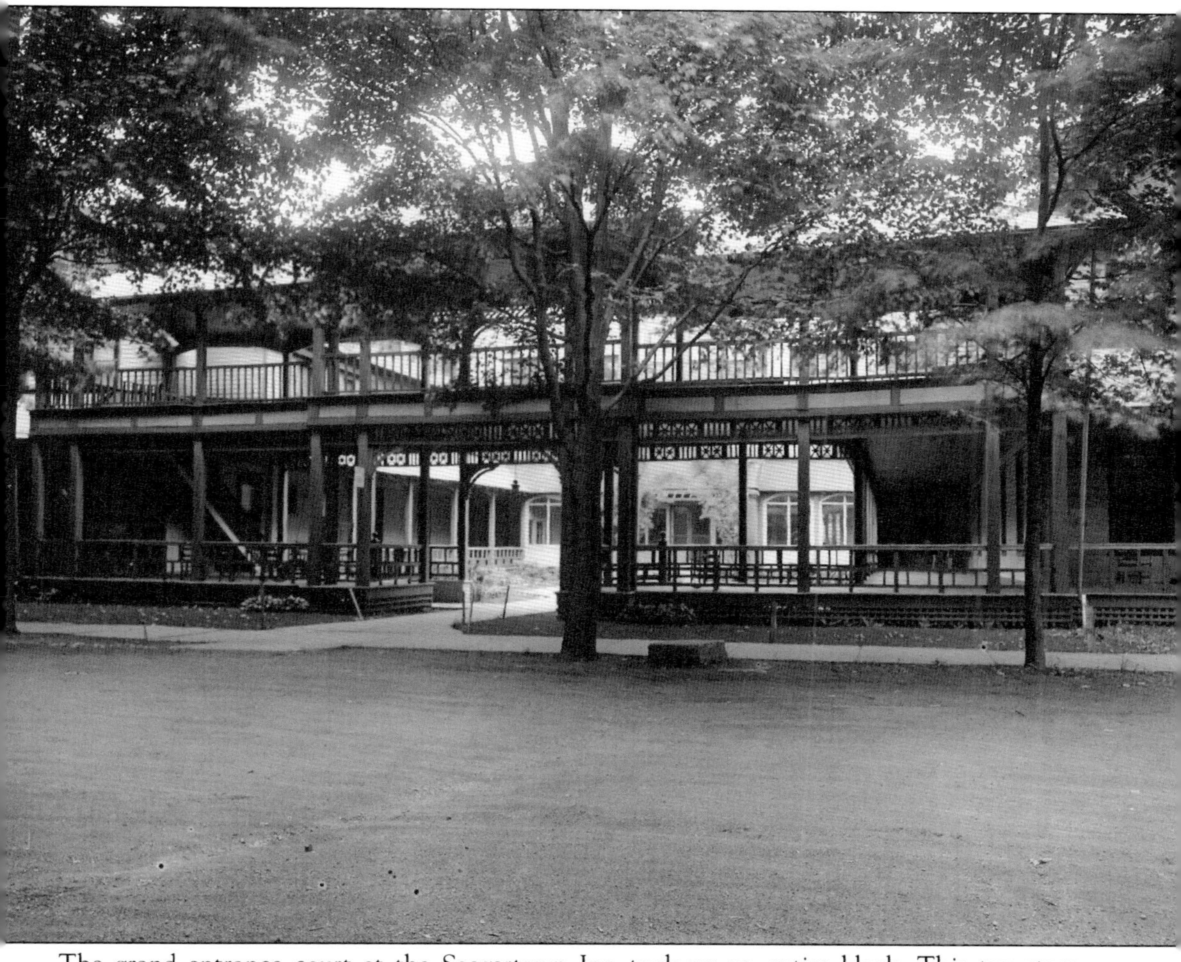

The grand entrance court at the Saegertown Inn took up an entire block. This two-story structure gives every room access to the open court or the grounds.

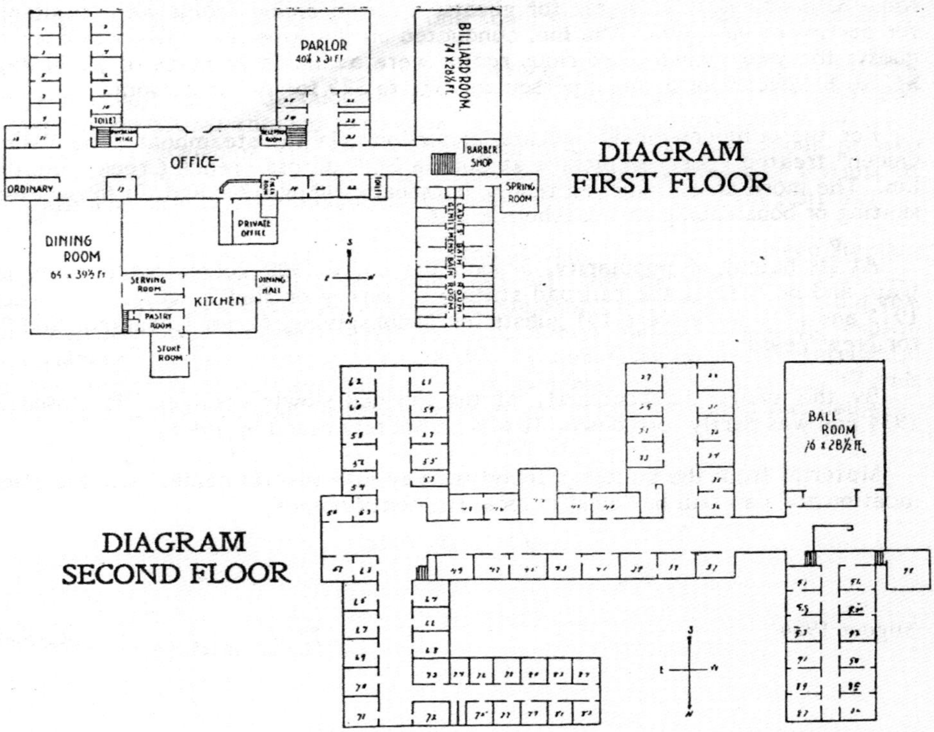

The floor plan for Ye Old Inn, Saegertown Inn's successor after a change in ownership, is seen here.

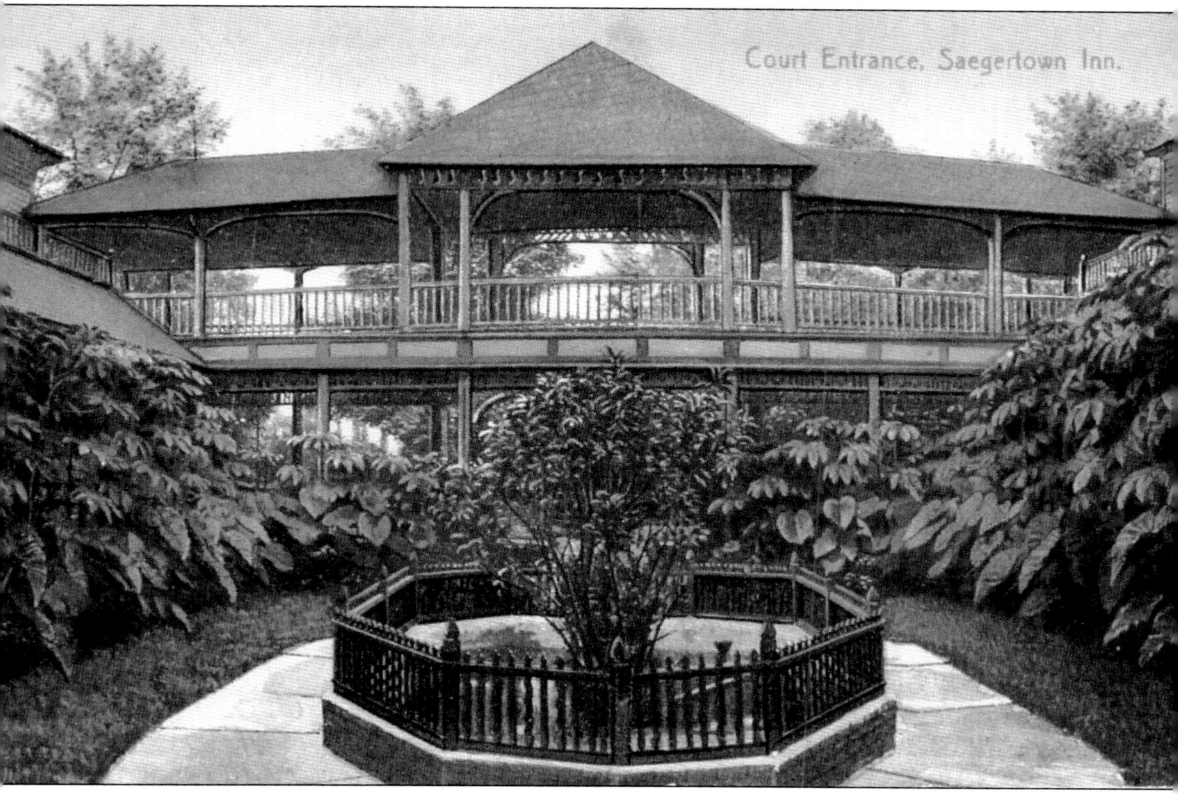

This attractive octagonal garden was one of the first things seen by visitors to the inn. The base of this structure still survives today and was recently found when a local resident was doing some digging on the property. All the greens and other vegetables served at the inn were grown in its gardens on the grounds.

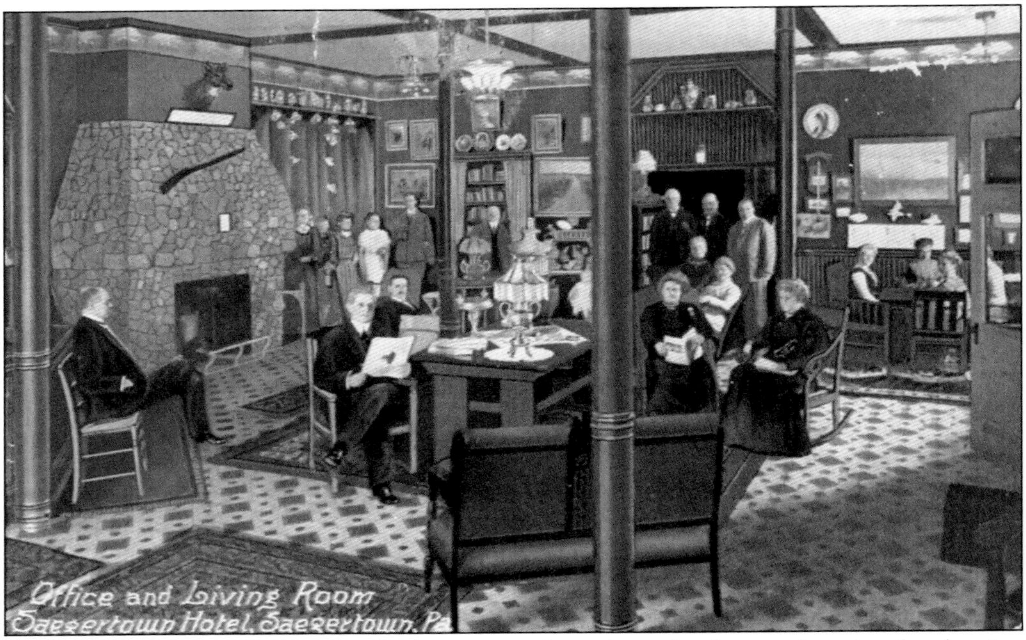

Large, homey, and guest friendly, the living room has a huge fireplace and seating for chatting with new friends. The infamous sign above the fireplace reads, "I am an old man and have had many troubles, but most of them never happened."

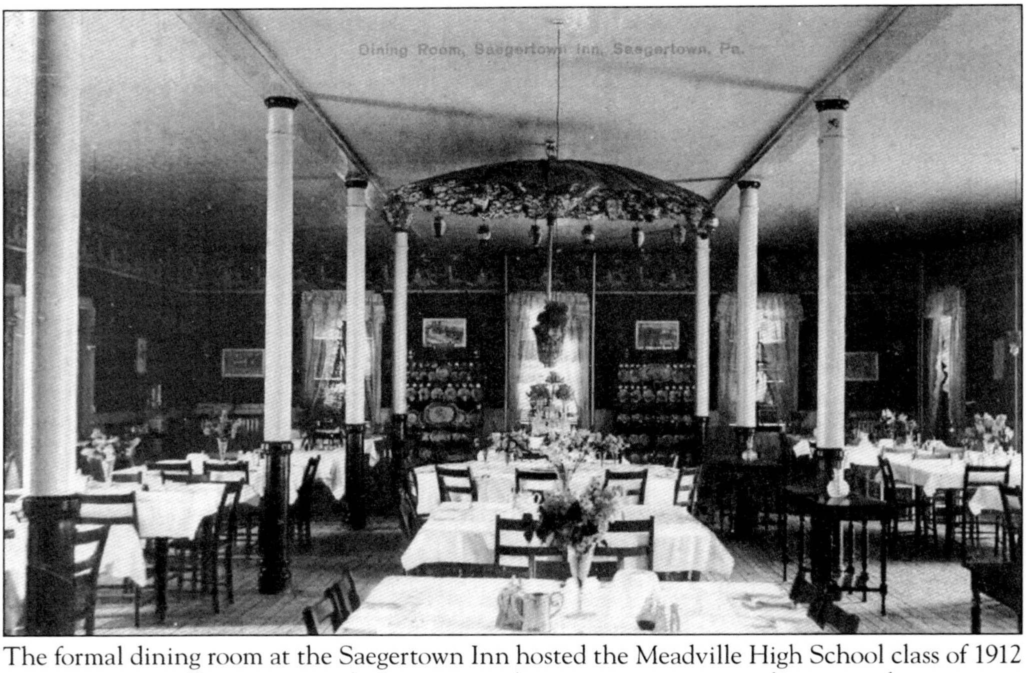

The formal dining room at the Saegertown Inn hosted the Meadville High School class of 1912 on January 12, 1912, with 75 students present. This gracious space served guests and community alike. Private fancy dining rooms were also available for parties or banquets.

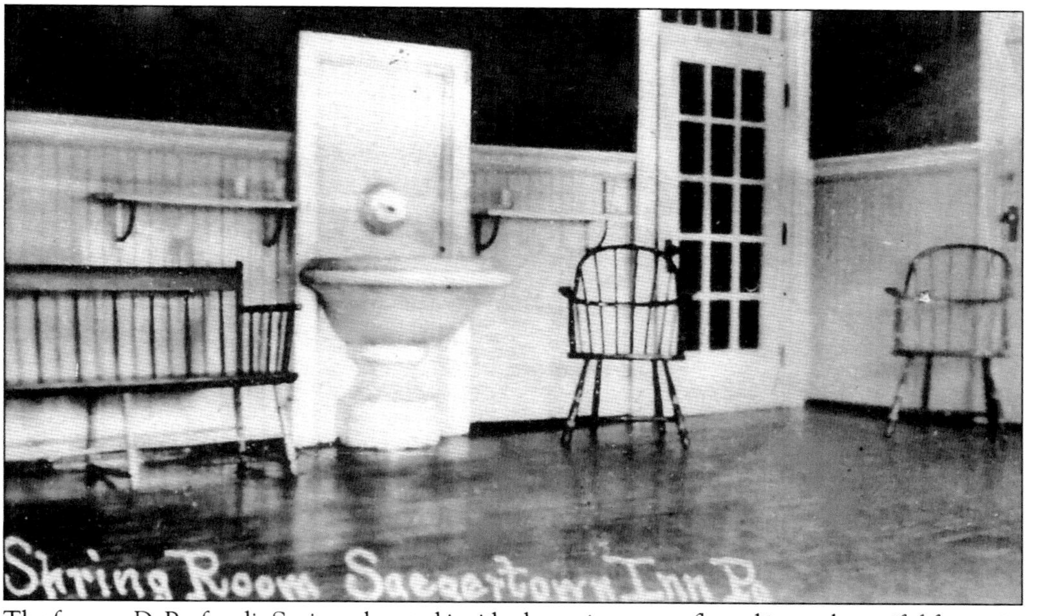

The famous DeProfundis Springs, located inside the spring room, flowed into a beautiful fountain along one wall. The water from the spring was served throughout the inn.

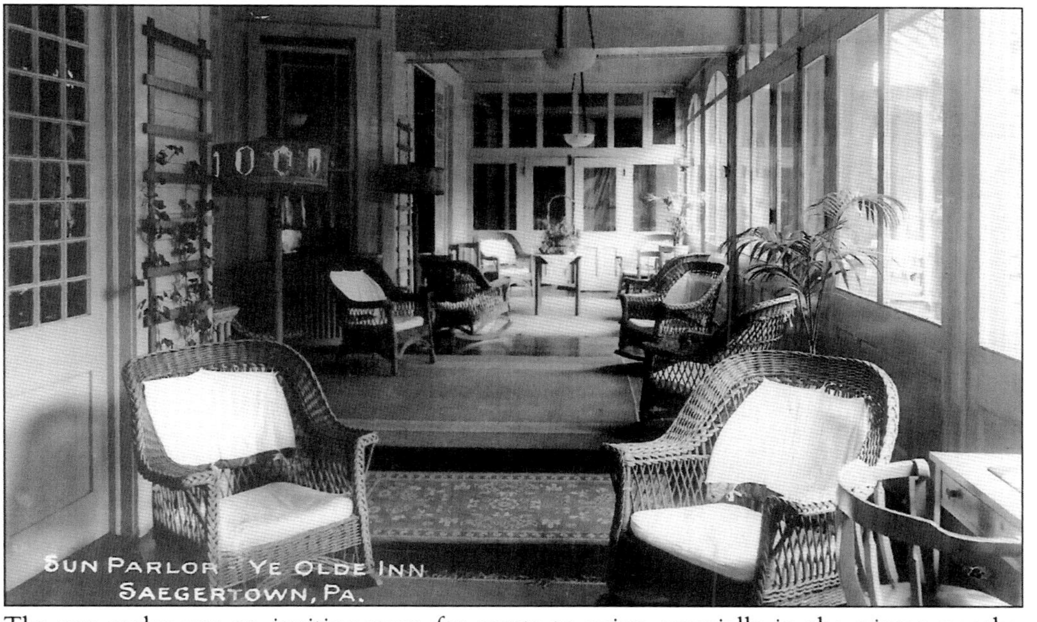

The sun parlor was an inviting room for guests to enjoy, especially in the winter months. Activities could take place here or just lounging in a wicker chair enjoying the sunlight.

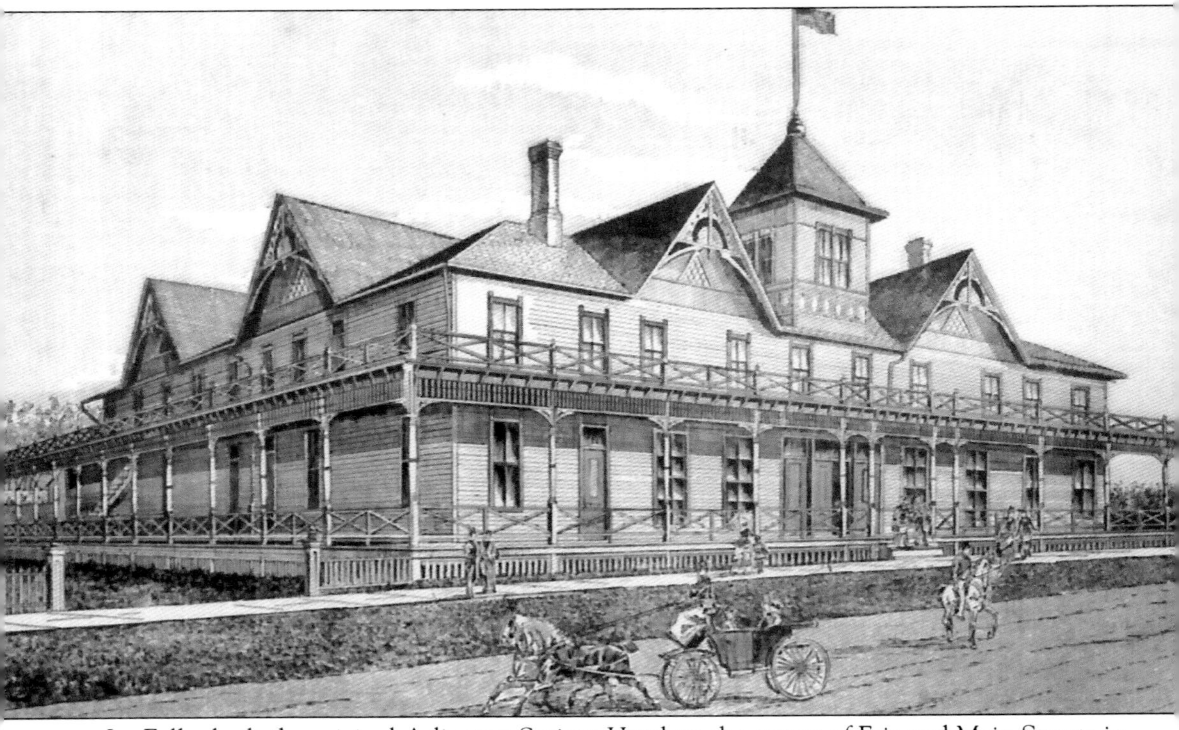

Ira Fuller built the original Arlington Springs Hotel on the corner of Erie and Main Streets in 1885. With a 125-guest capacity, the hotel was an elegant place to stay while enjoying Saegertown's mineral springs, boating on French Creek, or just taking the train to nearby Meadville for any occasion. The Arlington thrived for two years, until burning to the ground during the early hours of September 8, 1887. The fire's heat was intense enough to kill trees in yards across the street. It was rebuilt six months later and renamed the New Arlington Springs Hotel and later the Ponce de Leon and thrived through the early 1900s until the popularity of Saegertown as a resort area slowly faded.

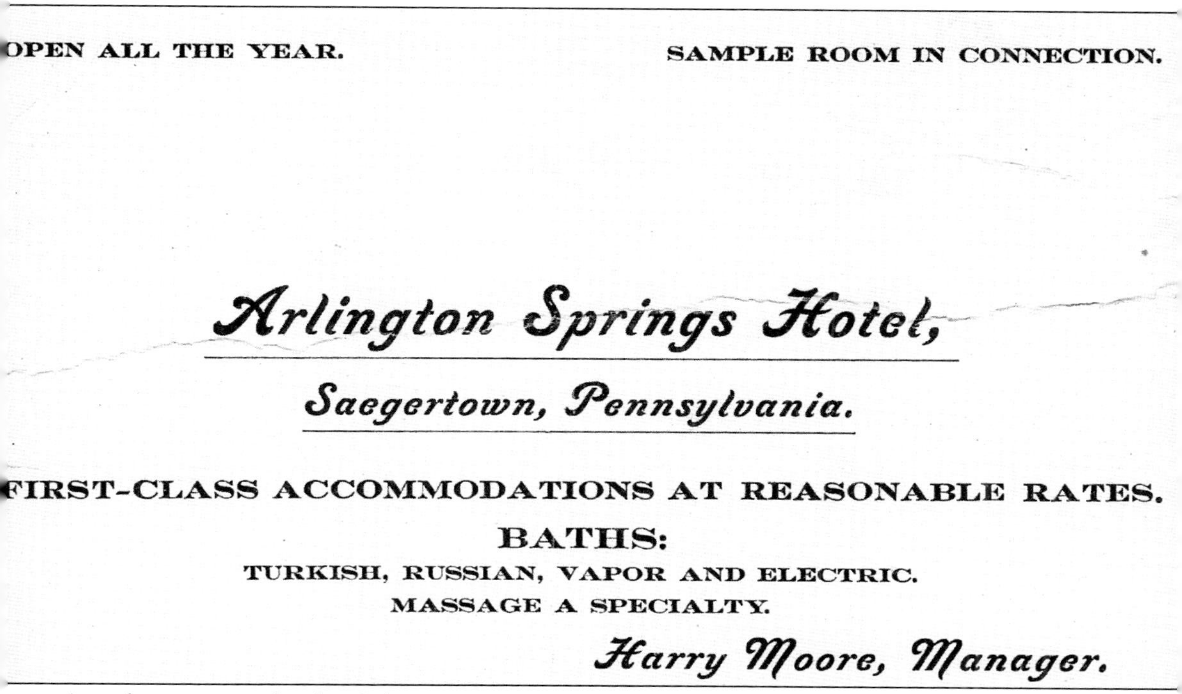

An advertisement for the Arlington Springs Hotel promoting its mineral baths is seen here printed on business card–size paper. Sized to fit in an envelope, these could travel fast with visitors to the hotel as well as local residents planning for visiting friends.

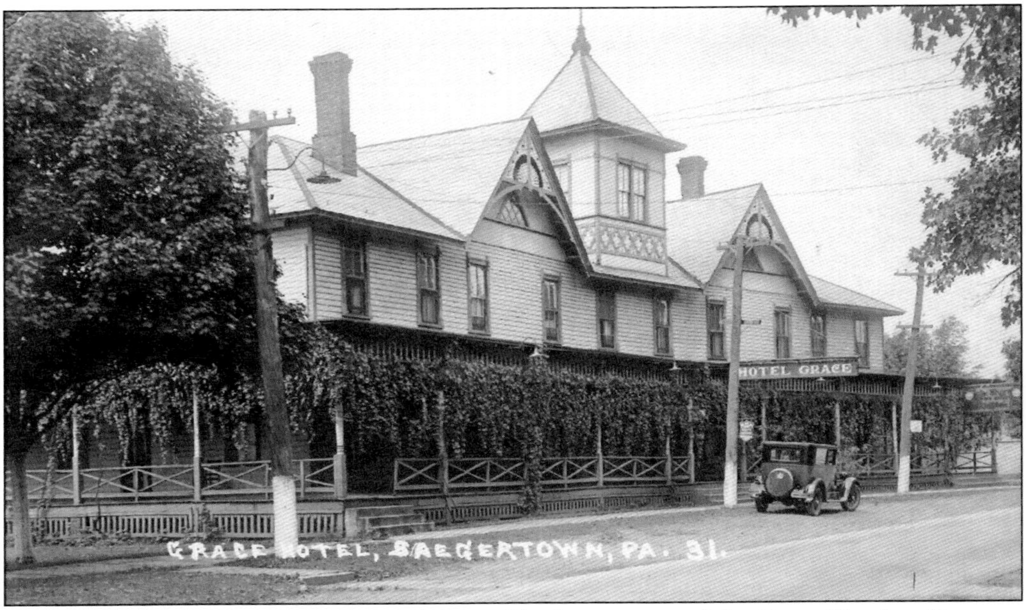

The New Arlington Springs or Ponce de Leon Hotel was renamed the Grace Hotel and became home to the Saegertown High School basketball team. It played on the ballroom dance floor, being careful not to run into the pillars in the center of the room. The Grace was demolished in 1935.

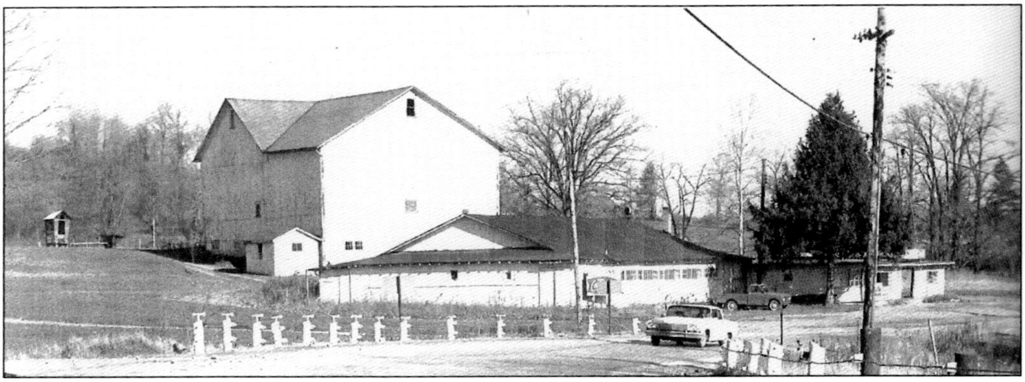

The White Inn was a moderately priced establishment. Community dances were held here at one time, as it had a "spring floor," making dancing more entertaining.

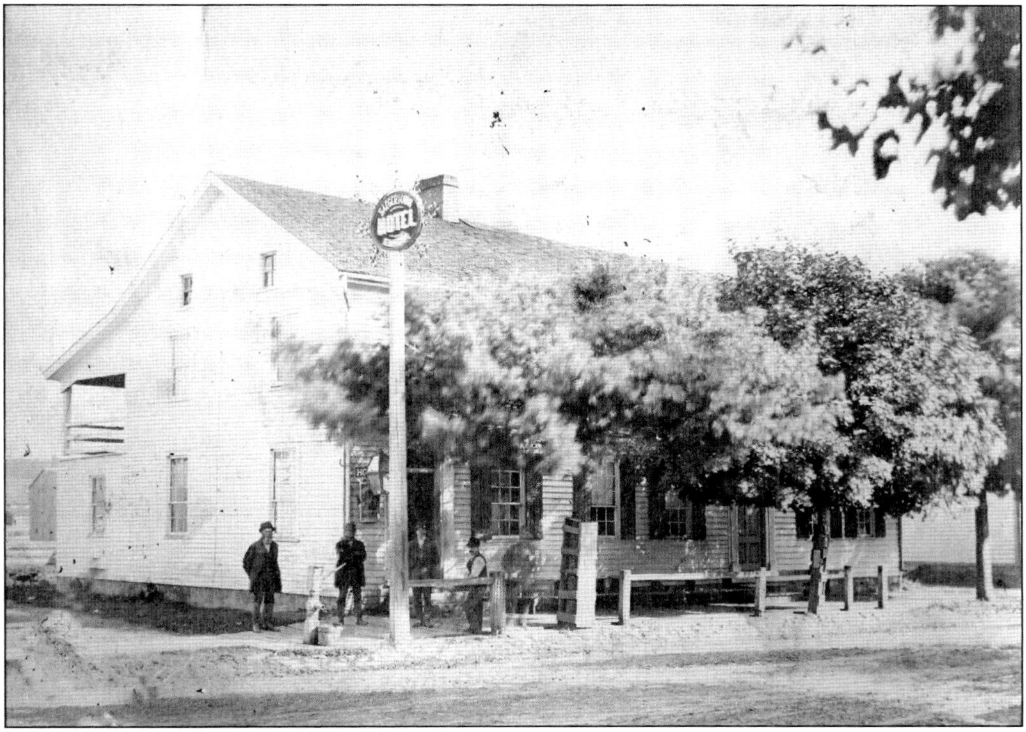

The Saegertown Motel, as seen here, was another more moderate sleeping establishment. Whereas cars pull into motels during the modern day, hitching posts line the front of this building for weary travelers to tie their horses.

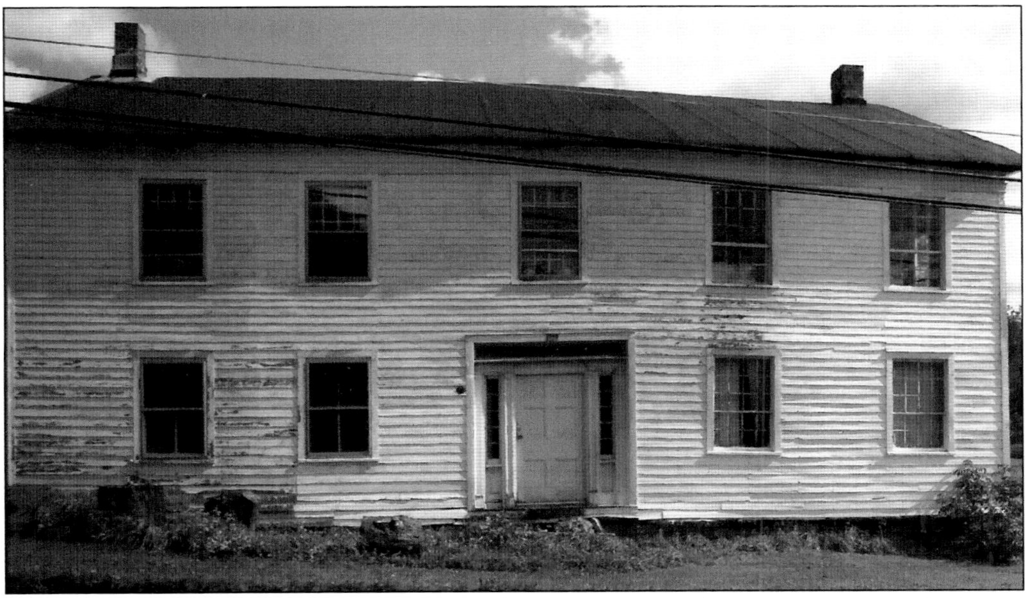

Almost every stagecoach stop, railroad town, and small community had at least one boardinghouse or hotel. The unidentified one shown here was under operation in Woodcock for years and is over a century old.

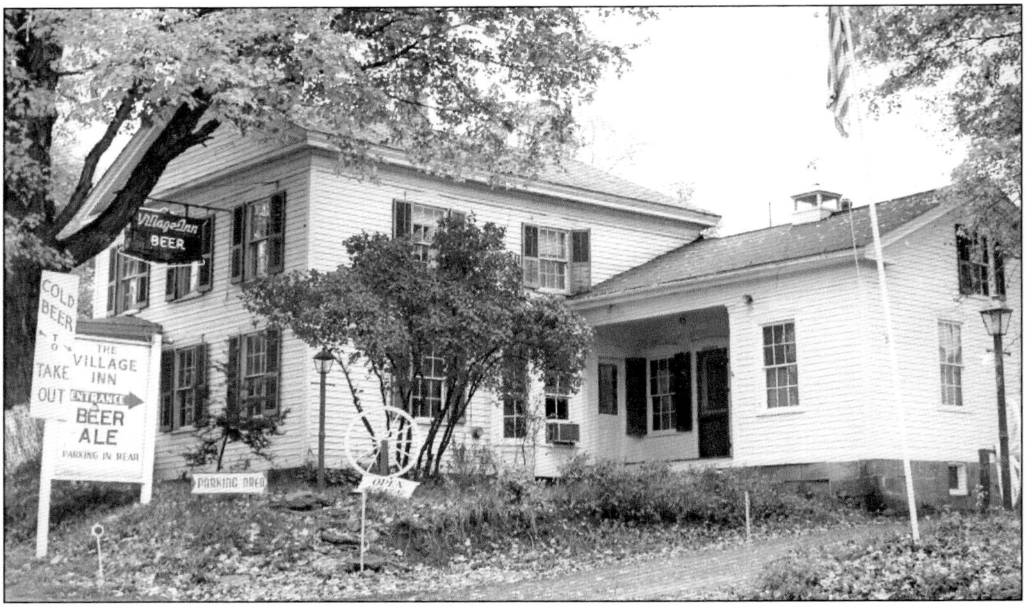

The Woodcock Village Inn, built in 1820, was one of the various inns and stagecoach stops on the busy Waterford Turnpike. The turnpike, being one of the first corduroy roads (lined with whole logs to make muddy areas accessible), figured greatly during the War of 1812. Harold Heist purchased the inn and restored it to its 1820s elegance in the latter half of the 1900s, as it is shown here, and it remained so until burning down in recent years.

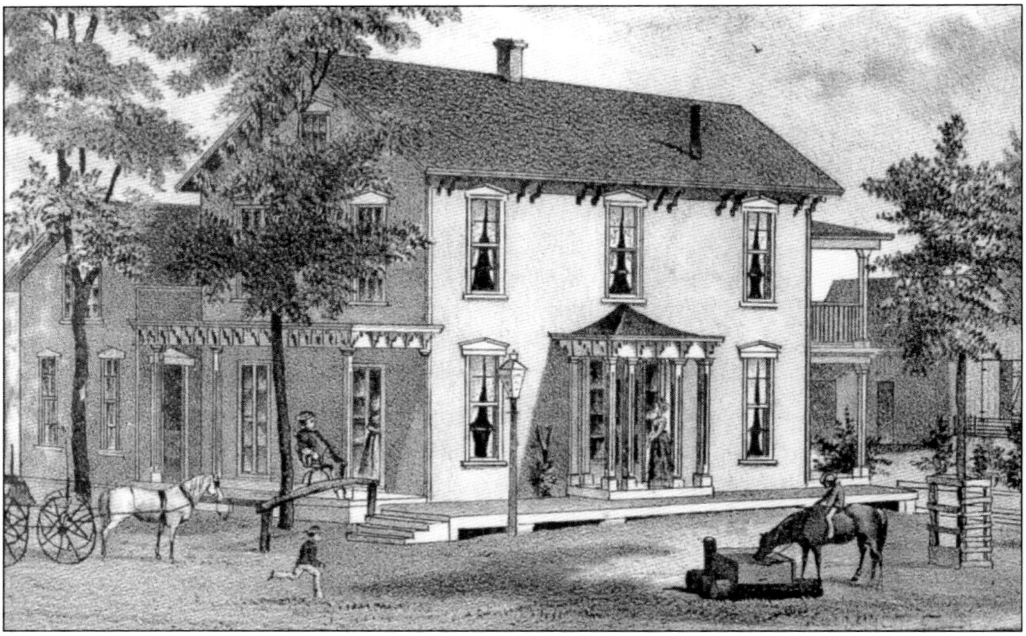

Fountain House Hotel was built on the southeast corner of tract No. 161 during the latter half of the 19th century by James McGill, quite possibly a relative of the Saegertown McGills. He used the building as a storehouse for sometime before converting it into a hotel along the Waterford Turnpike.

W. H. Hunter established a 15-room hotel with a magnificent ballroom in 1867. The ballroom was well known for its "spring" dance floor, having less than the normal number of floor joists to give the floor a bouncy feel when dancing. The building was later used as the Blooming Valley Grange hall.

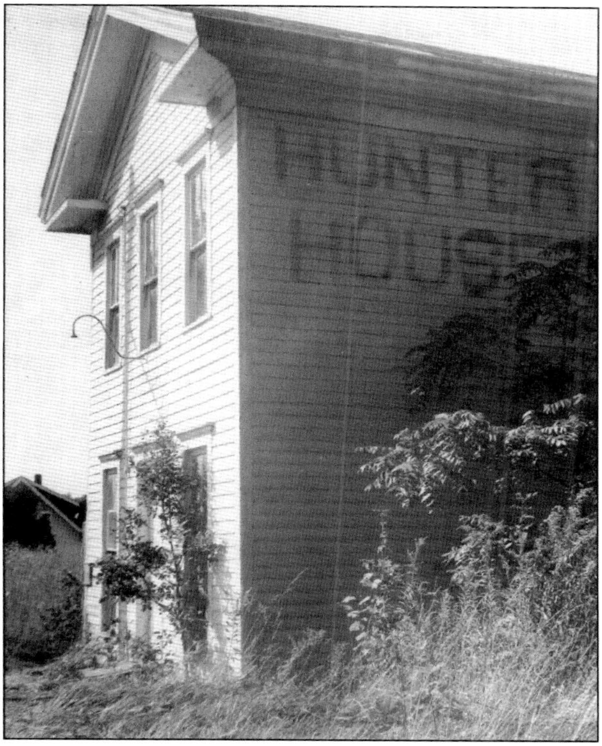

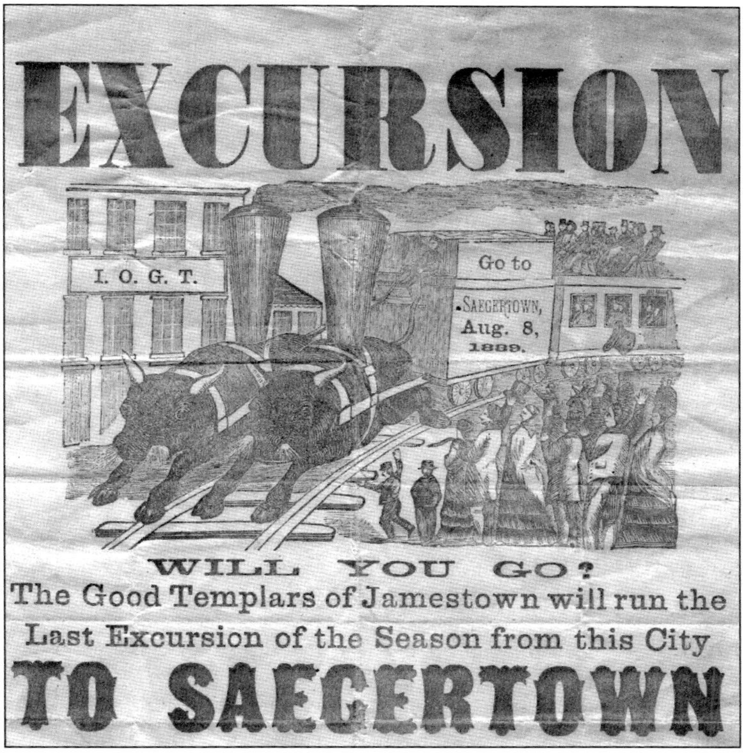

An advertisement for an 1889 excursion sponsored by the Good Templars of Jamestown is shown here. Round-trip tickets could be had for $1 with children riding for 50¢.